Of Fears and Foes

Of Fears and Foes

Security and Insecurity in an Evolving Global Political Economy

EDITED BY
JOSE V. CIPRUT

PRAEGER

Westport, Connecticut
London

Library of Congress Cataloging-in-Publication Data

Of fears and foes : security and insecurity in an evolving global political economy /
edited by Jose V. Ciprut.
      p.   cm
    Includes bibliographical references and index.
    ISBN 0–275–96855–3 (alk. paper)—ISBN 0–275–97575–4 (pbk. : alk. paper)
    1. Security, International.   I. Ciprut, Jose V.
  JZ5595.O38   2000
  327.1′721—dc21   99–045990

British Library Cataloguing in Publication Data is available.

Library of Congress Catalog Card Number: 99–045990
ISBN: 0–275–97575–4 (pbk.)

First published in 2000

Praeger Publishers, 88 Post Road West, Westport, CT 06881
An imprint of Greenwood Publishing Group, Inc.
www.praeger.com

Printed in the United States of America

The paper used in this book complies with the
Permanent Paper Standard issued by the National
Information Standards Organization (Z39.48–1984).

10 9 8 7 6 5 4 3 2 1

Copyright Acknowledgment

Every reasonable effort has been made to trace the owners of copyright materials in this book, but
in some instances this has proven impossible. The author and publisher will be glad to receive
information leading to more complete acknowledgments in subsequent printings of the book, and
in the meantime extend their apologies for any omissions.

For Vitali H. Ciprut and M. Suzan née-Naon

who were much less surprised than I
when I looked the condor in the eye

Dogs bark,
Caravan passes.
Where fears lurk,
Freedoms falter,
Foes retard,
Tyranny trespasses.

Contents

Preface

As the bloodiest of all centuries comes to an end, this volume enters the new millennium by recontextualizing and interconnecting certain military and non-military security dilemmas whose complex inputs and synergetic impacts elude and defy conventional analysis. In addition to reconsidering these complications at the national, international, and transnational levels of synthesis, we endeavor to assess their globalizing sociopolitical and geo-economic import from the perspectives of strategy and policy along a systemic approach.

We proceed in a frame of mind that seeks to link verifiable findings, generalizable insights, and theorizable practical action. We deploy an interdisciplinary mentality that seeks to understand the combinations and permutations of the newer constituents of the world's security equations. We reassess the outcomes of our joint endeavor in search of enlightened policies and effective responses.

The end of the Cold War was precipitated by the great comfort with which the West could and would have overwhelmingly outspent the East beyond a simple tilt of the balance of terror. Having all too successfully induced the implosion of its fears and the utter dismemberment of its foes, the West promptly engaged the East to elicit a relatively well-managed reciprocal program of gradual nuclear disarmament. Yet today, even as Asia installs additional intercontinental ballistic missiles pointing at the Americas, the planet's mightiest nation is proactively designing a "digitized" army of excellence, able to deploy crosslinked and intersustaining modules of unprecedented lethal precision. These modules are to be tailored, trained, and equipped to respond to a variety of more or less distal challenges with real-time efficacy, at a moment when the world remains hamstrung between two post–Cold War modes of deterrence that are neither exhaustive nor mutually exclusive: a minimum-deterrence doctrine, according to which a minimal nuclear arsenal ought to fend off all attempts of nuclear blackmail by any potential source of threat, and a discriminant-deterrence doctrine that advocates a gamut of flexibly combinable and adaptably lethal conventional munitions and precision-guided systems utilizable in preemptive or responsive stances.

As if the North's complexities along the East-West axis were not sufficient, nuclear proliferation and conventional armament build-ups in the South, by those unable or unwilling to reorder their priorities in ways reconcilable with the urgent vital needs of their large and expanding populations, continue to complicate matters. And an ever cheaper and easier global access to dual-use technologies now enables Third World plants to switch production from milk powder to biological toxins in no time, with unnerving effect. On one hand, the transfer of cheap lethal technologies to labile regimes with unsettled scores gives the latter the capacity to weaponize chemical, biological, and fissile materials simply by coupling them with acquirable or locally developed missiles; on the other hand, the threats from terrorists of diverse motivations and obediences promise to attain new thresholds if such perpetrators are successful in establishing rewarding relations of exchange with rogue states lacking the fortitude to engage in identifiable direct actions at the risk and peril of their own population.

If we add to this precarious state of international affairs a number of exacerbating factors, such as "othernesss," "alienation," economic "depletion," environmental "degradation," "modernization," "globalization," "ethno-nationalist" civil wars, terror, migration, "transnational" crime, and the lack of institutions designed to deal effectively with such extant and nascent realities on the ground, one would realize how urgent the need for new thinking has become and how crucial it is for us to redefine "security" in novel ways.

It is not our aim to shift the reader's focus from military options to non-military pursuits, let alone to advocate anti-military discourses as if military suasion were a reprehensible or futile alternative for security or self-defense. Rather, it is the very task of this book to substantiate the need to reconsider ultimate recourses to military latitudes in the light of the contextualized operational constraints imposed by the fast-ramifying non-military uncertainties under which the security equations of the new century will require to be solved.

Our findings favor the development of a globally sustainable ambit for international peace and security. Our analyses discover reason to encourage an inclusive and democratically participatory international effort capable of reconciling policy and action in matters of security that until recently were mainly the purview of countervailing industrial-military establishments, prodding the state harshly to pursue inordinately adversarial national interests.

There is an urgent need for fresh thinking and path-breaking research in the globalizing field of peace and security studies. All of us agree on the objectives; most of us agree also on the avenues of approach to them. We take pride in our resolve to initiate and sustain a conversation regardless of ideological differences, to uphold our right respectfully to disagree, to empower our readers to pick up and extend the debate in a manner to invigorate and even consolidate the polyphony on which such initiatives must depend. For only through inclusive debate, contradistinctive examination, and rigorous research can peace and security studies help to beget an inclusive and conclusive betterment of the human condition.

This book can bring no distress to those who find comfort in the certainties and clarities afforded through their long-standing convictions. Nor can it bring instant relief to those too perplexed to be decisive as to what dispositions to take in any direction. In a world where nothing remains the same for long, may our enterprise mark the humble beginnings of a conversation among many disciplines and leanings in need of each other on the way to sanity and wisdom. This is a project that seeks to encourage the joint search for, and the shared discovery of, unbeaten paths likely to open up to even more promising, felicitous, and secure futures for all.

To those who will easily recognize themselves for having so steadfastly stood by me through thick and thin in the delicate and demanding span of this collaborative project, I dedicate here and now my true gratitude, my collegial respects, and my cordial thanks.

The Quest for Certainty and the Newer Equations of Security

JOSE V. CIPRUT

THE SEARCH FOR CERTAINTY

Born to a universe he could not understand, man survived and prevailed by interpreting it. Fear and anger he would experience long before he could even tell the difference. Eager to peg cause unto effect, he would find solace in reducing his circular doubts into linear certainties. In short order, he would learn to master and dominate by destroying perceived threats and by assimilating or annihilating identifiable foes.

Elevation and centrality would serve him well. From the top, he would command; from the center, he would control. His castles would rise from the highest hilltops; his cathedrals would stand tall in the middle of his capitals. In times of peace as in times of war, horizontal formations would be led by vertical chains of command; central governments would engage in high politics, so as to extend their reach to the farthest-flung of dominions. Science would come to occupy the nucleus of military technologies. Only the tallest ramparts would deliver the remotest unimpeded views. And summit and core would in due course predetermine the divides between prince and pauper, and between center and periphery.

Man's discovery of time would raise questions of beginnings and ends, of changes and continuities, altogether creating doubts about the past and uncertainties about the future, therefore also leading to disquieting obsessions with identity and distressing preoccupations with direction. Discovery of space, on the other hand, would contribute to another scale of values—one placing worth on plentifully endowed, neatly divisible, retainably defendable territories, offering the certainties of bountiful locus and the reassurances of ownership—depending on the bearable risks, the acceptable sacrifices, and any other sustainable costs. One would learn to acquire, defend, and perpetuate such possessions through suasion, whether by decree or force. Notions of order and border, top and center; versions of inside and outside would in time and space come to affect thinking and dictate action. The expeditive convenience of deterministic reductionisms would permeate the design and conduct of pursuits and undertakings in all domains—whether ethnocultural, socioeconomic, technoscientific, or geopolitical.

Man's purposive determination and opportunistic emancipation would exact a high toll, however. His passage from subservience to the preordained unto obedience to the superimposed, his onward transition to a stewardship of the willfully envisioned and the participatorily accomplished, would prove a prolonged ordeal for the few who could endure the odyssey, remaining a remote prospect for those still too dormant, too weak, or too hesitant to embark.

Between the eleventh and sixteenth centuries, West European epidemics and demographics, migration, urbanization, industrialization, and economic expansion, among others, would fuel interests and kindle passions conducive to far-flung crusades and commerce. A nascent bourgeoisie empowered by new skills and wealth, numerate-literate and scheming, would come to rival a self-imbued aristocracy and a politically ambitious clergy. Merchants, astronomers, engineers, and military geometricians would contribute to the acceleration of social reorganization through their daily practice of applied rationality in varied social contexts to diversely gainful ends.

In 1231, the geopolitically expedient Pope Gregory IX issued "a bull recognizing the University of Paris as a corporation under papal protection, buttressing the Institution's claim of exemption from local [episcopal] authority" (Crosby, 1997: 72). And in the fifteenth and sixteenth centuries, the treaties of Tordesillas (1494) and of Saragosa (1529) exclusively and exhaustively split the formerly known and the meanwhile discovered expanses of the world between Spain and Portugal with the holy blessings of Rome.

In the sixteenth century, Aristotle and Ptolemy's universe was to be turned "inside-out" by Copernicus (1473–1543) "snatching the earth from the center and replacing it with the sun" (Crosby, 1997: 103). But it would be for Giordano Bruno (1548–1600) to go up in flames for offending a world that to this day finds it spiritually disquieting and emotionally disturbing to face up to the realities of infinity, zeroness, chance, and indeterminacy.

Long after the Enlightenment, man's unrelenting search for the absolute, the complete, and the perfect—in the battlefield as in the arts and the sciences—his search for a higher design deep down in the unintelligible, would spur his empirical quest for an all-encompassing order and for a single underlying logic. Antiquity's philosophical interest in continuity and change, in beginnings and ends, in deviations and cycles, would ultimately yield the place of honor to post-quantic preoccupations with "the paradox of time"—first stumbled upon by the physicist Ludwig Boltzmann no earlier than the late 1800s.

In casting fundamental doubt on the existence of a premise such as the "arrow of time," Boltzmann's "paradox of time" would do for modern physics (Prigogine and Stengers, 1993) what William James's "dilemma of determinism" (James, 1896) would accomplish in the spheres of modern thought. Both would contribute to existential and ontological asking-abouts that would interrogate "whether the future is given or in perpetual construction" (Prigogine, 1996).

Emulating the methods that consolidated the preeminence of the natural sciences, the social sciences would quickly develop a taste for politically "objective," morally "neutral," "precisely" measurable, "completely" explicable, "perfectly" predictable true knowledge. The "positivist" pursuits of nineteenth-century luminaries—Saint-Simon, Neurath, Carnap, and Hahn among them—would even push for the "scientization of politics" (Keat, 1981: 29) in an urge to "reform" education, to pursue a "scientific world conception," and to permit "the unification of mankind" by a "new organization of economic and social relations."

Since then, the natural sciences have learned to reckon with the "random fluctuations," the likely "bifurcations," and the shifty "instabilities" inherent to dynamic systems. They have reconciled themselves with the uncertainties of "chaos," the idiosyncrasies of "dissipative structures." Might one not expect that the social sciences and the budding field of peace and security research may therefore also begin to warrant the thorough revision of acquired certainties? The very ones that feed the foundations and meanings of our ontological givens, of our epistemological approaches, not the least of our empirical pursuits, and especially our explanations?

Classical physics privileged order and stability, the better to retrodict the past and so predict the future from prespecified initial conditions (Prigogine and Rice, 1997). For much too long, physics claimed total knowledge and perfect predictability. The virtue of a new social science, and of our new certainties regarding peace and security, may henceforth depend on our sincere recognition of their indefinite perfectibility. Such sobering notions as inbuilt uncertainty and pregnant indeterminacy, which have enriched both the content and extent of the hard sciences, could ameliorate approaches, queries, and resultant understandings in our pursuits of contextualized perspectives of peace in security as well. They could endow our findings, preferences, decisions, and actions with a vision of the new possibilities being offered us by all that is not predetermined—and encourage us to notice the long-overlooked when rewriting our systemic equations of the yet-to-be-imagined.

THE NEWER SYSTEMIC ELEMENTS OF SECURITY

For the less endowed of this world who constitute the masses that have never heard of the laws of physics, or of the good that indeterminacy can do for them, it ought not be less reassuring that "the future is not a given"; that "far from constituting a defeat for the human mind" what *might* be out there may hold unimaginable hope for humanity if only for permitting to discover new horizons and hitherto forbidden insights, indispensable to the pursuits of self-governance and the conduct of peace. The time may have come for the knowing few to shed those facile certainties mounted on adversarial dichotomies inimically built on Cold-War simplicisms.

On his quest for certainty, Descartes (1596–1650) would seek refuge in rationality in order to cogitate a way out of darkness. Newton (1642–1727) would find the light in "the Laws of Nature." But unable to judge and unwilling to condemn a humanity that had brought upon itself the atrocities of a war to end all wars, the astromathematician Louis Fry Richardson (1887–1953) would prefer to devise what he was certain would constitute a value-neutral model, to measure security beyond good and evil. Acting out of a premise that "what has happened often is likely to happen again, whether we wish it or not," concluding therefore that a "seeking for persistent quantitative relations" in issues of international security should lead to the discovery of "the more fated and the less freely choosable forms of international behavior," the good in him would make him look for man's relational and situational dilemmas in the observational comforts of "what was mechanical" (Richardson, 1960a: xxxv; Richardson, 1960b).

Yesterday's mechanistic determinants of hate and despair, of unforgettable turmoil and unforgivable bloodshed, are making way for the compound systemic elements of the complex dynamic models that shall compose tomorrow's security equations. These variables will need to satisfy an array of increasingly enmeshing dimensions in a web of jointly yet autonomously evolving units of analysis, across embedded, overlapping, and emerging intersocietal spans, along fluid intraregional perspectives in labile global settings.

The new security equations will feed on two major sources of change and continuity from which they will derive their normative justifications, their operational rigor, and their new contextual relevance. First, along the military dimension, they will reflect the dynamic tenor of the conceptual, attitudinal, functional, and structural reforms under way in the domain of military doctrine. They will also incorporate the new thinking already emergent at the sources that give life, content, and form to the new security strategies. And they cannot remain oblivious to the concomitant and consequent realignments or to the complex new configurations initiated by the military-industrial establishments now obliged to rethink their longer-term interests within, between, and across their once strictly nationally defined span of activities. It is these newer intimacies among doctrine, strategy, and technological innovation that will bestow the needed adaptive flexibilities so essential to future military readiness. It is also they that will confer legitimacy of recourse, and impart efficacy of execution, to military interventions—should such become necessary as a last recourse, in due restraint, but with all the decisive precision, timely efficiency, and effective finality that the many real-time exigencies of the new battlefields would most certainly require.

Second, and especially along the nonmilitary dimension, the new security equations will have to account for the deeper local and global transformations and reconfigurations already occurring in humanity's aged scale of values and priority rankings specific to the exigencies of its internal, external, transactional, and eco-societal environments, on which depends a better quality of life on earth. For it is in the dynamic overlaps among these now increasingly interdependent environments that will arise the complex interactive dimensions of our insecurities—upheld, among others, by language, religion, politics, economics, ecology, technology, development, modernization, globalization, ethnonationalist rage and fervor, migration, terror, criminality and law—each and all of which offer motive, opportunity, and locus for military action.

The Military Dimension

Although our theme focuses on context, and as such primarily on the interactive nonmilitary dimensions of insecurity, within which the military options of tomorrow may likely find themselves inextricably embedded, it might be helpful for our readers if the military dimension of insecurity were briefly surveyed here, in the light of the new relationships now arising between doctrine, strategy, and technology in the military spheres of security.

In the decades ahead, the world may very well develop into a uni-pluripolar, multi-centric landscape in which an international division of labor among major powers committed to a global regime of security, on one hand; and a community of advanced and nascent regions engaged in competitive cooperation focusing on buying and selling, on modern development and participatory self-governance, on the other, may jointly lower the chances for inter-state wars.

If the new currency, the Euro, meets its objective function, a "United Europe" may well emerge from the "European Union" (EU). And if meanwhile the United Nations, too, completes its overhaul, its new Permanent Security Council may well come to consist of the United States as first-among-equals, the "UE" (represented by a single seat to be held in rotation; for starters, among a foursome consisting of Italy-Britain-France-Germany), Russia, China, and Japan. The novel Permanent Security Council may find good cause in collaboratively developing the legitimate, powerful, and modern wherewithal needed for a voluntary, integrated, and intersustainingly operational, rapid deployment force—capable of redisposing itself at shortest notice and of meeting any threat with a decisive finality suited to each event and venue.

The accession of a non-nuclear power like Japan to Permanent Security Council membership may set a precedent for China and for the EU to emulate in an era when SALT III is meant to reduce even further the nuclear arsenals still held by the United States and Russia.

The greatest menace to a state in general, and to a non-democratic state in particular, is likely to arise from the very confines of its own civil society. The world's preoccupation with local peace, regional stability, and global order is likely to focus on the dangers inherent in the cheaper and easier access to weaponizable chemical, biological, fissile materials by restive regimes with unsettled scores; on the increasing affordability of missile technologies; on the self-styled martyrs, mercenaries, stringers, and part-timers who—unlike foreign enemy states—can eviscerate societies from within, without leaving footprints. After all, the deadly effects of silent biological offensives usually become evident only after uneventful lags of 50 to 70 hours. And a portable nuclear device, if parachuted to a blast (Pincus, 1997: A4), may wipe out not only dirty fingerprints but each and every victim, witness, culprit, and alibi as well.

The fact that countries like Afghanistan, Pakistan, and India; Iran, Iraq, Libya, Saudi Arabia, Syria, United Arab Emirates and Yemen; and North and South Korea, among others are acquiring and developing ballistic missiles capable of chemical, biological, and (possibly) nuclear payloads and warheads (Arms Control Association, 1996; Cato Institute, 1998), instead of catering to the urgent vital needs of their societies, does not augur peace within or among those who clearly need it most. In addition to the deadly panics which they are meant to suscitate, any threats to open societies from vicarious attacks by vengeful states are likely to capitalize on their inherent capacity to coerce democratic states into societal closure—a way of life at odds with the extended freedoms enjoyed in enlightened human communities. And there is not very much, if anything at all, that even the most modern of armed forces could do to combat isolated acts of terror neither timely nor directly traceable to countries generally known or specifically suspected to encourage, pay for, or orchestrate such infamy.

The success of international regimes, such as the Biological and Toxin Weapons Convention, the Chemical Weapons Convention, the Nuclear Suppliers Group, the Australia Group, and even of the Nuclear Non-Proliferation Treaty itself, has not been notable. Controls of global proliferation in materials, technologies, and equipment may continue to succumb to the lucrative pursuits of those who supply, and to the political machinations of those who for some reason remain intent on acquiring such by any means at any price. It is not simply or overnight that a range of credibly organized, jointly deployable military capabilities can be raised to institutionalize the solidary determination of the world's new leadership to conduct an activist collective security policy with the demonstrably clear intents of ensuring world stability, of deterring transnational threats to a region's longer-term peace, and of thwarting lowly death blows to the communal texture of any society's livelihood (cf. U.S. Defense Science Board, 1997; Cato Institute, 1998).

Ample literature exists on the military dimensions of change and continuity—whether in military doctrine, security strategy, or attending policy worldviews. Most writings on the sources and avenues of change in military doctrine (Johnsen, 1998; Dunnigan, 1996; Schneider and Grinter, 1995; Pfaltzgraff et al., 1988; Posen, 1984); those on modifications in strategic thinking (Kaufmann and Steinbrunner, 1991; Rearden, 1984; Westing, 1980); as well as on the issues of security strategy (Twining, 1992; Raevsky, 1993), cover a variety of perspectives—ranging from the national (White House, 1995) and regional (Ellings and Simon, 1996; Bellows, 1994; Gaertner 1992) to the collective (Chernoff, 1995) and conceptual (Carter, Perry, and Steinbrunner, 1992)—including many alternatives (Hollins, Powers, and Sommers, 1989).

Much of the extant literature on the future of security provides general, collective, or comparative perspectives useful to readers seeking to study security from military viewpoints (Butfoy, 1997; Dark, 1996; Davis, 1996; Murray and Viotti, 1994; Geiger et al., 1993). An even better grasp of the complex web of non-military settings in which the military dimension is intricately enmeshed will result from the chapters that follow. But whether viewed from specific national perspectives (Kokoshin, 1998; Brown, 1997; Bluth, 1995; Cimbala, 1995; Allison, 1993); seen from the angle of future order and stability (Scowcroft, Woolsey, and Etzold, 1988; Snow, 1994, 1995, 1999); of alliances (Gompert and Larrabee, 1997; Snyder, 1997; Colson, 1995); of institutional security compacts (Peters, 1996; Holland, 1997; Haftendorn, Keohane, and Wallander, 1999; Hong, 1997); or of regional considerations (Henk and Metz, 1997; Inoguchi and Stillman, 1997; Leifer, 1996; Lotter and Peters, 1996), the select literature on the military dimension—cited here in the intention of those who need to brush up on them, the better to appreciate the new exigencies of the non-military settings discussed in this volume—is useful.

No less relevant to our subject are the newer links between changing military doctrine, evolving security strategy, and the corresponding realignments within the military-industrial base. The literature here has grown in several directions to include the "peace dividend" perspective adopted in the aftermath of the Cold War, and the dismantlement and reconversion into civilian uses of decommissioned military bases (Cassidy and Bischak, 1993). The integration of civil-military potentials (OTA, 1991, 1994); the future interrelations among technology, strategy, and doctrine (Gordon,

1981; Pfaltzgraff et al., 1988; Margiotta and Sanders, 1985), the military significance of the new and emerging technologies (Gasparini, 1992; O'Neill, 1985; Gordon, 1981), and also of their international dynamics (Sanders, 1983) constitute other essential aspects that can provide even more insights for those interested.

Finally, over the last 25 years, concerns with the rise and demise of military-industrial establishments, with their ability to realign to the new realities, have been addressed from a range of theoretical (Rosen, 1973), conceptual (Sarkesian, 1972), even critical (Conca and Lipschutz, 1993; U.S. President's Council, 1992; Tolchin and Tolchin, 1992; Kemme, 1991; Tsagolov, 1985; Devkinandan, 1974; Lens, 1970) and contextual (Roberts, 1996) points of view. Clearly, these, too, should not be overlooked by those seeking broader understandings.

The Non-Military Dimension

Although the civilian society–security nexus has also been examined with an eye to the future (Schulz, 1998; Bebler, 1997; Rosecrance and Stein, 1993; Berki, 1986), non-military aspects of insecurity have been scrutinized mainly by those concerned with the fate of countries incapable of mustering effective military might (Singh and Vekaric, 1990), as well as by those opposing the military option on organizational (UNESCO, 1995) or philosophical grounds (Dunn and Staudenmaier, 1985). Our interdisciplinary volume attempts to fill this particular void, differently.

RATIONALE, ORGANIZATION, AND CONTENTS OF THIS VOLUME

It is the objective of this work to fill a gap, by engaging an array of experts, each from a different if related discipline, and to address the complex interactive dimensions of insecurity in a globalizing international political economy nearing a threshold.

We bring together all of the major contextual dimensions of change referred to in the aforegoing. We interrelate them in one and the same complex web that constitutes the human universe in which the quest for certainty and the search for security take effect. We entrust our experts with the responsibilities of free expression of the what, how, and why of past, present, and future, in virtue of their differing worldviews and perspectives. This collective effort seeks to engage our readership to join in that ongoing debate, lest what remains unspoken impede or retard the advent of the legal institutions, the collaborative regimes, and the multinational compacts urgently needed for transforming human exigencies and societal behaviors in ways essential to the timely design of a voluntarily peaceful, stably secure, and humane world.

Language and Theory

The road from implicit otherness to explicit alienation is often a short one, paved with the most reputable of theories in the social sciences. Chapter 1 shows how social theories can very often unsocially generate and shape the otherness of those they theorize into being. Is it not strange that political science has for so long found so little to say on this—ironically, eminently political—process, which the act of social theorizing constitues and embodies. Krippendorff shows how commonly the theorizing of an Other can engender distant otherness, even trivialize Others by reducing them into subservient mechanisms; how such practice can impose its monologism on everything that it touches; how it can nurture a culture of blindness vis-à-vis the political nature of social theory. The author touches upon the insecurities and the violent responses that such only seemingly benign theoretical practice can and does inflict on societal entities. He voices the urgent need for much greater accountability in the languaging of social science theory. He calls for an end to this unwarranted and unbecoming imposition of anachronic elitistic condescendence, reminiscent of an intellectual imperialism of sorts that results in little truth, if much alienation. Far from suggesting that the project of the social sciences is doomed, he sees an opportunity for a fresh start, for a new theoretical enterprise that would not dismiss or gratuitously silence the meek voices of those who impart life to the very phenomena which the social sciences seek to understand. This is a call for a more constructive dialogue between theorizer and theorized. It is an invitation for honesty to begin at home—on the theorist's own mind and computer screen.

The extant literature examines the language-security nexus from different points of view, including the implications for national security of language competence (Mueller, 1986); and the import of free speech in matters of national security (Shetreet, 1991) and culture (Smith, 1998; Wright, 1995). Rather, even a reader only barely familiar with the teachings of Saussure (1949, 1968) and Bakhtin (1984, 1990, 1993) will be able to savor in our first chapter a semioticist's security-pertinent allusions to "parole" as distinct from "langue," to the critical nexus between "speaker and situation," to the evolutionary nature of language as it shapes and it is shaped by culture through act, in dialogical relationships developed within polyphonic settings.

Diplomacy and War

Among a plethora of historic accounts ranging from the rise and fall of major powers to the advent of crises and war, once in a while a book appears that combines what Krippendorff and Conroy achieve in their chapters—dissecting the evolution of bad events from the point of view, and through the very words and acts, of the participants themselves (Hume, 1994; Cot,

1996; Danopoulos and Mersas, 1997). Chapter 2 offers a diplomatic historian's fine insights on the sweeping changes that have taken place over time and space in the perceptions, ideations, approaches, and pursuits of Realpolitik in (inter)national security-related matters. The example from East Asia illustrates the issues, fears, threats, and concerns of significance in the theory and practice of security diplomacy. A historian's grasp of global changes and continuities through the practice of diplomacy, subsumed in a subtle regional example, is shared with the reader in an often vibrant narrative of how deep alienation can turn into enmity, and contribute to hate and war, when international diplomacy is shaped by interpersonal chemistry. The diplomatic ties between Japan and Korea and those thereafter between Japan and the United States are insightfully interlinked.

Religion and Politics

The conjunction of religion and politics in national and in international settings is continuing to exhibit novel dimensions, auguring even newer implications for continuity and change in the evolving landscape of a globalizing political economy (Childress et al., 1991; Appelby, 1994; Haught, 1995; Wright, 1995; Turpin and Kurtz, 1997). The variegated impacts remain contingent on region and religion, even as the inputs continue to retain much in common (Choquette, 1975; Gernet, 1985; Levine, 1986; Ahanotu, 1992; Allen, 1992).

Across several chapters, we examine the security threats and promises embodied in the growing tensions and contentions between organized universal religions and worldwide secular developments. Except perhaps in theocracies, church-state relations have almost always created some tension inside national political boundaries. As transnational process and universal revolution, globalization now threatens the spiritual peace and religious identity of those who find solace in creeds that bond them beyond physical borders, and this is suscitating the opposition of the largest organized religions, which perceive a threat in the ongoing secularization. Comparatively tracing these potential conflicts to their origins and implications, one can see how anti-"Westernism" may follow.

Information and Power

The important societal inputs and political economic impacts of the Information Revolution has raised issues of security with many industrial, civilian, and military implications (Bohn, 1968; Clarkson, 1981; Schwartzstein, 1996).

In Chapter 3, Hart and Kim scrutinize the security-relevant societal effects of advanced technology. They conceptualize the threats, the new promises, and the ensuing implications of profuse information for the more traditional notions of "power" in times of swift and sweeping technological transformation, such as the period under way. They identify the institutional and cultural elements embedded in the information technologies. In addition, they examine why the transfer of technologies across national boundaries may become more problematic for, and more threatening to, the might of power across a globalizing international political economy.

Economics and Development

The security-related analysis of the links between economics and development provides a fascinating terrain for exploration in a field that has been known mainly to produce literature on gun-and-butter issues (Aganbegyan, 1988; Pascall and Lamson, 1991; Segal and Yang, 1996); Cold-War and post–Cold-War [re]configurations (Melman, 1974; Bischak, 1991; Markusen and Judken, 1992) and on the political economy of defense (Lee, 1995; Ross, 1991), with only exceptional or circumstantial attention to security in a global perspective (Kapstein, 1992).

Thus, in Chapter 4, Lord focuses on the rise of the younger economic powers in the post–Cold-War period, inquiring what is to be made of the older notions of "economic security"; what the new challenges of that concept may bode and why. She examines the few responses that states may possibly develop in addressing the new perceptions and interpretations of such threats. Compared to the purportedly alarming but in reality rather secure relative status of the more advanced nations, poor and developing countries are likely to set more difficult security challenges for themselves and for others on an interdependently evolving global marketplace.

Ecology and Peace

Their effect on intrasocietal development and intersocietal stability aside (Markley and Bagley, 1975; Conca and Lipschutz, 1993; Blake et al., 1997), security and ecology are often connected in writings about national insecurity (Renner, 1989; Rao and Sharma, 1991) and regional disorder (Hjort and Salih, 1989), as well as in relation to concerns with peace in a tumultuous world (Beckmann, 1983; Schuman and Sweig, 1991).

In Chapter 5, Dalby surveys the ongoing debates about environmental security and discovers that many of them are built on a range of presumptions, including those of the "efficacy" of states, the "expandability" of extant theory, and the "manageability" of even unsuspected threats through "simple" recourse to existing means. These gratuitous presumptions tend to underestimate and even overlook the complex and interactive causal mechanisms that underlie almost all symptomatic manifestations. In this chapter, Dalby demonstrates why a sweeping rethinking of our increasingly globalizing environmental problems is not only necessary but also urgent, lest what are now foreseeably serious threats ultimately transform themselves into life-threatening menaces conducive to violent crises, armed outbursts, and even full-fledged war.

Modernization and Democracy

Modernity, security, and order (Latham, 1997); the societal, (inter)national, and regional impacts of military modernization (Tamkoç, 1976; Demchak, 1991; U.S. General Accounting Office, 1995) and the effect of modernity on stable development (Plascov, 1982; Miklos, 1983); democracy, security, and development in specific countries (Thomas, 1996) or regions (Abdul Hafiz and Rahman Khan, 1990; Khanna, 1997); modern armaments and democratic rule of law (Russett, 1990; Michel, 1995; Roche, 1996); and the problems of modern security across a globalizing landscape (Mussington, 1994; Simon, 1997; Boissonnat et al., 1997; Garrett, 1998) are but a few of the myriad perspectives amply covered by this fecund branch of study.

In a cognizant stance, Teune's chapter observes that linked to freedom, "modernization"—the preeminent force for change in groups and markets for over three centuries—has tended to wane as democratic political development became ascendant amidst the processes of globalization. He suggests that this robust ascent tends to weaken national governments' proclivities to territorial control and war. He equates the dynamics of democratization to a second democratic revolution, which seems to have re-divided the world between the new-or-weak and old-or-readapting democracies: the former, preoccupied by the demand for institutions of popular sovereignty; the latter, by calls for far greater accountability. As conflicts seem to be shifting from among states to within and between groups, the spread of democracy, for Teune, presents a new and welcome occasion for globally replacing the more traditional institutions of international peacekeeping as well. He does not exclude, however, the element of war as a factor integral to change.

Globalization and Emancipation

In Chapter 7, Chase-Dunn offers an ideologized world-systems perspective on globalization. He engages the reader to compare the trajectories of several types of globalization over the last 100 years and to reconsider the factors at play in the increasing public references to "global" processes in everyday talk. We are shown how discrete dimensions of globalization may assume varying temporal paths, some progressing upward or downward while others undergo cyclical oscillations. Noting a lag between the economic and the political/cultural globalization processes, Chase-Dunn contends that an effective way of converting "casino capitalism" into a more humane transactional regime attuned to a sustainably more democratic and balanced world society would be to dissipate that lag on a truly global basis. He perceives a potential for redemption in the global practice of redefined social democracy. His radical ideological program is eminently debatable, however.

Migration and Order

Most of the security concerns about migration issues on a global basis (Weiner, 1993) involve especially center-periphery (Haglund, 1995), East-West (Waever et al., 1993) and North-South (Muni and Baral, 1996) relations. And many of these voice the North's viewpoints.

In contrast, Chapter 8, by Lohrmann and Guerra, provides us with a comparative analytic synthesis of international migration flows that only years of fieldwork—enabling the reconciliation of theory with practice—can so thoroughly afford. After a brief retrospective of the makings, trends, and implications of human displacement, emigration, and immigration across time and space, their chapter dwells on the recent debates that link international migration to national security issues. Existing measures and countermeasures are assessed, and the prospects for alternative means and untried strategies are debated in global context. Older definitions and perceptions—of fear, threat, security; and of development at the local, regional, and global levels of analysis—are challenged in the awareness of the new contexts and tenors of "security" now arising.

Ethnicity and Nationalism

In Chapter 9, Riggs discusses the role of the modernizing state as a driving force for industrialization, democratization, and nationalism. He observes the complex interdependencies that hinge each of these three processes on the other two, and he notes the permutations and combinations that can lead to mixed results and idiosyncratic consequences. Among the outcomes, he identifies the class conflicts and communist authoritarianisms ensuing from the Industrial Revolution and from urbanization—both of which he sees to be the consequences of raw capitalism in the service of imperialism, conducive to state nationalism and to the inevitable ultimate collapse of centrally planned despotic versions of state capitalism. Riggs argues that "quasi-democratic experiments"—by ethnic minorities in charge of weak authoritarian states enslaved to "para-modern" settings—can beget a variety of ethnonational countermovements pregnant of violent fundamentalisms that favor less or more active forms of dissent (from civil disobedience to ethnic cleansing). He submits that fuller recognition of the interactive complexities underlying such phenomena should provide a useful first step toward discovering viable solutions to these globally local and locally global problems, without waging war.

In the literature to date on the compound topic of security and (ethno)nationalism, the focus is usually on conflict (Brown, 1997), and most writings concentrate on a specific area (Brown, 1992; Misra, 1995; Brown and Ganguly, 1997; Chadda, 1997). Seldom is the query formulated along the all-encompassing security context thematically probed by Riggs in this chapter.

Transnational Terror and Organized Crime

There is a large body of literature on terror (Gearty, 1991) and terrorism (Guelke, 1995; Wieviorka, 1995; Combs, 1997); much material also exists on notorious terrorists and their acts. The meanings and implications of terrorism are no less belabored from myriad relational points, whether in connection to espionage and smuggling (Martin and Romano, 1992); to crimes affecting a state's security (Sinka, 1995); to proliferation (Tanter, 1998); to national security (Pelletiere, 1995); or to nuclear anarchy (Allison, 1996).

The link of terrorism to technology, too, has received ample attention (Kemme, 1991; Office of Technology Assessment, 1991, 1992; Tolchin and Tolchin, 1992; Wilkinson, 1993), although the connections between transnational terror and globalizing crime need even more elucidation than so far offered by international security-related reports on organized crime (Sterling, 1994; Webster et al., 1997).

In globalizing settings where criminality discovers formerly unimaginable paths of access to high technology, terrorism could even more affordably reward the less endowed among the vengeful. In Chapter 10, Johnston—who took part in the making of the Center for Strategic and International Studies Final Report on Global Organized Crime (Webster et al., 1997)—examines the nexus between technology and proliferation and its import for terror and organized crime on the global market. He analyzes the complex relations among terrorism, corruption and crime (black markets, money laundering, drugs-for-arms swaps) in periods of change when violent dissent stands to gain from crises that facilitate illicit complicities of real and potential threat to international security, regional peace, and global order.

The dual pursuits of marketization and democratization that have helped expand economic growth and political freedoms in the emerging markets have also weakened the authoritarian structures that used to suppress crime, corruption, and terrorism. In the absence of the institutions and mechanisms needed for effective and accountable enforcement of the rule of law, civic awakenings—in such emerging market nations as Brazil, China, Mexico, Poland, Russia, South Africa, and Turkey—are being retarded to the disadvantage of all.

For the industrialized world, the problems in the emerging markets represent more than just a greater risk for investment and commerce. The terrorist and criminal groups, which originate in the virtual safe havens incorporated by the emerging markets, take advantage of globalizing forces to collect far speedier and more substantive political and economic rewards in the democratic countries. Advances in communications technology, global economic deregulation, lowered borders, and correlated human displacements jointly facilitate the ascent of transnational networks of terror and organized crime of which singly they are not a direct source.

Networks of organized crime and transnational terrorism are spreading quickly not only because they breed faster in the law-defying environments provided by the emerging markets but because industrially advanced democracies have moved much too slowly in responding through transnational intelligence and law enforcement mechanisms and legal/judicial institutions of their own. The late progress marked by the appearance of transnational expert groups awaits the advent of meaningfully robust transnational mechanisms apt to counter these threats at a level still choked by vestigial national interests, misguided interpretations of sovereignty, and petty versions of trade advocacy. This domain of preoccupation is thus ideally suited for new configurations of collective defense, in verifiable forms of voluntary and participatory collaboration among the weak, the mighty, the rich, and the poor. And that may place the military dimension centrally within the compound non-military complexities of a globalizing international political economy.

International Law and Global Jurisdiction

Lastly, in Chapter 11, Hazard weighs the limitations of international laws and of multinational institutions (including their attendant law enforcement agencies) in the efforts made toward coping with the mounting challenges of transnational crimes in global theaters of operation. Dwelling on the new international exigencies of legal order and on the difficulties intrinsic to the globalization of jurisdictions, he draws general lessons and provides specific examples from the early U.S. experience with federalism, to suggest how a globalizing world community of nations might ultimately elect to handle specific transnational violations—ranging from money laundering to contraband of drugs and weapons to terrorism. At stake are shown to be the sustainable viability of national and international legislative institutions, and the very promise and meaning of order, stability, and peace—inside as well as outside of political borders, beyond the jealous purview of sovereignty.

And so ends our introduction to the 11 chapters that follow. Language, religion, and information can politically both integrate and fragment peoples within and beyond a state's confines. And so may industrialization, modernization, and globalization beget social and economic disparities likely to fan anger, foment violence, and foster terror inside and outside of political borders. Without the proper political organization, legislative/judicial institutions, and their law enforcement agencies, development and democracy are impeded, and globalizing settings remain vulnerable to the threats of newer transnational realities in a world equipped to address the national interest and to confront only the international crises endangering it (Stephan and Klimenko, 1991; Frank, 1992; Roberts, 1996). In a global setting, transnational threats to stable order and peace cannot be fought decisively on national or international military dimensions: The nature and future of war await to be reimagined.

REFERENCES

Abdul Hafiz, M., and Mizanur Rahman Khan (eds.) (1990). *Development, Politics, and Security: Third World Contest.* Dhaka: Bangladesh Institute of International and Strategic Studies.

Aganbegyan, Abel (1988). *Inside Perestroika.* New York: Harper and Row.

Ahanotu, Austin M. (ed.) (1992). *Religion, State, and Society in Contemporary Africa: Nigeria, Sudan, South Africa, Zaire, and Mozambique.* New York: P. Lang.

Allen, Douglass (ed.) (1992). *Religion and Political Conflict in Latin America.* Chapel Hill: University of North Carolina Press.

Allison, Graham T. (1996). *Avoiding Nuclear Anarchy: Containing the Threat of Loose Russian Nuclear Weapons and Fissile Materials.* Cambridge, MA: MIT Press.

Allison, Ray (1993). *Military Forces in the Soviet Successor States: An Analysis of the Military Policies, Force Dispositions and Evolving Threat Perceptions of the Former Soviet States.* London: Brassey's for International Institute for Strategic Studies.

Appelby, R. Scott (1994). *Religious Fundamentalisms and Global Conflict.* New York: Foreign Policy Association.

Arms Control Association (1996). *Arms Control Today* (March): 29–30.

———, and Systems Planning Corporation (1992). *Ballistic Missile Proliferation: An Emerging Threat,* re-edited in Cato Institute (1998), *Policy Analysis,* No. 309, June 22.

Bakhtin, Mikhail Mikhailovich (1984). *Problems of Dostoevsky's Poetics* (Cary Emerson, ed. and trans.) Minneapolis: University of Minnesota Press.

——— (1990). *Art and Answerability: Early Philosophical Essays* (Michael Holquist and Vadim Liapunov, eds). Austin: University of Texas Press.

——— (1993). *Toward a Philosophy of the Act* (Michael Holquist and Vadim Liapunov, eds.). Austin: University of Texas Press.

Bebler, Anton A. (ed.) (1997). *Civil-Military Relations in Post-Communist States: Central and Eastern Europe in Transition.* Westport, CT: Praeger.

Beckmann, Arnim (ed.) (1983). *Umwelt braucht Frieden.* Frankfurt: Fischer Verlag.

Bellows, Michael D. (1994). *Asia in the 21st Century: Evolving Strategic Priorities.* Washington, DC: National Defense University Press.

Berki, R. N. (1986). *Security and Society: Reflection on Law, Order, and Politics.* New York: St. Martin's Press.

Bischak, Gregory (ed.) (1991). *Toward a Peace Economy in the United States*. New York: St. Martin's Press.

Blake, Gerald et al. (eds.) (1997). *International Boundaries and Environmental Security: Frameworks for Regional Cooperation*. London and Boston: Kluwer Law International.

Bluth, Christoph (1995). *The Collapse of Soviet Military Power*. Aldershot, UK, and Brookfield, VT: Dartmouth Publishing Co.

Bohn, Lewis C. (1968). *Information Technology in Development*. Croton-on-Hudson, NY: Hudson Institute.

Boissonnat, Jean et al. (1997). *Entre Mondialisation et Nations: Quelle Europe?* Semaines Sociales de France. Paris: Bayard Editions/Centurion.

Brown, J. F. (1992). *Nationalism, Democracy, and Security in the Balkans*. Aldershot, UK, and Brookfield, VT: Dartmouth Publishing Co.

Brown, Michael E. (1997). *Nationalism and Ethnic Conflict*. Cambridge, MA: MIT Press.

————, and Sumit Ganguly (eds.) (1997). *Government Policies and Ethnic Relations in Asia and the Pacific*. Cambridge, MA: MIT Press.

Butfoy, Andrew (1997). *Common Security and Strategic Reform: A Critical Analysis*. Basingstoke, UK, and New York: St. Martin's Press.

Carter, Ashton B., William J. Perry, and John D. Steinbrunner (1992). *A New Concept of Cooperative Security*. Washington, DC: Brookings Institution.

Cassidy, Kevin J., and Gregory A. Bischak (eds.) (1993). *Real Security: Converting the Defense Economy and Building Peace*. Albany, NY: SUNY Press.

Cato Institute (1998). Theater Missile Defense. *Policy Analysis* No. 309, June 22.

Chadda, Maya (1997). *Ethnicity, Security and Separatism in India*. New York: Columbia University Press.

Chernoff, Fred (1995). *After Bipolarity: The Vanishing Threat, Theories of Cooperation, and the Future of the Atlantic Alliance*. Ann Arbor: University of Michigan Press.

Childress, James F. et al. (1991). *The American Search for Peace: Moral Reasoning, Religious Hope, and National Security*. Washington, DC: Georgetown University Press.

Choquette, Robert (1975). *Language and Religion: A History of English-French Conflict in Ontario*. Ottawa: University of Ottawa Press.

Cimbala, Stephen J. (1995). *Collective Insecurity: US Defense Policy and the New World Disorder*. Westport, CT: Greenwood Press.

Clarkson, Albert (1981). *Toward Effective Strategic Analysis: New Applications of Information Technology*. Boulder, CO: Westview Press.

Colson, Bruno (1995). *Europe, Repenser les Alliances*. Paris: Institut de Strategie Comparée (Economica).

Combs, Cindy C. (1997). *Terrorism in the Twenty-First Century*. Upper Saddle River, NJ: Prentice-Hall.

Conca, Ken (1997). *Manufacturing Insecurity: The Rise and Fall of Brazil's Military-Industrial Complex*. Boulder, CO: Lynne Rienner.

————, and Ronnie D. Lipschutz (eds.) (1993). *The State and Social Power in Global Environmentatl Politics*. New York: Columbia University Press.

Cot, Jean, with Cecile Monot (1996). *Dernière Guerre Balkanique? Ex-Yougoslavie—*

Témoignages, Analyses, Perspectives. Fondation pour les Etudes de Defense. Paris: L'Harmattan.

Crosby, Alfred W. (1997). *The Measure of Reality: Quantification and Western Society, 1250–1600*. New York: Cambridge University Press

Danopoulos, Constantine P., and Kostas G. Mersas (1997). *Crises in the Balkans: Views from the Participants*. Boulder, CO: Westview Press.

Dark, Ken R. (ed.) (1996). *New Studies in Post–Cold War Security*. Aldershot, UK, and Brookfield, VT: Dartmouth Publishing Co.

———, with A. L. Harris (1996). *The New World and the New World Order: US Relative Decline, Domestic Instability in the Americas and the End of the Cold War*. Basingstoke, UK: Macmillan Press; New York: St. Martin's Press.

Davis, M. Jane (ed.) (1996). *Security Issues in the Post–Cold War World*. Brookfield, VT: Edward Elgar.

Demchak, Chris C. (1991). *Military Organizations, Complex Machines: Modernization in the U.S. Armed Services*. Ithaca, NY: Cornell University Press.

Devkinandan, S. (1974). *How China May Use Atom Bomb: 7 Military Scenarios*. Delhi: New Century Books.

Dunn, Keith A., and William O. Staudenmeier (eds.) (1984). *Military Strategy in Transition: Defense and Deterrence in the 1980s*. Boulder, CO: Westview Press.

Dunnigan, James F. (1996). *Digital Soldiers: The Evolution of High-Tech Weaponry and Tomorrow's Brave Battlefield*. New York: St. Martin's Press.

Edgar, Alastair D., and David G. Haglund (1995). *The Canadian Defence Industry in the New Global Environment*. Montreal: McGill–Queens University Press.

Ellings, Richard J., and Sheldon Simon (1996). *Southeast Asian Security in the New Millennium*. Armonk, NY: M. E. Sharpe.

Frank, Thomas M. (1992). *Political Questions/Judicial Answers: Does the Rule of Law Apply to Foreign Affairs?* Princeton, NJ: Princeton University Press.

Gaertner, Heinz (1992). *Wird Europa Sicherer? Zwischen Kollektiver und Nationaler Sicherheit*. Wien: Braumueller fuer Oe.I.I.P.

Garrett, Geoffrey (1998). *Partisan Politics in the Global Economy*. Cambridge: Cambridge University Press.

Gasparini, Alves Pericles (1992). *Access to Outer Space Technologies: Implications for International Security*. New York: UN Institute for Disarmament Research.

Gearty, Conor A. (1991). *Terror*. London and Boston: Faber and Faber.

Geiger, Michaela and associates (1993). *Strategien fuer die Zukunft: Brauchen wir ein neues Denken in der Sicherheitspolitik?* Gruenwald, Germany: Atverb. Verlag (for Hans Seidel Foundation).

Gernet, Jacques (1985). *Chine et Christianisme*. Paris: Editions de la Maison des Sciences de l'Homme.

Gompert, David C., and F. Stephen Larrabee (eds.) (1997). *America and Europe: A partnership for a New Era*. Cambridge, UK, and New York: Cambridge University Press.

Gordon, Don E. (1981). *Electronic Warfare: Element of Strategy and Multiplier of Combat Power*. New York: Pergamon Press.

Guelke, Adrian (1995). *The Age of Terrorism and the International Political System*. London and New York: Tauris Academic Studies, I. B. Tauris Publications.

Haftendorn, Helga, Robert O. Keohane, and Celeste A. Wallander (eds.) (1999).

Imperfect Unions: Security Institutions over Time and Space. New York: Oxford University Press.

Haglund, David G. (ed.) (1995). *The Center-Periphery Debate in International Security*. Kingston, Ontario: Center for International Relations, Queen's University and L. B. Pearson CIPTC.

Haught, James R. (1995). *Holy Hatred: Religious Conflicts of the 90's*. Amherst, NY: Prometheus Books.

Henk, Dan, and Steven Metz (1997). *The United States and the Transformation of African Security: The African Crisis Response Initiative and Beyond*. Carlisle Barracks, PA: Strategic Studies Institute, U.S. Army War College.

Hjort, Anders, and M. A. Mohamed Salih (1989). *Ecology and Politics: Environmental Stress and Security in Africa*. Uppsala, Sweden: Scandinavian Institute of African Studies.

Holland, Martin (1997). *Common Foreign and Security Policy: The Record and Reforms*. London and Washington, DC: Pinter.

Hollins, Harry, Averill Powers, and Mark Sommers (eds.) (1989). *The Conquest of War: Alternative Strategies for Global Security*. Boulder, CO: Westview Press.

Hong, Ki-Joon (1997). *The CSCE Security Regime Formation: An Asian Perspective*. Basingstoke, UK: Macmillan; New York: St. Martin's Press.

Hume, Cameron R. (1994). *The United Nations, Iran and Iraq: How Peacemaking Changed*. Bloomington: Indiana University Press.

Inoguchi, Takashi, and Grant B. Stillman (eds.) (1997). *North-east Asian Regional Security: The Role of International Institutions*. Tokyo and New York: United Nations University Press.

James, William (1896). The Dilemma of Determinism. In *The Will to Believe*. New York and and London: Longman's.

Johnsen, William Thomas (1998). *Force Planning Considerations for Army XXI*. Carlisle Barracks, PA: Strategic Studies Institute, U.S. Army War College.

Kapstein, Ethan B. (1992). *The Political Economy of National Security: A Global Perspective*. New York: McGraw-Hill.

Kaufmann, William K., and J. Steinbrunner (1991). *Decision for Defense: Prospects for a New Order*. Washington, DC: Brookings Institution.

Keat, Russel (1981). *The Politics of Social Theory: Habermas, Freud and the Critique of Positivism*. Chicago: University of Chicago Press.

Kemme, David M. (1991). *Technology Markets and Export Controls in the 1990s*. New York: New York University Press.

Khanna, D. D. (ed.) (1997). *Sustainable Development: Environmental Security, Disarmament, and Development Interface in South Asia*. New Delhi: Macmillan India.

Kokoshin, Andrei A. (1998). *Soviet Strategic Thought, 1971–91*. Cambridge, MA: The MIT Press.

Latham, Robert (1997). *The Liberal Moment: Modernity, Security, and the Making of Postwar International Order*. New York: Columbia University Press.

Lee, David (1995). *Search for Security: The Political Economy of Australia's Postwar Foreign and Defence Policy*. St. Leonard's, NSW, Australia: Allen and Unwin in collaboration with RSPAS, ANU.

Leifer, Michael (1996). *The ASEAN Regional Forum: Extending ASEAN's Model of*

Regional Security. Oxford and New York: Oxford University Press, for International Institute of Strategic Studies, Adelphi Paper No. 302.

Lens, Sidney (1970). *The Military-Industrial Complex*. Philadelphia: Pilgrim Press.

Levine, Daniel H. (ed.) (1986). *Religion and Political Conflict in Latin America*. Chapel Hill: University of North Carolina Press.

Lotter, Christof and Susanne Peters (eds.) (1996). *The Changing European Security Environment*. Weimar: Boehlau (Jenaer Beitraege: Bds. zur Politikwissenschaft).

Margiotta, Franklin D. and Ralph Sanders (eds.) (1985). *Technology, Strategy, and National Security*. Washington, DC: National Defense University.

Markley, O. W., and Marilyn D. Bagley (1975). *Minimum Standards for Quality of Life*. Washington, DC: Office of Research and Development, U.S. Environmental Protection Agency 600/5-75012.

Markusen, Ann, and Joel Judken (1992). *Dismantling the Cold War Economy*. New York: Basic Books.

Martin, John M., and Anne T. Romano (1992). *Multinational Crime: Terrorism, Espionage, Drug and Arms Trafficking*. Newbury Park, CA: Sage Publications.

Matthews, Lloyd J. (ed.) (1998). *Challenging the United States Symmetrically and Asymmetrically: Can America Be Defeated?* Carlisle Barracks, PA: Strategic Studies Institute, U.S. Army War College.

Melman, Seymour (1974). *The Permanent War Economy*. New York: Simon and Schuster.

Michel, Andre (1995). *Surarmement, Pouvoirs, Democratie*. Paris: L'Harmattan, 1995.

Miklos, Jack C. (1983). *The Iranian Revolution and Modernization: Way Stations to Anarchy*. Washington, DC: National Defense University Press.

Misra, S. S. (1995). *Ethnic Conflict and Security Crisis in Sri Lanka*. Delhi: Kalinga Publications.

Mueller, Milton (1986). *The Currency of the Word: War, Revolution, and the Temporal Coordination of Literate Media in England, 1608–1655*. Master's Thesis in Communication, Annenberg School of Communication, the University of Pennsylvania.

Muni, S. D., and Lok Raj Baral (eds.) (1996). *Refugees and Regional Security in South Asia*. New Delhi, India: Konark Publishers.

Murray, Douglas J., and Paul R. Viotti (eds.) (1994). *The Defense Policy of Nations: A Comparative Study*. 3rd ed. Baltimore, MD: The Johns Hopkins University Press.

Mussington, David (1994). *Arms Unbound: The Globalization of Defense Production*. Washington, DC: Brassey's.

Office of Technology Assessment (OTA), U.S. Congress (1991). *Adjusting to a New Security Environment: The Defense Technology and Industrial Base Challenge*. Washington, DC: U.S. Government Printing Office.

——— (1992). *Technology Against Terrorism: Structuring Security*. Washington, DC: U.S. Government Printing Office.

——— (1994). *Assessing the Potential for Civil-Military Integration: Technologies, Processes, and Practices*. Washington, DC: U.S. Government Printing Office.

O'Neill, Robert J. (ed.) (1985). *New Technology and Western Security Policy*. Hamden, CT: Archon Books.

Pascall, Glenn R., and Robert D. Lamson (1991). *Beyond Guns and Butter: Recapturing America's Economic Momentum after a Military Decade.* Washington, DC: Brassey's.

Pelletiere, Stephen C. (ed.) (1995). *Terrorism: National Security Policy and the Home Front.* Carlisle Barracks, PA: Strategic Studies Institute, U.S. Army War College.

Peters, Ingo (ed.) (1996). *New Security Challenges: The Adaptation of International Institutions—Reforming the UN, NATO, the EU, and CSCE since 1989.* New York: St. Martin's Press.

Pfaltzgraff, R. L., Jr., et al. (eds.) (1988). *Emerging Doctrines and Technologies: Implications for Global and Regional Political-Military Balances.* Lexington, MA: Lexington Books.

Pincus, Walter (1997). *Washington Post,* December 23, p. A4.

Plascov, Avi (1982). *Modernization, Political Development, and Stability.* Montclair, NJ: Allanheld; Osmun: Gower.

Posen, Barry R. (1984). *The Sources of Military Doctrine: France, Britain, and Germany between the World Wars.* Ithaca, NY: Cornell University Press.

Prigogine, Ilya (1996). Une Nouvelle Rationalité. In *La Fin des Certitudes: Temps, Chaos et les Lois de la Nature.* Paris: Editions Odile Jacob.

———, and Stuart A. Rice (eds.) (1997). *Resonances, Instability and Irreversibility.* New York: John Wiley.

———, and Isabelle Stengers (1993). *Das Paradox der Zeit.* Muenchen: R. Piper.

Raevsky, Andrei (1993). *Development of Russian National Security Policies: Military Reform.* New York: United Nations.

Rao, D.V.L.N. Ramakrishna, and R. C. Sharma (eds.) (1991). *India's Borders, Ecology, and Security Perspectives.* New Delhi: SPF.

Rearden, Steven L. (1984). *The Evolution of American Strategic Doctrine: Paul H. Nitze and the Social Challenge.* Boulder, CO: Westview Press and FPI, SAIS, Johns Hopkins University.

Renner, Michael (1989). *National Security: The Economic and Environmental Dimensions.* Washington, DC: Worldwatch Institute.

Richardson, Louis Fry (1960a). *Statistics of Deadly Quarrels* (Q. W. Right and C. C. Lienau, eds.). Pittsburgh, PA: Boxwood Press; Chicago: Quadrangle Books.

——— (1960b). *Arms and Insecurity* (N. Rashevsky and E. Trucco, eds.). Pittsburgh, PA: Boxwood Press; Chicago: Quadrangle Books.

Roberts, Brad (1996). *Weapons Proliferation and World Order: After the Cold War.* Boston: Kluwer Law International.

Roche, Jean-Jacques (1996). *Un Empire Sans Rival: Essai sur la pax democratica.* Paris: Editions Vinci.

Rosecrance, Richard, and Arthur A. Stein (eds.) (1993). *The Domestic Bases of Grand Strategy.* Ithaca, NY: Cornell University Press.

Rosen, Steven (comp.) (1973). *Testing the Theory of the Industrial-Military Complex.* Lexington, MA: Lexington Books.

Ross, Andrew L. (1991). *The Political Economy of Defense: Issues and Perspectives.* Westport, CT: Greenwood Press.

Russett, Bruce M. (1990). *Controlling the Sword: The Democratic Governance of National Security.* Cambridge, MA: Harvard University Press.

Sanders, Ralph (1983). *International Dynamics of Technology,* Westport, CT: Greenwood Press.

Sarkesian, Sam C. (ed.) (1972). *The Military-Industrial Complex: A Reassessment.* Beverly Hills, CA: Sage Publications.

Saussure, Ferdinand de (1949). *Cours de Linguistique Générale* (Charles Bally and Albert Sechehaye, eds.). Paris: Editions Payot.

―――― (1968). *Saussure et le Structuralisme sans le Savoir* (Georges Mounin, ed.) Paris: P. Seghers.

Schneider, Barry R., and Lawrence E. Grinter (1995). *Battlefield of the Future: 21st Century Warfare Issues.* Montgomery, AL: Maxwell AFB, Air University Press.

Schulz, Donald E. (ed.) (1998). *The Role of the Armed Forces in the Americas: Civil-Military Relations for the 21st Century.* Carlisle Barracks, PA: Strategic Studies Institute, U.S. Army War College.

Schuman, Michael, and Julia Sweig (eds.) (1991). *Conditions of Peace—An Inquiry: Security, Democracy, Ecology, Economics, Community.* Washington, DC: Expro Press.

Schwartzstein, Stuart J. D. (ed.) (1996). *The Information Revolution and National Security: Dimensions and Directions.* Washington, DC: Center for Strategic and International Studies.

Scowcroft, Brent, R. James Woolsey, and Thomas H. Etzold (eds.) (1988). *Defending Peace and Freedom Toward Strategic Stability in the Year 2000.* Lanham, MD: University Press of America.

Segal, Gerald, and Richard H. Yang (1996). *Chinese Economic Reform: The Impact on Security.* London and New York: Routledge.

Shetreet, Shimon (ed.) (1991). *Free Speech and National Security.* Dordrecht and Boston: Martinus Nijhoff.

Simon, Denis Fred (ed.) (1997). *Techno-Security in an Age of Globalization: Perspective from the Pacific Rim.* Armonk, NY: M. E. Sharpe.

Singh, Jasjit, and Vatroslav Vekaric (eds.) (1990). *Non-Provocative Defence: The Search for Equal Security.* London: Tri-Service Press.

Sinka, Rajeev Kumar (1995). *Crimes Affecting State Security: Problems and Recent Trends.* New Delhi: Deep and Deep Publs.

Smith, Michael G. (1998). *Language and Power in the Creation of the USSR, 1917–1953.* Berlin and New York: Mouton de Gruyter.

Snow, Donald M. (1994). *The Shape of the Future: The Post–Cold War World.* 2nd ed. Armonk, NY: M. E. Sharpe.

―――― (1995). *National Security: Defense Policy for a New International Order.* 3rd ed. New York: St. Martin's Press.

―――― (1999). *The Shape of the Future: World Politics in a New Century.* 3rd ed. Armonk, NY: M. E. Sharpe.

Snyder, Glenn Herald (1997). *Alliance Politics.* Ithaca, NY: Cornell University Press.

Stephan, Paul, III, and Boris Klimenko (eds.) (1991). *International Law and International Security—Military and Political Dimensions: A US-Soviet Dialogue.* Armonk, NY: M. E. Sharpe.

Sterling, Claire (1994). *Thieves' World: The Threat of the New Global Network of Organized Crime.* New York: Simon and Schuster.

Tamkoç, Metin (1976). *The Warrior Diplomats: Guardians of the National Security and Modernization of Turkey.* Salt Lake City: University of Utah Press.

Tanter, Raymond (1998). *Rogue Regimes: Terrorism and Proliferation.* New York: St. Martin's Press.

Thomas, Raju G. C. (1996). *Democracy, Security, and Development in India*. New York: St. Martin's Press.

Tolchin, Martin, and Susan Tolchin (1992). *Selling Our Security: The Erosion of America's Assets*. New York: Knopf.

Toulmin, Stephen (1990). *Cosmopolis: The Hidden Agenda of Modernity*. New York: The Free Press.

Tsagolov, Georgii Nikolaevich (1985). *War Is Their Business: The US Military-Industrial Complex* (Dmitry Belyavsky, trans.). Moscow: Progress Publishers.

Turpin, Jennifer, and Lester R. Kurtz (eds.) (1997). *The Web of Violence: From Interpersonal to Global*. Urbana: University of Illinois Press.

Twining, David Thomas (ed.) (1992). *Beyond Glasnost: Soviet Reform and Security Issues*. Westport, CT: Greenwood Press.

U.S. Congress, Commission on Security and Cooperation in Europe (1995). *Readings on Chechnya: Hearing before the C.S.C.E.* 104th Congress, 1st Session, May 1.

U.S. Defense Science Board (1997). *The Defense Science Board 1997 Summer Study Task Force on Department of Defense Responses to Transnational Threats— Final Report*. Washington, DC: U.S. Department of Defense.

U.S. General Accounting Office (1995). *National Security: Impact of China's Military Modernization in the Pacific Region—Report to Congressional Subcommittees*. Washington, DC: General Accounting Office.

U.S. President's Council (1992). *Science, Technology, and National Security: A Report Prepared by the President's Council of Advisors on Science and Technology*. Washington, DC: The Council.

Waever, Ole et al. (eds.) (1993). *Identity, Migration, and the New Security Agenda in Europe*. New York: St. Martin's Press.

Webster, William H. et al. (1997). *Russian Organized Crime/Global Organized Crime Project*. Washington, DC: Center for Strategic and International Studies.

Weiner, Myron (ed.) (1993). *International Migration and Security*. Boulder, CO: Westview Press.

Westing, Arthur (1980). *Warfare in a Fragile World*. London: Taylor Francis.

White House (1995). *A National Security Strategy of Engagement and Enlargement*. Washington, DC: The White House.

Wieviorka, Michel (1995). *Face au Terrorisme*. Paris: Eds. L. Levi.

Wilkinson, Paul (ed.) (1993). *Technology and Terrorism*. London and Portland, OR: Frank Cass.

Wright, Stuart A. (ed.) (1995). *Armageddon in Waco: Cultural Perspectives on the Branch Davidian Conflict*. Chicago: University of Chicago Press.

CHAPTER 1

On the Otherness
That Theory Creates

KLAUS KRIPPENDORFF

INTRODUCTION

The urge to theorize has been a driving force of Western intellectual tradition. It underlies academic discourse, giving the scientific enterprise its vitality. Without systematic theorizing much of contemporary culture, particularly technology, would be virtually unthinkable.

Naturally, theorizing has not been without critics. The skeptics have raised their voices against the ability of theory to describe anything at all. Radical empiricists, such as Francis Bacon, and even some logical positivists, have had stories to tell of the "blindness of abstraction." Now, postmodernists, poststructuralists, constructionists, deconstructionists, and many others, are questioning the intelligibility of master narratives and querying the ability of unifying theories or logical/mathematical systems to represent reality. From their perspective, science, literature, and law are just three of many literary genres, each cultivating its own reading of texts.

The most recent critique comes from feminist scholars. Although feminism is not a unified perspective, feminist thought has grown far beyond its early advocacy of equal rights, be it by conceptualizing patriarchal society, exploring gender differences, or even contributing scathing critiques of male rationality, of technological world constructions, and of the oppressive consequences of theory. Along its path, feminism has emphasized the embodied nature of knowledge, for example, by accounting for voices instead of texts. Feminism has also advocated relational epistemologies, insisted on the participation of emotions, and discovered validation in practical actions that could lead to personal liberation.

Narrower in scope, but no less important, is the opposition to theory by philosophers concerned with ethics. Dwight Furrow (1995), for instance, influenced by a rereading of Aristotle, questions the capacity of normative ethical theory to provide guidance on normative questions and challenges its relevance to the lived experience of moral agents. Such critiques are fueled by a need to understand the Holocaust, and other atrocities committed since World War II, by people with theories to live by.

Within literary scholarship, writers continue to reexamine their own foundations by questioning the intelligibility of texts in terms of the theory-driven distinction between meanings and an author's intentions. To them there is nothing in a text that could point to the difference between the two and no method that could shed light on what this distinction creates. For Knapp and Michaels (1985: 30): "[theory] is the name for all the ways people have tried to stand outside [the] practice [of reading and interpretation] in order to govern [that] practice from without. . . . [N]o one can reach [such] a position." This leads them to propose that "the theoretical enterprise should therefore come to an end."

The foregoing critiques have very different histories and little in common with each other except for their opposition to systematic theorizing. Often they even oppose each other. For example, feminists have been criticized for essentializing the very gender differences that they oppose; and proponents of postmodernism, for being silent on moral questions that undermine the intelligibility of moral experiences.

Many of these critiques rely on what I would call deficiency arguments—a rhetorical strategy that seeks to show the failure of a theory by pointing to what it blatantly omits or to what it surreptitiously distorts without recognizing that such critiques are based on another theory—usually one closer to these critics' heart and therefore more "real" to them. Critiques of ideology, Marxists, for example, excel in this. They argue against theories of knowledge from a perspective that is assumed to be "free" of ideological biases, more encompassing in scope, capturing a broader territory, or offering a greater number of distinctions. Yet, using one theory to criticize another remains entirely within the practice of theorizing and cannot therefore reveal the blind spots of theorizing. Worse, unable to recognize these blind spots makes theorists blind to their own blindness.

The following examines the social role of theory and the particular relation that theorizing entails between theorists and the theorized others who are the natural focus of social scientific inquiries.

SOME ENTAILMENTS OF THEORIZING

Etymologically, theory comes from the Greek *theoria*, the meaning of which comprises not only the process of "looking at," "viewing," "contemplating," or "speculating," but also the very object perceived, "a sight," "a tableau," or "a spectacle." These meanings imply a distinct attitude vis-à-vis what is theorized. Spectacles are created to be seen and discussed, not to be altered. Spectacles are in front of the viewer''s eye. In such accounts of theorizing, the use of ocular metaphors entails a tacit *preference for sight* over sound, touch, and feelings, and it assigns secondary importance to voices, stories, oral traditions, and practical knowledge. It is no accident that we speak of scientific "observers," not of scientific listeners. There is no auditory or tactile analogue to "observation," and, although reading and writing would be difficult without sight, we tend to exclude them when we speak of observing things.

As spectators, *theorists observe but do not allow themselves to enter their domain of observation.* Consequently, theorists endow facts, naively conceptualized as residing outside of us, with the power to determine which theories are valid. It is the belief in this ontology, and nothing but that, which ultimately justifies claims of being able to theorize facts for what they are, without preconceptions and without accountability to those who may be affected by these theories.

Since the seventeenth century, science has become increasingly "successful" in disconnecting theory from facts and observation from practice, notwithstanding that etymology links "fact" to manufacture. Perhaps with the exception of hermeneutics and constructivism, all scientific methods somehow operationalize the derivation of theories from observational data. Aside from the rare admission that data depend on theory, I know of no formalization of this reverse dependency or of any interactions between the two (see Woolgar, 1993: 36, 53–66).

Ethnographic analyses of scientific practices reveal the cherished uni-directionality in proceeding from observations to theories to be a myth (see Garfinkle, 1967; Garfinkle, Lynch, and Livingstone, 1982). But overcoming this uni-directional conception would seem quite impossible as long as theories are stated in terms of an extensional logic, such as the logic of propositions, or modeled by computers, which are sequential machines that embody the very same logic. To preserve this uni-directionality of scientific discourse against the threat of vicious paradoxes, Bertrand Russell invented his famous Theory of Logical Types, which has the effect of outlawing self-reference. It is this restricted notion of logic and of language that places scientific observers at the top of logical hierarchies, that thereby conceptualizes description top-downwards, that thus leads theorists to believe *they could observe their world without being observed by the objects of their observation.*

The ocular metaphor is so prevalent within the scientific community that theorists are encouraged to keep their distance not just to the observed but to their theories as well. A case in point is the very distinction between theories and beliefs. In scientific texts, theories appear as more or less confirmed hypotheses—each having a calculable probability, however small, of being invalid. Not so for beliefs: When we theorize, we theorize *about* something; but when we believe, we believe *in* something. In beliefs, the emotional detachment that theorists claim to have vis-à-vis their theories is erased in favor of the virtual certainty that things are the way they are *seen and spoken of.* In the words of Stanley Fish (1985: 116),

[A] theory is a special achievement of consciousness; a belief is a prerequisite of being conscious at all. Beliefs are not what you think *about* but what you think *with* . . . it is within the space provided by their articulations that mental activity—including the activity of theorizing—goes on. Theories are something you can have—you can wield them and hold them at a distance; beliefs have *you*, in the sense that there can be no distance between them and the acts they enable. (emphasis added)

The truths of theories may be pondered, but the truths of beliefs are held.

Contrary to popular conceptions of theories as accurate representations, theories are attractive because they exceed their domain of observation in at least five ways: (1) Theories *generalize* to cases claimed to be similar to those observed. Yet, without further observations, no assurance is available that the unobserved cases would support a theory's claim. Therefore, generalizations rely on a good deal of belief. (2) Theories *predict* under the assumption that the patterns observed in the past will persist into the future. Belief in such continuities have much practical value, but, as Francis Bacon already noted, they are ascertainable only in retrospect. (3) Theories *integrate* several propositions into a single coherent network, and (4) they *generate empirical hypotheses* from a very small number of quasi-axiomatic propositions. Note that (3) and (4) are predicated on the belief that the logic of propositions truly corresponds to the logic of the world. According to Carl Hempel (Mitchell, 1985: 7), (5) theory tends to be taken as "a complex spatial network [that] floats, as it were, above the plane of observation and is anchored to it by rules of interpretation." Yet rules of interpretation always are the rules of a theorist or of a community of theorists, not of an observed nature. They allow theorists to justify omitting details deemed irrelevant, accidental, unique, inconsistent, or subjective; filling in of the gaps of missed observations; or smoothing the rugged curves—none of which is derivable from observation and measurement.

Politically, the more territory a theory covers, the more it is preferred, the better it will be remembered, and the more likely it will be applied. Thus, theorizing supports a *conceptual imperialism*; the urge to oversee, predict, control, and govern ever-growing territories (Krippendorff, 1993)—an inkling that science shares with other forms of government in national, spiritual, or commercial spheres of life. True, theories by themselves neither reign nor rule. Once institutionalized, however, they do encourage their users to "survey," "capture," "represent," "monitor," and ultimately "manage," where they do not even "discipline" what they claim to describe. The underlying logic of propositions, especially its Theory of Logical Types, encourages the construction of logical hierarchies of ever-increasing levels of abstractions, from objects to language, to meta-language, to meta-meta-language, and so forth, with theorists finding comfort only at the top.

Foucault's (1977) famous metaphorical use of the *panopticon* to give an account of how knowledge works in society is telling. The panopticon is an ideal prison design that enables centrally located guards to monitor the behavior of all inmates, who in turn can see only the guards observing them but not each other. Here discipline is assured by the efficiency of observation. In taking this design as a metaphor to explore power relations in society, Foucault equates knowledge and theory and carries the built-in ocularity to its ultimate sociological conclusion: government of one view at the expense of all others.

Theories are also expected to be rational and consistent, ideally in the form of mathematical expressions, as systems of equations, for example. Formalizations of this kind have the double advantage of being computable in principle and of sparing one the complications of context and meaning. Mathematical theories provide the backbone of the natural sciences but have made inroads also in efforts to explain social phenomena, in economics, linguistics, psychology, and systems science, for instance. While rationality and consistency are considered twin values of scientific explorations, they are also two different aspects of the monologism that theory implies. Being "rational" is tantamount to speaking in the voice of one's community, a voice that is assumed common to all of its members and sanctioned as such. Rationality defers one's own voice to a fictional authority. Being "consistent," on the other hand, is tantamount to avoiding contradictions among the propositions of a theory. Consistency entails the belief that a single overarching logic could govern the phenomena that a theory claims to be about. The requirement that theories be both rational and consistent thus reduces them to *monological* constructions in the dual sense of being the product of a single *voice* and of being cast in terms of *one (coherent) logic*. This has considerable implications for social theorizing.

THE LANGUAGING OF THEORIES

Consider the following rather typical propositions, which could be found in any social science writing:

(a) *Institutions have four functions.*
(b) *Nationalism is an outgrowth of modernism.*
(c) *Terrorism is caused by a breakdown in political structures.*
(d) *Unemployment feeds crime.*

In the context of the foregoing, these four propositions should be troublesome: None of them indicates whose truths they state, attesting to their complete disembodiment. All hide the fact that they are fundamentally about what people do. Institutions, nationalism, terrorism, unemployment and crime do not exist without their performers. Yet, their voices are silenced in each of these generalizations. There is no indication of how their behaviors end up being so categorized. Even the voice of the theorist remains hidden, perhaps deliberately, behind an objectivist language.

Language is implicated here in even more fundamental ways, however. Of the four propositions: (a) asserts that a concept "has" or is "in possession of" properties, which lends an almost physical existence to this concept, to institutions as it were. (b) applies an agricultural metaphor to two rather high-level abstractions from a complex nexus of human behaviors without referring to any particular group of people or locale; but metaphors reside in language, not in nature. (c) claims two abstractions—a category of human behavior and a stable pattern abstracted from a process—to be causally related. But how could that be? Next, (d) accounts for what probably is a statistical correlation in terms of nutrition between two variables, of which one is an agent and the other its target. A casual reading of these propositions gives the impression that they state facts. However, such a reading overlooks their metaphorical nature. How could concepts cause anything analogous to how billiard balls bounce against each other? And measurement variables "act," let alone interact? In what sense could non-material structures break? The failure to recognize the metaphorical nature of language, even in the most rigorous scientific discourses, attests to a remarkable unawareness of how language directs the world we theorize.

Clearly, theories are formed in language, but they also must be languaged into being and be fit to survive in processes of human communication. In the context of their communication, the notion of theory suffers from *two illusions*:

1. The first stems from the belief that the form of theory could be separated from what language makes available and that, by the same token, human communication has no influence on how and where theories come into being. Theories are not merely found. They are constructed, proposed, promoted, published, discussed, and either adopted or rejected. Their reality lies in stating them, in understanding them as such, and in enacting them into actual practices (see Chapters 2, 7, 9, and 11 in this volume). These are the acts of real people, actors who see some virtue in promulgating what they speak of. It follows that theorizing cannot be understood from a notion of language as a neutral medium of representation (as a formalization in pure propositional logic) or from the corollary that theories can be justifiable by observations (of objects outside language) only. The notion of languaging as a dialogical process permits us to recognize theories as mediating between their stakeholders and residing as such in processes of communication (see Chapters 3, 6, and 10). From this perspective, theories cannot be found in the contents of statements or inside individual minds; rather,

they are discovered in processes of their continuous rearticulations. Theories that fail to compel people to reproduce, to recirculate them within their community, simply fade away.

As communications, theories serve a variety of social functions. They can define a theorist's identity. They can form the basis of particular research programs or schools of thought. They can become institutionalized in disciplines that require adherence to or belief in them from its practitioners. Linguists, psychologists, biologists, indeed all academic disciplines, distinguish themselves by the theories they believe in. Sometimes theories take the form of abstract paradigms that privilege particular scientific explorations. At other times, they certify practitioners and protect them against criticisms from other disciplines. In either case, theories are political phenomena.

2. The second illusion arises from the conviction that social theories have invariant and single meanings. But unlike natural scientific theories, social theories, once published, can reenter and touch the lives of the very people about whom they speak (Krippendorff, 1996). When such a reentry occurs, theories and those theorized in them begin to interact and modify each other in ways that violate the idea of theory as a descriptive account of stable facts, as a representation of an unintelligent world. Those who discover themselves to be theorized might use the publicity in ways to enhance their status. They can also see it as a threat to their identity. When known, a theory can thus affect the behavior of the theorized in ways that can strengthen or invalidate it. At the time, Black Power and feminist movements effectively countered prevailing theories about them by circulating theories of their own. Theories may also be adopted by people who find new meanings in living through their propositions, by enacting their stereotypes, preserving their distinctions—thus making a theory truer simply through its practice.

The mass media, by catering to audiences conceptualized in terms of size and attractiveness, "mainstream" the public. They cause more people to become similar to each other, thereby also enhancing their attractiveness to advertisers. Taking theories, especially predictive ones, as prescriptions for action can turn them into self-fulfilling prophecies. In social reality, which depends on the knowledge people have of it, this is the norm, not the exception.

Thus, *theories* of social phenomena do not simply represent but, rather, also *transform their objects in the process of their communication*. Positivists have reasons to worry that the reentry of theories into their domain of observation could undermine the validity of those theories. This is why they take considerable methodological precautions to protect their ontology from such challenges.

If theorizing is, indeed, a political process and if the dissemination of social theories does change their validity, one might think that political science would have much to say about the politics of theorizing; that the theories created in the *social sciences* would, at least, *account for their own social consequences*. This, however, seems not to be the case. Inspired by the successes of the natural sciences and convinced that the social sciences, too, could discover and accumulate a body of theories, social theorists have effectively succeeded in making social theory "unsocial," political theory "apolitical," and so forth. The widespread practice of theorizing the social conceals its communicative and political nature. *Theorizing the social seems to work only where theorists, the institutions using their theories, and the theorized others collude—in holding the theorized reality constant, while collectively denying that alone or together any one of them had anything to do with it.*

This grand self-deception correlates well with the myth that theorists could stay outside of the language they use to explain the world—a world portrayed as if inhabited by people devoid of any linguistic intelligence of their own, if only because the theorists themselves take a "God's eye view" (Putnam, 1981) of the universe they try to explain.

Scholars daring to question such monological views can be seriously sanctioned. This has happened to several philosophers of science—Popper, Lakatos, and Kuhn, for instance—among whom the late Paul Feyerabend was to be singled out by phycisists as "*The Worst Enemy of Science*" (Horgan, 1993).

It would seem that the foregoing offers us a choice. We can continue practicing natural science methods of theorizing our domain of observation, hiding ourselves behind an objectivist language, and losing touch with the social world we unwittingly transform. Or we can deliberately and responsibly involve ourselves in the very politics that our inquiries set in motion. To underscore the urgency of this choice, let me explore how fellow humans fare in the theories of social science about them.

THEORIZING THE OTHER

1. *Theorizing gives birth to distant otherness.* As ideated generalizations, theories classify observations and theorize people in terms of third-person plural. "They" are the subjects of experiments, the interviewees of surveys, and the respondents to mail questionnaires. "They" also are the conservatives, the unemployed, the Catholics, and the terrorists. All of "them" are neatly labeled and assigned to particular classes on account of characteristics that all members of such classes are assumed to share. Classification already begins at the data-generating stage of social research. In interviewing, for example, neither the identity of the interviewee nor that of the interviewer becomes data. For fear of biasing the data, personal knowledge, which could emerge when experimenters come too close to their subjects, is systematically repressed.

In the theater, spectators have no problem in distinguishing between actors and the characters they impersonate on stage. But in social research, individuals are the very categories that a theory provides for. Where individuals identify with a group, belief, or trait, theorists are not prohibited from dismissing such declarations as subjective, as lacking abstraction, or as irrelevant to their theory. And when quoted, individual voices are taken to exemplify the voice of a class. This is accomplished by channeling a plurality of voices into a single, artificially constructed voice—one for each class, one for each category, of the theorist's choosing. But classes never speak; individuals do, usually always to others, even when they are virtual in nature. In the reality of everyday life, collective monologues, choruses, for example, are extremely rare. To take such exceptions as a norm for social scientific insights attests to the artificial and unsocial nature of theorizing.

In everyday languaging, third-person pronouns refer to those absent. Theorizing makes this absence a seeming virtue that gives theorists the freedom to characterize others in ways radically different and inferior to themselves. Whether one calls this a professional disability (a deafness to individual voices or an institutionalized disrespect for otherness), theorizing is responsible for estranging others from us.

2. *Theorizing trivializes others by reducing them to obedient mechanisms.* As spectators, social theorists observe human behaviors, including verbal interactions, from outside the spectacle. From this perspective, behaviors appear as linear sequences, temporally ordered chains of events, or trajectories in a Cartesian space within predefined coordinates. To understand the trajectories, natural scientists would seek to discover their regularities. However, the very mention of "regularities" assumes that trajectories are followed without much choice in the matter. And talk of their "discovery" tends to suggest that they existed prior to their observation and measurement. Such assumptions are not only built into mathematical theories of behavior, but also inscribed into computational techniques for analyzing behavioral data. They can also enter less formalized conversations on social causation. For example, plays are usually scripted; and scripts explain much of what theater audiences end up seeing. But for the strict determinacy of machines, scripts are to performances much as computer programs are to computations. They are in control of the plot. Describing human behavior in terms of scripts, rules, and grammars, or even as being reactive to messages, conjures the determinism of obedient mechanisms. Since spectators can never be sure whether, when, and to what extent an observed behavior is an act or a response—minutely scripted or improvised—to unobserved conditions, deterministic accounts have no observational basis. They are the fruit of preferences—unless theorists step out of their observer's role and ask pertinent questions. However, even the Turing Test, designed to distinguish machine from human intelligence, is never quite conclusive. Its use has taught us that interaction is a necessary but not a sufficient condition

to determine the presence of human intelligence or agency. Commonly, theorists cannot afford this interaction—because it would shift the authority for theorizing to the subjects being observed and thus erode the theorist's objective observer status. Hence, theorizing remains stuck in causal and mechanistic explanations of human behavior, from which that of the theorists is excluded.

Without even engaging theorized others in conversations on the theories being developed about them, social theorists remain remarkably free to explore any theory that would be of interest to their own community. Although novel conceptualizations may not come easy, from the convenient position of an outside observer it is all right for sociologists like Goffman (1959, 1963) to describe social interactions in dramaturgical categories; for psychologists like Schank and Abelson (1977) to interpret the same behavior in terms of individuals following rules and scripts; for literary scholars like Hirsch (1967) to extract intentions from an author's writings; for cognitive scientists to develop algorithms that are presumed to govern individual actors' processing and exchange of information; or for economists and political scientists to measure the efficacy with which actors apply available resources. Without consulting the constituents of the social phenomenon of interest, almost anything goes.

3. *Theorizing creates the very unsocial conditions in which theories can survive, if only by inscribing its monologism into its observational data.* At moments of contact between theorist and theorized, social research greatly depends on collaboration and dialogue. Human subjects are used in scientific experiments only on the basis of informed consent. Yet, after signing the consent form, their ability to understand the nature of their involvement and to say "no" to practices they might consider unconscionable is rarely ever called upon again, does not enter the data, and has therefore little chance to inform a theory that speaks to these subjects' capabilities. To uphold the notion that theory is responsive to observations only, the dialogical nature of the actual contact must be hidden; the very collaboration needed to conclude an experiment, concealed.

Or consider interviewing. In this asymmetrical interaction, the interviewer asks questions and the interviewee is expected to answer them. Interviewees are allowed to speak only within the narrow confines of what is relevant. In effect, interviewees are being *used* to support the point that researchers intend to make, and in the course of this exploitation, the inbuilt asymmetrical power relations are necessarily and irretrievably inscribed in the data on which theories are constructed.

The deception of informants with regard to the purpose of their participation in a research project, the expectation of answers to questions that are irrelevant to an interviewees' life, and the contrived stimulus conditions to which subjects are asked to respond affirm the essential asymmetry, artificiality, and unsocial character of the experimental conditions that spawn the data for social and psychological theories. It is these power relations that creep into the data-generating process in evident violation of the idea of theory as observer-independent. In fact, *theorizing subjects its subjects.* It renders them *serviceable* (Sampson, 1993) *to theories that end up demonstrating little more than how well theorists have managed to disable the social nature of human beings.* True, submitting to authorities and following instructions are part of what we can do. But replicating these less than desirable human conditions at the expense of human agency, for the sake of theorizing, amounts to political suicide for the social sciences.

4. *Theorizing nurtures a culture of blindness to the political nature of theory—for theorist and theorized alike.* The social sciences are concerned with the ways human beings *can* live together (see Chapters 4, 5, and 8): Sociology, with how people organize themselves into larger wholes and coordinate their actions in ways that sustain these wholes (see Chapter 7); Political Science, with how people create publics (see Chapters 6, 9, and 10), arrive at consensus on agendas (see the Introduction), and mandate their leaders to form governments (Chapter 11); International Relations, with how peoples perceive each other across national boundaries (see Chapter 2), seek to resolve international conflicts and regulate the myriad of interactions (see Chapter 3) between diverse constituencies of nation-states; Communication Research, with how people construct, sustain, and transform their social realities by communicating with each other. But none of these social phenomena can be understood by straightjacketing people into mechanistic preconceptions or by taking away from them the spaces in which they interact with one another. The celebration of theory, the use of ocular metaphors for knowing, the reliance on extensional logic for understanding, and the naturalness with which people accept confinements during data-making processes, all have become part of a culture that suppresses the awareness of the political nature of theories—not only for theorists but also for all those who see each other in these terms. The culture of theorizing makes it difficult for the social sciences to reflect on its social nature.

But this self-defeating consequence of theorizing is not recognizable from within a representational notion of language—the one notion, which philosophers—Wittgenstein, Austin, Searle, Bakhtin, and Rorty among them—have systematically challenged in preference to less abstract and dialogical conceptions. Critiques here center largely on the fact that words are actions, too, and that languaging accomplishes things beyond describing actions. Reentry adds a cybernetic spin to these critiques, showing that languaging is recursive. Where language informs action, theories are likely to become self-validating. Under these conditions, generalizations of others, whether published in scientific journals or disseminated in the mass media, provide fertile ground for social prejudices to arise and to become truths that easily can subordinate, discipline, marginalize, and criminalize others for their otherness.

It is always possible to contest and reject a claim. But in view of the authority that scientific theories conjure in modern culture, contesting them would go against a whole complex array of deep-rooted cultural beliefs. Among them is the conviction that theories have but one legitimate interpretation and that theories are shaped by observations, not by theorists. The latter belief leaves no real target for challenges; the former makes political considerations seem irrelevant.

Whenever scientific accounts concern specific populations—be they the homeless, the followers of a particular religion, or women, homosexuals, Afro-Americans, teachers, consumers, Arabs—they can achieve two things: in the immediate, they can entice "us" to treat "them" in the categories these accounts employ. In the long run, this treatment can transform "them" into the neatly homogeneous groups which we claim "they" are. Self-validation or reification is typical in the social sciences. As Giddens (1984) observed, has not the mere metaphorical use of the term *market* in nineteenth-century academic writings about economic activities ended up materializing that reality in ways that, today, neither CEOs nor economists would dare to question? Has not our conception of "the public" shifted from what was discussed in salons and side street cafes to what scholars first theorized as public opinion, then encouraged pollsters to measure? And has not the use of hydraulic and archeological metaphors in Freud's writing of the human psyche produced a whole industry of psychotherapists and their clients for all of whom mental disorders have become as real as they can be? Have not the theories of consumer behavior and of mass media consumption, so avidly embraced by advertising agencies, brought forth the very consumerism that these theories needed in order to survive by creating the passive audiences that theories of mass communication are so good at describing? Do not correlations reported between intelligence, ethnicity, and crime, when supported by genetic explanations, inform our educational policies and hiring practices that keep such correlations real—well beyond published data? And do not statistics of cultural, racial, sexual, and national population characteristics inform and reify the very distinctions that statisticians build into their survey instruments and then naively "discover?" Is it then not likely that theories, which cannot but describe human nature in mechanistic terms, create the cultural dupes needed in order for television culture to work, abet the very behaviors necessary for certain institutions to persist, discourage some people from contesting scientific theories about them, and create obedient citizens who might well differ in whom they vote for, but not in how or how much they could be influenced in one way or another?

This is the reality we face. I am not suggesting that the project of the social sciences is doomed. Rather, what I submit here is that, in the sense and to the extent that theorizing does continue to dominate our understanding of other human beings, it unwittingly also installs an intellectual imperialism in our social world that silences the voices of the theorized, prevents us from engaging in meaningful conversations with those who constitute the social phenomena that we wish to understand, and risks depriving us of the only source for understanding how social phenomena come to be. It is in this awareness that we can learn profitably to redefine our fears and foes, to remodel our security, to redirect our future, and to safeguard the individual and societal well-being and dignity of the generations yet to be born, in an increasingly crowded world.

REFERENCES

Fish, Stanley (1985). Consequences. Pp. 106–131 in W.J.T. Mitchell (ed.), *Against Theory*. Chicago: University of Chicago Press.

Foucault, Michel (1977). *Discipline and Punish: The Birth of the Prison*. New York: Pantheon Books.

Furrow, Dwight (1995). *Against Theory: Continental and Analytic Challenges in Moral Philosophy*. New York: Routledge.

Garfinkle, Harold (1967). *Studies in Ethnomethodology*. Englewood Cliffs, NJ: Prentice-Hall.

———, M. Lynch, and E. Livingstone (1982). The Work of a Discovering Science Construed with Materials for the Optically Discovered Pulsar. *Philosophy of the Social Sciences* 11: 131–258.

Giddens, Anthony (1984). *The Constitution of Society*. Berkeley: University of California Press.

Goffman, Erving (1959). *The Presentation of Self in Everyday Life*. New York: Doubleday.

——— (1963). *Behavior in Public Places*. New York: The Free Press.

Hirsch E. D., Jr. (1967) *Validity in Interpretation*. New Haven, CT: Yale University Press.

Horgan, John (1993). The Worst Enemy of Science: Paul Karl Feyerabend. *Scientific American* (May): 36–37.

Knapp, Steven, and Walter Benn Michaels (1985). Against Theory. Pp. 11–30 in W.J.T. Mitchell (ed.), *Against Theory*. Chicago: University of Chicago Press.

Krippendorff, Klaus (1993). Conversation or Intellectual Imperialism in Comparing Communication (Theories). *Communication Theory* 3, 3: 252–266.

——— (1996). A Second-order Cybernetics of Otherness. *Systems Research* 13, 3: 311–328.

Mitchell, W.J.T. (1985). Introduction: Pragmatic Theory. Pp. 1–10 in W.J.T. Mitchell (ed.), *Against Theory*. Chicago: University of Chicago Press.

Putnam, Hilary (1981). *Reason, Truth and History*. New York: Cambridge University Press.

Sampson, Edward E. (1993). *Celebrating the Other; A Dialogic Account of Human Nature*. Boulder, CO: Westview Press.

Schank, Roger C., and Robert P. Abelson (1977). *Scripts, Plans, Goals, and Understanding*. Hillsdale, NJ: Lawrence Erlbaum.

Woolgar, Steve (1993). *Science, the Very Idea*. New York: Routledge.

CHAPTER 2

From Otherness to Alienation, to Enmity, to War: A Case—or Two

F. HILARY CONROY

APOLOGIA

If there are lessons to be learned from history, then I as a diplomatic historian must here confess to have retained some good lessons of direct relevance to this apologia. For one thing, in 1960, even as political scientists were busy expanding political theory and international economists were absorbed in developing econometrics with too little time and regard for the craziness of historical events and the people that shaped them, the title of my book, *The Japanese Seizure of Korea: A Study of Realism and Idealism in International Relations* (Conroy, 1960) should have read "Realism and Idealism in International Relations: The Japanese Seizure of Korea, a Case Study." Not simply because diplomatic history and case studies were far more in fashion then than they are now. But especially because my book might have been read not merely by historians of East Asia in general, and by the select few who studied Japan–Korea relations in particular, but by many political scientists interested in international affairs and more international economists attracted to East Asia. The study, which tried to be "objective"—impartial, fair, understanding—on both Japan and Korea, and no less "reasonable and realistic" about the problems that they were facing as East Asian nations coming into the wider world of the late nineteenth and early twentieth century, did not reverberate—I would admit—in the wider community of scholars in International Relations at the time, as it might have otherwise.

Also, instead of vouching to show why "Dr. Conroy believes," the jacket of the publication should have assured the reader that the author "concludes" [from his Japan–Korea study] "that this particular configuration of events is a remarkably clear example of the [problems inherent in the] 're-alist' approach to international relations that is currently advocated by many leading authorities in the field." Yes, "languaging" (see Chapter 1) does matter.

Though it can capture what is unique in time and space, does not—cannot—history also liberate the generalizable, the similar, and the comparable, helping to clarify the makings, meanings, and implications of what ceases to appear as random across space and time, once contexts and perspectives can be studied and compared?

Could the anger, fury, and madness that fueled the political pressures, which—from the seizure of Korea to the raid on Pearl Harbor—pushed Japan to disaster despite the semi-realist efforts of realist politicians to avert the "assassinate America" drive, find an echo in the efforts that a very few did make under Nazi rule, in an attempt to deflect the Fuehrer's venomous folly?

Have the intense hatred and the absurd hostility hurled by Imperial Japan's "Conquer Korea" advocates upon their "betrayers" inside Japan not had parallels in the racial, ethnic, political, and religious confrontations occurring elsewhere, in other periods of history, or in the tensions that have surrounded the Crusades, the Jihads, the Thirty-Years' and Hundred-Years' wars, the Joan of Arc and Salem witchcraft trials, Hitler's evil, Mideastern terrorism, the Oklahoma City bombing, and the Serb-Croatian-Bosnian tragedy in a land once and perhaps all too briefly called Yugoslavia?

What did the American leaders, Secretary of State Hull and President Roosevelt, do (if anything at all) to help those among the Japanese who were trying to find ways to avoid a Pacific war? Might there be any implications or lessons here for mistakes made elsewhere in properly and timely addressing pathological threats from the Hitlers, Stalins, Saddams, and Milosovics of the world?

Before enacting the good old American idea of "containment," how many had the wisdom to consider the haunting implications of the similarity between Japan's war in China and America's war in Vietnam? And is it not ironic that, during that Vietnam War era, the best place to talk about that dilemma was "elsewhere," mostly in Canada? Was McCarthyism in America as potentially poisonous as "Greater East Asia-ism" had been in Japan? Handling fears, foes, and insecurity in historical time and space under leaders who are unable to say "no," mainly for being "afraid to be cowards" (to quote from Shakespeare's *Falstaff*) is not exactly "securizing."

The United States did get away from Vietnam without triggering a third world war, and the "Evil Empire" has "collapsed" since. But are there not still thousands of "land mines" to clear up? And if international treaties, international trade, leagues of nations, international "laws," and institutions have, indeed, made notable progress, is a great deal more "realistic diplomacy" not needed?

Since the world is evolving, probably in the direction of globalism or at least "transnationalism," it must respond to the changes with suitably positive measures and helpful attitudes. Many of the changes and possible responses are discussed in the chapters to follow. These challenging discourses, while pointing out the flaws and difficulties in achieving democracy, do not in general suggest that such is impossible or unworkable. However, *Atlantic Monthly* Contributing Editor Robert D. Kaplan may have already sounded the need for a Volume 2 of *Of Fears and Foes* through his troubling query, "Was Democracy Just a Moment?" (Kaplan, 1997) for which he uses historical examples, from the fall of Athens to his personal experience in 1980s Sudan, whereupon he concludes: "If a society is not in reasonable health, democracy can not only be risky but disastrous."

As historians ought not to disregard, Hitler and Mussolini were not only elected but approved and hailed for their momentous "achievements" by millions of grateful supporters (Klein, 1998). And we have to ask, "Wasn't Yugoslavia better off with Tito than it has been with Democracy?" Another worrisome placard that Kaplan agitates reads: "Corporations are like the feudal domains that evolved into nation states; they are nothing less than the vanguard of a new Darwinian organization of politics." True?

Of course, today's panorama of democracies is not all gloom and doom. South Africa has risen from Apartheid to Reconciliation through Archbishop Desmond Tutu's "Healing Approach" to history. Instead of forgetting the past—something that recordkeepers and historians will never permit us do—should leaders and followers who did "bad things" not "sort of" semi-apologize? And ought not their many victims in turn, at least "sort of" semi-forgive? A great such semi-idea seems to be almost working in South Africa to the delight of many a peace searcher and researcher like me.

Although most of my academic research career has been devoted to the study of modern East Asian history with special attention to Japan and to its course toward the Pacific War, in 1969 I was privileged to be invited to participate in a lecture series on "peace research" celebrating the fiftieth anniversary of the Hoover Institution at Stanford University. Participants included (former British Foreign Secretary and briefly Premier) Anthony Eden, (the President of the Norwegian Parliament, the Chair of the Nobel Peace Prize Committee) Bernt Ingvaldsen, (Australian diplomat-statesman and former Vice-President of the United Nations General Assembly) Sir Claude Spencer, (the U.S. Assistant Secretary of Defense for International Security Affairs) G. Warren Nutter, and a number of academic scholars with an expertise in international relations.

The volume in which our lectures were published (Tompkins, 1971) voiced the reasoning of Anthony Eden, urging "practical"—realistic if at times power political—approaches to peacemaking: The United Nations was too "diffuse and unwieldy" to handle the real problems. Badly needed was a strong coalition of democratic countries (such as NATO) to hold off communists and crush would-be dictators. Security specialist Nutter insisted that pragmatic solutions to power conflicts required "defensive armaments," and even Nobel Prize awarder Ingvaldsen advocated "keeping the sword in the sheath"—just in case. The professors attending expressed rather negative feelings about the prospects of peacekeeping by means other than military police control mechanisms. University of Paris Professor Bertrand de Jouvenel emphasized a "drive to power" as the key element in world politics, and Professor Robert Scalapino of the University of California (Berkeley) referred to "congeries of difficulties" afflicting the Third World with cross currents of tribalism, racialism, neocolonialism, and ethnicity—all of which promised a future bedeviled with "small wars."

My lecture entitled "Man's Natural Desire for Peace" placed me in the role of "Pollyanna of the Conference," and the only way I could justify my optimistic lecture title was humbly to invoke Tibetan Buddhism's emphasis on an "eye of wisdom" conducive to "loving kindness" and to a "pitying mind"—thoughts that had been expressed by the Dalai Lama as he reviewed the Chinese Communist takeover of his homeland from his place in exile. Of course, from other Asian and Western philosophies and religions, I could find additional examples of wonderful appeals to "forgive and forget" bad things in history and of peaceful paths to peaceable change—from Gandhiism to sit-down strikes (prominent in the 1960s)—but in general I came away from that conference feeling that the time had not yet come to celebrate "Peaceful Change in Modern Society"—the title of our publication celebrating that occasion.

As indicated in my conclusion, cultural interchange with a sense of mutual appreciation—applied with some sense of humor—would seem to be necessary if fears and foes and wars are to be avoided in the future. Peace research is still sorely needed and although our standard journals in the History field, such as *The American Historical Review* and the *Journal of Asian Studies* have been making some progress in this direction, new titles—such as *Amerasia Journal, Journal of World History, Peace and Change*—are helping break even newer ground.

Could the Asian Pacific wars have been avoided? This chapter exposes the history of Japanese expanionism from the Early Meiji "Conquer Korea" argument to Pearl Harbor as a basis for analysis of the difficulties diplomats face in trying to be sensible and "realistic" in the sensitive domain of nation-state diplomacy. It considers not only the Japanese but also the American side in the Pearl Harbor syndrome, and it goes on to apply some of the "lessons" learned to such concepts as "domino theory" and "containment" in the Vietnam War. Then it alludes to ways in which peace research might contribute to the avoidance of conflict, whether national, ethnic, or religious, primarily by changes in attitude and focus.

For a historian used to dealing with the specifics of people and events within precise time spans, it is difficult to explain why an East Asian historical account of Japan's journey to Pearl Harbor or an interpretation of the aftermath of the U.S.-Vietnam War are relevant to the broader global concerns of international insecurities, and to the fears and foes that animate them across time and space—especially where the temporal need not be limited to 1870–1970; and the spatial ought to span more than East Asia. But I shall try—and this time around, would that I even succeed.

FROM OTHERNESS TO ALIENATION, TO ENMITY, TO WAR

The foundations of the findings in my research on the likely relationship between the configuration of the mentalities and the events conducive to the wars conducted by Japan in the Pacific—over Korea, in China, and later on, against the United States—remain all too unshaken, since my first publication in 1960, to this day.

I was much surprised to discover in 1960 that the oligarchic leaders of post-1873 Meiji Japan had not been acting out a deep-seated Japanese imperialistic ambition to "seize Korea", to set a course toward further Japanese expansionism that would eventually lead to the Pacific War, but that they were cautious proponents of realism in international relations—in the sensible, defensive style of diplomacy advocated by such as Metternich, Morgenthau, and at my time of writing certainly the most respected "realist" in international policy circles, Mr. X (George F. Kennan), not to mention U.S. Secretary of State Henry Kissinger some years later.

Yet in the Japan–Korea case, realism had been "frustrated." Why and how? It took two chapters to explain this (Conroy, 1960), but in brief, I intimated that the realist oligarchs in charge of Japanese foreign relations had sought a "safe and sane" policy for Korea, which need not have meant an "annexation" of Korea.

My Japanese "realists" were several times Prime Minister and Resident General of Korea (1905–1910), Ito Hirobumi, his various cabinet ministers—and among them, especially Mutsu Munemitsu and Inoue Kaoru. They were merely following in the footsteps of Meiji Restoration leader Okubo Toshimichi who, with Imperial Council headman Iwakura Tomomi, had vetoed and defeated "Conquer Korea" advocates led by Saigo Takamori and other belligerent samurai types in the "Great Debate" (or the "Great Divide"), over *seikan* ("conquering Korea") in Japan's Meiji government, in 1873.

A brief discussion of this episode is important and relevant, for it casts a lingering cloud over Japanese foreign policy making as it tried to be truly "realistic" in the best sense of that word—doing what was necessary and right for Japan's survival and progress as a newly modernizing nation entering the real world of nation-state politics. In summary, while the key members of the Emperor's Imperial Council, charged with formulating and carrying out long-range policies for Japan in the new age, were abroad on the world-touring Iwakura Mission, Council Member and samurai hero Saigo Takamori, empowered as absentee Chargé d'affaires in Tokyo, decided to launch an invasion of Korea. His reason or excuse was the Korean King's refusal to acknowledge the elevation in 1868 of the Japanese Emperor to "Imperial" status, and to abide by the newly instituted Japanese rules regarding Korean relations.

Fortunately, though he had already received the tentative approval of his youthful Emperor, Saigo waited until the return of the Iwakura mission before "going to Korea"—expecting fullest approval of his heroic project, especially since a leading member of the Iwakura Mission, Okubo Toshimichi, was his fellow Satsuma clansman and "friend-since-childhood." But to Saigo's surprise, and chagrin, Okubo and the other Iwakura-missioners, following Iwakura's advice, refused to go along with his "already approved" plan, forcing the Emperor to retract. Okubo's grand presentation of his "Seven Reasons for Opposing the Korean Expedition" would be followed by Saigo's resignation from the Imperial Council and his return to Satsuma to sulk, then lick his samurai wounds, and eventually lead (and die in) the Satsuma rebellion of 1877. The introduction to Okubo's "Seven Reasons for Opposing the Korean Expedition" reads as follows: "In order to govern . . . [our] . . . country and protect the people, it is necessary to have a flexible policy and to watch the world situation; always watching the situation we go forward or retreat. If the situation is bad, we simply stop. . . ." As his reasons for "stopping" the Korean expedition, he cites government expenditures, industrial development needs and problems, diplomatic relations with Britain and Russia, Britain's "watching Asia with a tiger's eye," and Japan's "unequal" treaties with Europe and America. He is fully cognizant that "of course, we cannot overlook the arrogant attitude of Korea, but we have no clear reason to attack Korea" (Conroy, 1960: 47–49).

Realism had prevailed, but the scars left were many: Saigo's return to Satsuma, the Satsuma rebellion, and the assassination of Okubo who was literally cut to pieces by Saigo-istic samurai as he was being transported to an Imperial conference on May 14, 1878. But Okubo's "safe and sane" Korean policy had been firmly established and seemed likely to be carried forward indefinitely. Indeed, it survived many difficult and delicate problems, such as Chinese meddling in the politics of Seoul and the long tenure as advisor (1885–1894) to the Korean King of Yuan Shih-k'ai (Yuan Shikai) who was considered a man of infamy by the Japanese. In the interim, Saigo was becoming something of a folk hero in Japanese samurai culture, while other Japanese such as Fukuzawa Yukichi were making friends among Koreans seeking progress and freedom for their country.

At great risk and difficulty for themselves, Iwakura and Okubo had placed Japan on a realistic course in its international relations. Although both were dead within the decade following the Great Debate of 1873, their designated successor, Ito Hirobumi, and his associates remained dedicated to realism in theory and in action almost to the end—in 1912—of the long and eventful Meiji era. Even Saigo Takamori's "Conquer Korea" associates—including his own younger brother, Saigo Tsugumichi, and Mutsu Munemitsu who had been jailed for supporting the Satsuma rebellion—would come around to supporting the "safe and sane" Korea policy and to propagating careful "sanity" in foreign relations generally.

This does not mean that there were no crises, expeditions, or wars. There were many of these, including a "Formosa expedition," which resulted in Japan's acquisition of the Ryukyu Islands in return for temporarily conceding Formosa to China. Also, there was a very delicate handling of the Unequal Treaty Revision issue vis-à-vis Western countries, by literally obtaining permission from Britain and a look-the-other-way sort of semi-approval from Russia and the United States to hit back at China for overaggressiveness in Korea. Whence the victorious Sino-Japanese War (1894–1895) but then the humiliating return to China of the Liaotung peninsula area of southern Manchuria conquered by Japan during the war—no sooner than Russia, France, and Germany requested it by the so-called Triple Intervention. These events were, of course, all tied to "Chosen Mondai" (the Korean Problem) as the Japanese had come to call it. The way in which the Japanese specifically handled the Treaty Revision problem would greatly influence the foreign policy of Japan in the Meiji period. Professor Richard T. Chang's analysis of "The Question of Unilateral Denunciation" of these unequal treaties comes to the conclusion that even though the unequal treaties violated Japan's sovereign rights as a nation, Japan's policymakers in the 1880s–1890s "elected not to resort to any form of denunciation" and that, indeed, "this election was a realistic, wise, and statesmanlike decision" (see Conroy, Davies, and Patterson, 1984). My own analysis of the "Western Parameters of Sino-Japanese Relations" shows how Japan's leaders gave the highest importance to the realistic preservation on an even keel of broadest-based international relations with Western powers, in an effort to obtain their acceptance, if not cooperation, regarding Japan's various foreign policy moves in those decades (see Conroy, Davies, and Patterson, 1984). Not only did Ito Hirobumi pursue such diplomacy very effectively but, as a study by Louis G. Perez (1999) quite conclusively shows, the reformed former supporter of Saigo, Mutsu Munemitsu, conducted some very brilliant diplomacy as well.

Japan's relationship with Hawaii and with Americans residing there, up to Hawaii's annexation by the United States in 1898, provides an excellent example of the realistic diplomacy pursued by Ito, Mutsu, and their fellow foreign policymakers during this period. In a study begun in the aftermath of Pearl Harbor, which drew on experience gained as a Japanese-language specialist in the Occupation of Japan, I explored this peculiar Japan–Hawaii relationship in long-range documentary detail (Conroy, 1953) to find out whether Japanese leaders had harbored any "schemes to seize Hawaii" in those earlier years. Originally, I had even planned to give that study the suggestive title "The Japanese Expansion to Hawaii." Much to my surprise, I was to discover that it was the American planters in Hawaii who needed, wanted, and arranged to obtain Japanese immigrant labor; that the Japanese government had refrained from quarreling over "troublesome issues," such as the American-dominated Hawaiian government's new "democratic" constitution of 1887, which gave all male residents of Hawaiian, American, or European birth or descent, meeting the requisite age, tax, and other requirements, the right to vote—with the exclusion of Asiatics, therefore of the Japanese. Albeit reluctantly, Japan resigned itself to this exclusion, to the very extreme of acknowledging "with pleasure" the invitation received for its representative to attend the ceremony celebrating the U.S. annexation of Hawaii, held in Honolulu in 1898—despite the fact that, at the time, the Japanese residents by far outnumbered the community of Americans residing in Hawaii.

Regarding Hawaii, it is also interesting and important to note that Japan's leaders developed realistic restraint from very early on. In 1881, while visiting Tokyo on a world tour with his suite of American advisors, Hawaiian King Kalakaua would not only offer Japan an "equal treaty" that could have made a tiny, if not wholly insignificant, dent in the unequal treaty system which kept Japan away from international equality, but—slipping away from his American advisors—he would secretly propose to the Emperor an "Asiatic Federation" between Japan and Hawaii as well. It was the Emperor's realistically cautious advisors who would encourage their master politely if firmly to demur on both counts, short of causing much trouble for Japan in the wider international system.

After 1900, things would become a bit more complicated. When through the Anglo-Japanese Alliance of 1902, Britain would sway Japan to stand up to Russia, Ito Hirobumi would travel to Saint Petersburg, in search of a way to avoid hostilities. The Russian-Japanese war settlement would be handled in a way that would ease Russian-Japanese tensions quickly and easily. And, finally, with the installation of the system of "Residency General," in Korea, and with Ito Hirobumi in place as the "Resident General," Japan would attain the climax of its well-oiled realistic diplomacy.

But by 1910, with Ito assassinated and Korea annexed, such realistic diplomacy would be in shambles. Why? Because even Ito himself—in the year or so before his assassination by a Korean, on October 26, 1909—had almost given up on realistic diplomacy. Pressured by younger political rivals like Katsura Taro in Tokyo who were presumed to be more patriotic, he chose to turn over his Residency Generalship to his assistant, Sone Arasuke. But though he would try hard to follow Ito's style of diplomacy, Sone was less adept. And back in Tokyo, even Ito was beginning to respond to what might be called "patriotic pressures."

Where did this pushy "patriotism" come from? The sources are important as they illustrate the problems that realism in general and realists in particular face—not just in that Japanese-Korean context but wherever such pursuits still prevail in international relations. In the Japan–Korea setting of the time, and following Saigo's death, the "Korean question" stayed dormant for a while. But by the mid-1880s, there was an anti-oligarchic "People's Rights Movement"—*Jiyu Minken Undo*—afoot in Japan. Also by 1885, the Chinese were pressuring Korea to maintain its long-standing conservative "tributary" status. Japanese human rights leaders, namely, the well-known liberal organizer Fukuzawa Yukichi and his Korean and Japanese friends and followers, began scheming ways to bring "people's rights" to Korea. In 1885, in a rather spectacular "Osaka Incident," a band of idealistic young Japanese led by one Oi Kentaro gathered in Osaka, almost ready to launch a Liberate Korea movement, when the Japanese police arrested them. In this regard, it should not be overlooked that Japanese "people's rights" advocates including Fukuzawa had looked on the Sino-Japanese war as a struggle to "liberate" Korea from negative, old Chinese-style customs and political structure.

But after that war there was a subtle change, almost back to Saigo-style samurai-ism. To some it was still Liberate Korea, but there was another, even more ambitious program advocated first by the so-called Dark Ocean Society—*Genyosha*—organized in 1881, a mere four years after Saigo's death, to honor his memory and the "dark ocean" that led to Korea; then, upon the Genyosha's merger with a much more activist and grandiose organization, by what came to be called the Amur River or Black Dragon Society—*Kokuryukai*. Its leaders, Uchida Ryohei and Toyama Mitsuru, and increasingly large numbers of critics of Ito-style realism began to urge a greater mission for Japan—not just "liberating" Korea but "revitalizing" a much larger area and why not all of Greater East Asia, *Dai Toa*—not in some Western-style people's rights direction but in one where Imperial Japan would take upon itself a mission to rule the world (cf. Chapters 6 and 7 on globalization). It was they who, by exerting a huge amount of pressure on Ito and on his "realistic" Residency General, had brought about its collapse and—in 1910—the very annexation of Korea, which Ito-ist realism had deemed so utterly unnecessary for so long. In addition to the Kokuryukai Society, their specific vehicle to that end had been the *Ilchin* (in Japanese, *Isshin*) Renovation-Restoration society, which were after something they called *Gappo*, a word literally meaning not quite an "annexation"— still much too Western a concept—but, rather, a "merging," very much like "lips and teeth," into a great Oriental Federation. It would fall on the Japanese government officials to finalize the annexation, by using the term *heigo* for the very first time, thereby quite unambiguously signifying that Japan now would simply "annex," nay, even more clearly, "take over" Korea.

Although it was not realized in the wider world at the time, the annexation of Korea marked the very origin of the subsequent ultranationalist movement in Japan, which ultimately would lead to the Pacific War. And this took place in spite of the fact that there lingered on numerous "realistic" political leaders in Japan who, over the next 30 years, would continue very often to resort to their "realistic style." Perhaps most notable among these was Shidehara Kijuro. He was a principal architect of the Washington Conference treaty system of 1922. But like Ito in 1909, he would be incapable of standing up to the pressure from Greater East Asia-style "patriots" by the time the Manchurian Incident of 1931 (Conroy and Takemoto, 1974) took place.

The pressure from what could probably best be defined as the Japanese form of ultranationalism continued to build up during the 1930s, leading to the Pacific War despite the efforts of the likes of Ito and Shidehara to be more realistic than Pearl Harbor Premier, General Tojo Hideki. Tojo had admonished the ambivalent and vacillating former Premier Prince Konoe Fumimaro that there might come a time in a man's life when he must take a huge risk and "with his eyes closed, jump from Kiyomizu temple [a literally and figuratively high temple in Kyoto] into the ravine below."

There is little doubt (Conroy and Wray, 1990) that the war in the Pacific was eminently avoidable: During negotiations in the summer of 1941, and before General Tojo became premier, the Japanese side and the American side were not willing to tone down the antagonistic rhetoric or to negotiate realistically. Premier Konoe who had offered to come to Hawaii or Alaska to negotiate with President Roosevelt, would not (could not?) say publicly and in advance that Japanese troops would be, indeed, fully withdrawn from China, as U.S. Open Door policy demanded.

Therefore, it is surely not unfair to conclude that

postwar history would seem to mock an inevitability theory [of the war in the Pacific] of any kind. Japan has learned to live [very well] without controlling China or Southeast Asia and the United States learned not only to do without its Open Door policy in China but also to favor a strong Japan as a good balance in Asia. So why the [Pacific] war at all. (Conroy and Wray, 1990: 184)

Of course, this was written in 1990, and it could probably be argued that the Japanese economy has not been doing so well since then and that the United States is trying to resume some kind of "open door" trade with China. But these developments would suggest that, once again, a cautious, temperate, and sensible realism, shunning unwarranted and undue excesses in the finer realms of international politics, is still very much needed.

Why is realism so difficult to achieve and maintain? Let us for a moment return to the case of pre–World War II Japanese imperialism–expansionism. In the late 1930s, one Okawa Shumei—later to be indicted as a war criminal but ultimately not convicted as such on grounds of "mental instability"—published a history of Japan titled *Nippon Nissen Roppyaku Nenshi* [Japan's 2,600-Year History] which went through 18 printings between July and December 1939. By 1941, it had become the most popular introductory history text in Japan's schools. Very ultranationalistic, to put it mildly, it was a kind of abbreviated culmination of the half century of Japan's "merging with" Korea—then Manchuria and then China—that had begun with the *Seikan Ron* (Conquer Korea) argument in 1873, and had been dramatically advocated and publicized by the Black Dragon Society and its adherents as both a symbolic and concrete, necessary, expression of Japanese national interest and Japanese patriotism. This movement had already produced a huge, two-volume, *Nikkan Gappo Hisshi* ["Secret History of the Merger of Japan and Korea"] in 1936 and a two-volume non- (and anti-) official history of Japan–China negotiations—*Nishi Kosho Gaishi*—by Kokuryukai, in 1939, dedicated to Black Dragon leader Toyama Mitsura's ideal of a "Brighter Asia" under the decisive leadership of Japan.

Okawa's "2,600-Year History" carried Japan's "mission" back to First Emperor Jimmu Tenno's descent from the gods to assume the rulership of Japan and to begin to lead it on to (expansionism)—great(er) things. True, the Tokugawa had interrupted that thrust through their faint-hearted seclusionist policy. But Okawa's deep research uncovered a great Tokugawa anti-seclusionist in one Sato Shinen. As early as 1924, Okawa admitted that "If I were to write a history of modern Japan, I should begin with a description of Sato Shinen's ideas." Indeed, this statement was presented at Okawa's War Crimes trial (IMTFE, Exhibit 2182A: 10–11), citing Okawa's *Dai Toa Chitsujo Kensetsu*—the Establishment of Order in Greater East Asia.

What were Sato Shinen's great ideas? Sato had written *Kondo Hisaku*—Secret Absorption Plan—in which Japan, "the first state created and the foundation of the world," naturally was destined to rule it. He advised the "taking" of Korea and Manchuria, for starters; next, the "absorption" of China; then the "invasion" of British-, French-, Dutch-, and Spanish-controlled territories to the south, the Russian-controlled areas to the north, altogether eventually conducive to Japanese control of the whole world—a truly new global order to every unprecedented extent of the term.

Even before Okawa could incorporate Sato's ideas into his textbook, the Black Dragon Society had also discovered Sato along with some other premodern advocates of Japanese expansionism. It would publish laudatory biographies on them, in several volumes, titled *Toa Senkaku Shishi Kiden* [Biographies of Pioneer Exponents of Asiatic Expansion]. Thus the "right and duty" of Japan to save Asia by Japanese expansion was not only well-articulated but had become a key factor in Japan's national pride by the late-1930s.

Why, we may ask, could not Japan's realistic politicians and diplomats counter this? In the Japanese situation, it is easy to say that Japan's leaders had all been weaned on a samurai ethic. Nitobe Inazo had written (and even become world-famous for) his book *Bushid'o* ("The Way of the Warrior: The Soul of Japan"), as early as 1905. And though he was only trying to explain "The Way" rather than to promote it, Nitobe may be said to have succumbed to the samurai ethic in the end. His story, at once interesting and ironic, is told by Sharlie C. Ushioda in a collection of "historical and sociological studies of Japanese immigration and assimilation" (Conroy and Miyakawa, 1972). In brief, Nitobe, a man influenced by American missionaries and Christianized when still a student at Japan's Sapporo Agricultural College (1877–81), went to the United States for further study. He would marry an American girl from a Philadelphia Quaker family. Though he and his American wife would make their residence in Japan, they traveled so very frequently to the United States that Nitobe would become a "Bridge Across the Pacific"-cum-"A Man of Two Worlds," seeking to reconcile his samurai heritage and Christian/Quaker conversion in his book. He would almost succeed, by becoming a professor-teacher of mutual understanding, an undersecretary-general in the League of Nations, as well as an activist with the Institute of Pacific Relations. But in the late 1920s and early 1930s, he became disillusioned, first by the U.S. Japanese Exclusion Law of 1924, but also by the heavy-handed U.S./European "propaganda" about the Manchurian Incident of 1931 and Japan's penetration of Manchuria, which he would defend as a preemptive "buffer against Russian communism" and a reach for the industrial and agricultural "life line of Japan." Nitobe was, however, still advocating conciliatory negotiations when he died in 1933, while attending an Institute of Pacific Relations conference in Canada. One cannot say what his evaluation of Japanese militarism in the late 1930s would have been, but in the later 1930s editions of his by-now-famous *Bushid'o*, his criticisms of samurai bravado were either deleted or softened, implicitly to portray even this grand internationalist Christian/Quaker as a full-fledged advocate of Japanese expansionism.

Japan's path to Pearl Harbor offers a splendid historical instance of political/diplomatic realism being thwarted by what Tokyo University Professor Maruyama Masao (1963) deems to be an "underlying pathology" (cf. Maruyama, 1997). In 1965–1966, I spent a year at the East-West Center in Hawaii studying its document collection on Japanese expansionism and reading Maruyama and other postwar reflections on Japanese behavior patterns that led up to and into the Pacific War. I concluded (Conroy, 1966) that they divulged a

constant feeling of "nervousness" in the upper echelons of the [Japanese] power structure where "leaders" were afraid of seeming weak in the eyes of their subordinates. By [about 1940,] the vocabulary of subordinates, both among the infamous Young Officers and to a lesser degree [also among] officials in the civilian government establishment, as well as that of the general public, was heavily laden with the sort of terminology first used by the patriotic societies vis-à-vis the Korean annexation question. [Cf. chapter by Krippendorff, this volume.] Matters pertaining to "imperial benevolence" and "Greater East Asia" were simply not negotiable issues; attempts by governmental officials to negotiate on them especially in western languages with "alien" [un-Asian] diplomats were not only branded as weak, but [viewed, and therefore harshly dealt with, as] treasonous.

Now let us inquire whether this sort of pressure to derail diplomacy applies peculiarly to Japan and to its samurai–bushido tradition. First, in the pre-Pacific War scenario, the American diplomatic leadership was not subjected to any similar pressure. For sure, there were pressures on Secretary of State Cordell Hull not to let Japan get away with aggressions likely to violate the U.S. "open door rights" in China. In December 1937, there took place a very provocative Panay Incident—a Japanese attack on an American river boat on the Yangtze River—and by 1941, Hull's State Department expert on China, Stanley K. Hornbeck, and his associates, were convinced that only "by turning the screws we could force the Japanese into submission, that a tough attitude would cause them to abandon their aims in Asia." After speaking with Hornbeck in late October 1941, John K. Emmerson, who had served under Ambassador Joseph Grew at the U.S. Embassy in Tokyo, would conclude (see Emmerson, 1990, p. 41) that this was the position of Hornbeck's clique of China experts, noting that Hornbeck had reassured Hull as late as November 27, 1941, that the Japanese government did not "desire or intend or expect to have armed conflict" with the United States.

Convincing evidence (Klein, 1977) has been found that Hull was on the verge of offering an ad hoc temporary modus vivendi to Japan in late November 1941, which might have allowed discussion of Japan's "withdrawal from China" in lieu of the preconference guarantee, which his position had previously demanded. But this was derailed when, upon learning of such a potential ad hoc arrangement, British Prime Minister Churchill had Britain's ambassador in Washington, DC, rush a terse one-paragraph reply to U.S. President Roosevelt, which ended with the words: "We are sure that the regard of the United States for the Chinese cause will govern your action." This response reached Washington on November 25. The next day, Hull simply broke off negotiations with Japanese ambassador Nomura Kichisaburo (Klein and Conroy, 1990). Hence, it could be argued that at a crucial moment, Churchill reminded Hull through Roosevelt that he must stand strong on the China question. Of course, it could be also argued that, by the end of November 1941, Japan was already on the warpath anyway— and that the "kaffee-klatsch" over the modus vivendi would have made no difference in the manner that the course of events was steadily, rapidly, and inexorably coming to a head.

Before we put Pearl Harbor to rest, we should not disregard the fact that

Cordell Hull might have had a serious chance at negotiating a peaceful settlement, more than even he ever realized, owing to the peculiar relationship between the Japanese Ambassador Nomura and his direct "superiors" in Tokyo, especially during the summer of 1941, while the ambivalent Prince Konoe was still Japan's premier. True, Konoe had inherited a respect, even an enthusiasm, for the patriotic-expansionist jargon popularized by the Black Dragon Society and its advocates, from his father, Konoe Atsumaro, who in the days of talk about "merging lips and teeth with Korea" had supported their ideas. But Konoe had also been influenced by the elder statesman Genro Saionji Kinmochi, whom he had followed to the Versailles Conference in 1919 and who had recommended (in fact, chosen) him to be premier in the crucial times between 1937 and 1941. Prince Konoe had appointed a virulent foreign minister, Matsuoka Yosuke, who went on to ratify Japan's Tripartite (Axis) Alliance with Germany and Italy in September 1940. But by far not less important had been his appointment of a "friend of President Roosevelt," an enemy of Matsuoka, Nomura Kichisaburo, as Japanese ambassador to Washington, DC. A feud had been developing between Nomura and Matsuoka since February 14, 1941—the date of Nomura's arrival in Washington as ambassador. Nomura was, as he wanted to be, ambivalent Premier Prince Konoe's top peacemaker. He saw in Matsuoka the very protagonist of Konoe's Axis Alliance. Noteworthy is the fact that Nomura, a retired admiral of highest repute and prestige, had accepted the ambassadorial assignment to the United States on the condition that he be spared Tokyo's restraints on his negotiations for peace. Nomura's "strange diplomacy" (Burns and Bennett, 1974; Conroy, 1970a; Conroy and Wray, 1990) has been attributed by some scholars (Butow, 1974) to his lack of professional expertise as a diplomat and his reliance on the assistance of a "strange" clique of unofficial peacemaking advisors, whom Stanley Hornbeck would satirically refer to as Nomura's "John Doe Associates."

Without going into all the details of this, let me say that my own analysis gives more credit to Nomura for at least trying to "give peace a chance" in defiance of his Axis-pursuing "boss" in Tokyo, Foreign Minister Matsuoka. Nomura succeeded in that task to the extent of ultimately getting Matsuoka ousted as foreign minister and replaced by a Nomura friend and supporter, Admiral Toyoda Teijiro, on July 12, 1941. Under these circumstances, with such opportunities, the way should have been opened up for peace. Unfortunately, however, there is more to the story. In the course of his several months' quarrel with Matsuoka over the direction of Japan-U.S. relations, Nomura had frequently softened the inflexible instructions received from Tokyo when relaying them to Cordell Hull. This he would do also on the advice of his peace-pursuing John Doe Associates (two American Catholic priests, a Japanese army colonel, and a Japanese banker who reputedly "had the ear" of Premier Konoe). His softening of Tokyo's tough words would lead to Nomura's undoing in Washington, however. Hull's code breakers in the State Department would not hesitate to provide him with the harsher Tokyo originals of Namura's less brusk "proposals." Although, by July 1941, Matsuoka was ousted and the climate in Tokyo was changing for the better, Hull could not overcome his impression of Nomura as an untrustworthy, "devious Jap." The unforgiving outcomes of that categorical disapproval would follow in quick succession: the oil embargo; FDR's refusal to meet Konoe unless or until Japan publicly accepted Hull's Four Principles, including a promise of withdrawal from China; and Konoe's decision to resign and to leave all matters in the hands of General Tojo and of the Japanese military.

It could be concluded that, as with the annexation of Korea, here, too, realism failed, by hardening the path of an otherwise possibly well-avoidable war. In retrospect, might there have been anything more helpful to realism that could have been undertaken in a situation that threatened to turn into a syndrome? Was there any way that the "samurai ethics," which made Tojo take the "leap into the ravine below" could have been deflected? How about some sense of humor? When Hull learned that Nomura was softening the hard-line rhetoric from Tokyo, what if he had said, "Mr. Nomura, we have broken your diplomatic code. We are decoding the messages that you receive from Tokyo. Should we not discuss any problems of translation? And, by the way, if you are trying to get rid of that crazy Matsuoka fellow, perhaps I could even help you."

The psychology of Matsuoka's "craziness" is an interesting point that may be worth a brief glance, in this analytic context: His boyhood experience in Oregon, which seems to have led him to hate Americans, led to his derision as "the delegate from Oregon" in the Japanese Diet from which he moved on to arrange and forge Japan's withdrawal from the League of Nations and entry into the Axis Alliance. At any rate, following Matsuoka's ouster from the Konoe cabinet, Hull might have suggested to Nomura that all such matters be discussed at the conference Konoe had wanted with FDR, instead of harping on his "Four Points." Is it possible then that Konoe might not have resigned, but instead would have summoned the courage to do some peacemaking from the softer side of his ambivalence?

The earlier-mentioned Fukuzawa Yukichi, the famous people's rights advocate of the earlier Meiji era, once, while addressing a graduating class of Keio University, which he had founded, went so far as to suggest that they should all remember what he called "The Ujimushi Principle." In colloquial Japanese, *Ujimushi* means literally "bugs and worms." In Japanese slang, however, it is a reference to children as "small fry." We should never forget, Yukichi advised, that we are all ujimushi in this world, even when we are grown up. We should always think of life as kid's games and refrain from taking things too seriously. Good advice for realist negotiators? In sum, it would seem that good-natured humor can be useful in helping the cause of realism in international affairs.

Years ago, I compared Japan's war in China and America's war in Vietnam (Conroy, 1970b). In my deep probe of the "Lessons from Japanese Imperialism" (Conroy, 1966), during my research at the East-West Center in the mid-1960s, I had felt duty-bound to say something about that comparison as I realized more and more that Vietnam—a quagmire for the United States in the 1960s—was too unnervingly similar to the Japan-in-China situation in 1937–1941: Most Japanese in that era had thought they were "saving China" from bad things, especially from communism, and that their main objective was to bring about a Greater East Asia Co-Prosperity Sphere—*Dai Toa Kyoeiken*. Years later, the well-meaning President Lyndon Johnson and his advisors would deem they had an even more urgent reason to save South Vietnam—"the Domino effect," which presumed that communism would spread through Southeast Asia like a disease if it were not stopped. However, even if it had spread, there is little indication that in the longer run it would have survived.

What did realism have to say to this? Interestingly enough, the *ichiban* (number one) realism expert, George F. Kennan (1951), father of Containment and latter-day Ito Hirobumi, came to the opinion that the Domino theory might have been an exaggeration. In 1967, I heard him tell an American Historical Association meeting in Toronto, Canada, that his idea for the containment of communism had been conceived for Europe, that it had not included Communist China and its border countries—for, that was "another problem." Fortunately, a few years later, after Lyndon Johnson threw in the towel, and newly elected President Nixon's realist advisor Henry Kissinger took it upon himself to "solve" the Vietnam (and the China) problem, I would find good reason to revise my "Historical Parallel to Vietnam," under the new title "Comparing America's War in Vietnam and Japan's War in China" (Conroy, 1982). This time around, I could contrast the outcomes: An anti-war movement inside the United States had ended in "peace" and full withdrawal from Vietnam. Yet, in the case of Japan in China, the effort had escalated into a war in the Pacific. But I did find it rather noteworthy that a "peace with honor" arrangement had been necessary for the Nixon–Kissinger withdrawal from Vietnam—the release of American prisoners of war and their well-publicized, red-carpeted, return to the United States; the transferral of any further responsibility for the "saving of South Vietnam" to the dubious know-how and wherewithal of the Thieu government forces; and the truly heroic airlifts of Americans, even some of the "good" South Vietnamese, moments before the fall of Saigon.

Could Japan have gotten out of its "War in China" in similar fashion if realism had prevailed? Very possibly: It had a Japan-friendly Wang Ching-wei (Wang Jingwei) "puppet government" in Nanking, "ruling" half of China even as Mao's Communists and Chiang K'ai-shek's own Kuomintang had the remainder engaged in a "unified" resistance of sorts. Many Japanese, probably including Premier Prince Konoe, would have liked to exit and leave their "better China" to Wang, who might or might not have been able to survive. Some scholars (Lin, 1978) give Wang considerable credit for survival skills. But no Japanese Kissinger would rise to the occasion, at that unique moment in the history of the Land of the Rising Sun.

A FEW REFLECTIONS IN THE GUISE OF CONCLUSION

In this chapter, I have used the historic course of Japanese expansionism— from "Scizure of Korea" and war "in" (not against) China to the Pacific War—in comparative contrast with the U.S. war "in" (not against) Vietnam, to illuminate the problems that realistic diplomacy faces in trying to avoid wars while striving to deal also with "fears" and "foes." As a historian duty-bound to objectivity and balance in interpretation and presentation, I have had some reluctance to go beyond the specifics of my studies of Asian Pacific history into the broader realms of international politics, but the extensive and exciting nature of this volume has encouraged me to develop my argument along complex diplomatic dimensions relevant to the thematic concerns of this volume.

In my introduction to this chapter, I submitted that peace research is still sorely needed and that some new journals in the field of history have been making even greater progress in that direction. The multidisciplinary perspectives brought together on the common theme of fears and foes in this volume, I believe, break yet another original path through an inclusive, sincere, and polyvalent conversation in a constructive direction of promise.

There are many ways of approach to world history: One could westernize or deliberately de-westernize (Bingham, Conroy, and Ikle, 1974) it. Much as I admire Toynbee's fecund output, I remember having once characterized his Westernization of "A History of the World" as an effort starting with ancient civilizations and ending with the Church of England. One can also nationalize "world" history, dissecting each nation into "ancient, medieval, early modern, and modern"; or even ideologize it with the provocative brilliance of a Hobsbawm (1994). Ah, if only historians looked at world history from the moon: they would certainly acquire a truly global view.

NOTE

Among the "peacemaking" journals mentioned, the *Journal of World History* grew out of the Chicago School's emphasis on "Great [Western] Books," begun by University of Chicago President Robert Maynard Hutchins, developed by Professors William. H. McNeill, Marshall Hodgson, Akira Iriye, and others, including Franklin D. Scott (Northwestern, specialist in "Migration"). Iriye went on to Harvard, where he helped to expand "great books" beyond Western civilization and to emphasize the multiplicity and importance of cultural factors in international relations, about which he and his former students (Robert D. Johnson, ed.) have written. The work of Philip Curtin, Jerry Bentley, Daniel Kwok, Judith Zinsser, and Ray Lorantas have also been of special importance in this World History enterprise.

The *Peace and Change* journal had its origin in the worries of Professor Merle Curti, Univerity of Wisconsin, and some 50 other scholars, who gathered at a Philadelphia Quaker Meeting House in December 1963 to discuss why there was so much talk on "Causes of War" and so little on "Causes of Peace" at the American Historical Association. Charles Chatfield, Blanche Cook, Lawrence Wittner, Charles Barker, Sandi Cooper, Charles DiBenedetti, Arno Mayer, Barton Bernstein, and Hansheng Lin and their writings did enhance peace research and do deserve to be in the bibliography.

The *Amerasia Journal* owes its origins to Professor Chitoshi Yanaga and his Yale students Lowell Chun-Hoon and Don Nakanashi. Others who have helped develop it at UCLA include Glenn Omatsu, Franklin Ng, Russell Leong, Yuji Ichioka, Arif Dirlik, as well as L. H. Shimagawa and T. Scott Miyakawa.

Recent studies of Japanese imperialism which I have reviewed and which I intend to include in my future bibliographies are by Peter Duus, Donald Calman, Louise Young, John Stephan, Germaine Hoston, Walter McDougall, Ian Nish, and W. G. Beasley, and should provide further good readings for those more directly concerned.

All in all, yes, history does have a future.

REFERENCES

Amerasia Journal (Asian American Studies Center, University of California, Los Angeles).

American Historical Review, The (Journal of the American Historical Association).

Bingham, Woodbridge, Hilary Conroy, and Frank W. Ikle (1964–1965; rev. ed. 1974). *History of Asia* (2 vols.). Boston: Allyn and Bacon.

Burns, Richard D., and Edward M. Bennett (eds.) (1974). *Diplomats in Crisis: United States-Chinese-Japanese Relations, 1939–1941.* Santa Barbara, CA: ABC-Clio Press.

Butow, Robert J. C. (1974). *The John Doe Associates: Backdoor Diplomacy for Peace, 1941.* Stanford, CA: Stanford University Press.

Conroy, Hilary (1951). Government versus Patriot: The Background of Japan's Asiatic Expansion. *Pacific Historical Review* 20, 1: 31–42.

——— (1952). Japan's War in China. *Pacific Historical Review* 21, 4: 367–379.

——— (1953). *The Japanese Frontier in Hawaii, 1868–1898.* Berkeley: University of California Press. [Cf. Conroy, Hilary (1973). *The Japanese Expansion into Hawaii: 1868–1898.* San Francisco: R & E Research Associates.]

——— (1955). Japanese Nationalism and Expansionism. *American Historical Review* 60, 4: 818–829.

——— (1960). *The Japanese Seizure of Korea: A Study of Realism and Idealism in International Relations.* Philadelphia: University of Pennsylvania Press; paperback, 1974.

——— (1966). Lessons from Japanese Imperialism. *Monumenta Nipponica*, 21, nos. 3–4: 334–345. [Cf. Institute of Advanced Projects, East-West Center, Humanities no. 1.]

——— (1970a). The Strange Diplomacy of Admiral Nomura. *Proceedings of the American Philosophical Society* 114, 3 (June 1970): 205–216.

——— (1970b). Japan's War in China: Historical Parallel to Vietnam? *Pacific Affairs* 43, 1 (Spring 1970): 61–72.

——— (1982). Comparing America's War in Vietnam and Japan's War in China. In David J. Lu (ed.), *Perspectives on Japan's External Relations*. Bucknell University, Center for Japanese Studies.

———, Sandra Davies, and Wayne Patterson (eds.) (1984) *Japan in Transition: Thought and Action in the Meiji Era, 1868–1912*. London: Associated University Presses.

———, and T. Scott Miyakawa (1972). *East Across the Pacific; Historical and Sociological Studies of Japanese Immigration and Assimilation*. Santa Barbara, CA: ABC-Clio Press.

———, and Toru Takemoto (1974). An Ounce of Prevention: A New Look at the Manchurian Incident. *Peace and Change* 2, 1 (Spring 1974): 42–46.

———, and Harry Wray (eds.) (1990). *Pearl Harbor Reexamined: Prologue to the Pacific War*. Honolulu: University of Hawaii Press. [Cf. Wray, H., and H. Conroy (1983). *Japan Examined: Perspectives on Modern Japanese History*. Honolulu: University of Hawaii Press.]

Coox, Alvin D., and Hilary Conroy (eds.) (1978). *China and Japan: Search for Balance*. Santa Barbara, CA: ABC-Clio Press.

Davies, Wallace E. (1955). *Patriotism on Parade*. Cambridge, MA: Harvard University Press.

Emmerson, John K. (1990). Principles versus Realities: U.S. Prewar Foreign Policy toward Japan. P. 47 in H. Conroy and H. Wray (eds.), *Pearl Harbor Reexamined: Prologue to the Pacific War*. Honolulu: University of Hawaii Press.

Hobsbawm, Eric J. (1994). *The Age of Extremes: A History of the World, 1914–1991*. New York: Pantheon Books.

IMTFE (International Military Tribunal for the Far East). Exhibit 2182A, pp. 10–11 (Okawa's War Crimes Trial).

Journal of Asian Studies (Journal of the Association of Asian Studies).

Journal of Pacific Affairs (University of British Columbia, Canada).

Journal of World History (World History Association, University of Hawaii Press).

Kaplan, Robert D. (1997). Was Democracy Just a Moment? *Atlantic Monthly* (December): 73.

Kennan, George F. (1947). The Sources of Soviet Conduct (by Mr. X). *Foreign Affairs* 25, 4: 566–582.

——— (1951). *American Diplomacy, 1900–1950*. Chicago: University of Chicago Press, Mentor Books.

Klein, David H. (1977). Anglo-American Diplomacy and the Pacific War: The Politics of Confrontation. Ph.D. dissertation, University of Pennsylvania.

Klein, David H., and Hilary Conroy (1990). Churchill, Roosevelt and the China Question. In H. Conroy and H. Wray (eds.), *Pearl Harbor Reexamined: Prologue to the Pacific War*. Honolulu: University of Hawaii Press.

Klein, Julia M. (1998). On John Lucacs' "Hitler as History." *The Philadelphia Inquirer*, January 13.

Kuzuu Yoshihisa (ed.) (1933–1936). *Toa Senkaku Shishi Kiden* [Biographies of Pioneer Exponents of Asian Expansion]. 3 vols. Tokyo: Kokuryukai.

———— (1936). *Nikkan Gappa Hisshi* [Secret History of the Merger of Japan and Korea]. Tokyo: Kokuryukai.

Lin, Han-sheng (1978). A New Look at Chinese Nationalist Appeasers. In Alvin D. Coox and Hilary Conroy (eds.), *China and Japan: Search for Balance*. Santa Barbara, CA: ABC-Clio Press.

Lu, David J. (ed.) (1981). *Perspectives on Japan's External Relations*. Bucknell University, Center for Japanese Studies.

Maruyama, Masao (1963). *Thought and Behavior in Modern Japanese Politics*. Oxford: Oxford University Press.

———— (1997). Obituary-Memorial. *Japan Echo*, 24. Special Issue.

Meskill, Johanna (1966). *Hitler and Japan: The Hollow Alliance*. New York: Atherton.

Nishi Kosho Gaishi [Japanese-Chinese Negotiations]. (1939). Tokyo: Kokuryukai.

Nitobe, Inazo (1905). *Bushid'o: The Soul of Japan; An Exposition of Japanese Thought*. Enlarged 10th ed. London and New York: G. P. Putnam and Sons.

Okawa Shumei (1939?). *Nissen Roppyaku Nenshi* [2,600-Year History of Japan]. Tokyo: Dai Ichi Shoten.

———— (n.d.) *Dai Toa Chitsujo Kensetsu* [Establishment of Order in Greater East Asia]. IMTFE Exhibit 2182A, International War Crimes Tribunal.

Peace and Change (Journal of Peace History Society). Boston: Blackwell Publishers.

Perez, Louis G. (1999). *Japan Comes of Age: Mutsu Munemitsu and the Revision of the Unequal Treaties*. Madison, NJ: Fairleigh Dickinson University Press; London: Associated University Presses. [See also: Perez, Louis G. (1998). *History of Japan*. Westport, CT: Greenwood Press.]

Sato Shinen (ca. 1800). *Kondo Hisaku* [Secret Absorption Plan]. In *Dai Toa Shiso Zenshu* [Collection of Japanese Ideas], Vol. 8, pp. 146–149. Tokyo, 1933. [Cf. Yoshi S. Kuno, *Japanese Expansion on the Asiatic Continent*. Vol. 2, pp. 227–228, 351–358. Berkeley: University of California Press, 1940.]

Stephan, John (1984). *Hawaii under the Rising Sun: Japanese Plans for Conquest after Pearl Harbor*. Honolulu: University of Hawaii Press.

Tompkins, E. Berkeley (ed.) (1971). *Peaceful Change in Modern Society*. Stanford, CA: Stanford University Press.

Ushioda, Sharlie C. (1972). Man of Two Worlds: An Inquiry into the Value System of Inazo Nitobe, 1862–1933. In H. Conroy and S. Miyakawa (eds.), *East Across the Pacific: Historical and Sociological Studies of Japanese Immigration and Assimilation*. Santa Barbara, CA: ABC-Clio Press.

CHAPTER 3

Power in the Information Age

JEFFREY A. HART AND SANG-BAE KIM

INTRODUCTION

Power and technology are closely related to one another. The assessment or measurement of power generally takes into account this interdependence. In *The Peloponnesian Wars*, Thucydides was careful to tell us how many *hoplites* (armored foot soldiers) and ships each side had prior to an important battle. After the end of World War II, most of the attempts to assess relative national strengths had to take into account the possession of nuclear weapons and nuclear weapon delivery systems.

We want to go beyond the more limited question of assessing military power in terms of military technology, to discuss the cognitive and conceptual underpinnings of power. Our interest is not in the mere measurement of the military/strategic power of nation-states at the international level but also in the factors, which may be affecting the distribution of all types of power, within and across nations, in the information age. In this chapter, however, we will focus primarily on the impact of information technologies on the conceptualization of technology itself, and we will discuss some important implications of the changed conceptualization regarding the assessment of power.

It is necessary first to take a step back and ask about the relationship between information and knowledge. We assume that the creation and dissemination of knowledge require the analysis and restructuring of information; that information, by itself, does not constitute knowledge. In fact, too much information in the context of confusion leads to what some call "infoglut." One must possess some cognitive filtering and structuring mechanism to sort out what is relevant information from among what is not and to incorporate the new information productively into the old synthesis. However, without accurate and timely information, even the best conceptual structures are useless. Thus, there exists an interdependency between information and knowledge, just as there exists one between knowledge and power. Power can often enable actors to acquire both the information and the conceptual tools needed to devise effective strategies; knowledge helps actors to define goals and objectives in a more informed and, potentially, more rational manner.

Knowledge power, according to Francis Bacon, was the quest of science in its search to discover "the knowledge of Causes, and secret motions of things; and the enlarging of the bounds of Human Empire, to the effecting of all things possible" (Bacon, 1624: 36). This was a succinct, confident, ambitious statement of the nature and purpose of science; it brought together the previously separate notions of scientific knowledge, power, and progress. Bacon's two new aims of academic work were "control of nature" by means of science, and "advancement of learning." Bacon wanted scientists to pursue progress rather than individual fame, to cooperate with one another in order to bring about a speedier progress of civilization. In Bacon's conception, scientists were neither scholarly disputants nor literati greedy of glory. Until then, knowledge had been considered an end in itself, and the quiet contemplation of truth had been deemed the highest vocation to which man could aspire. Not so, Bacon suggested—the purpose of man was action and the aim of knowledge, utility—whereby he became known as an early champion of utilitarianism.

Since Bacon's time, the scientific/technological project, exemplified by the academic study of the natural sciences and engineering, has triumphed. Most contemporary governmental R&D programs share the premises in Bacon's writings that science and technology are useful for the betterment of the human condition, but also for the advancement of the interests of the nation-state in which technology is invented. Bacon's idea of knowledge power is, therefore, a useful starting point when seeking to understand power in the information age. But Bacon's formulation needs some updating when accounting for the altered nature of the processes by which knowledge is created and embedded in technology, in view of the shifts in the conceptualization of technology and the many changes in the acquisition of technological knowledge that have taken place since the recent beginnings of the information age.

TOWARD A NEW CONCEPTUALIZATION OF TECHNOLOGY

The word "technology" was first used in the seventeenth century, when it began to replace the more elementary idea of "technics." According to the *Oxford English Dictionary*, its original English meaning, dating back to the early seventeenth century, was "a discourse or treatise (a *logos*) on art or the arts"; and "the scientific study (a *logos*) of the practical or industrial arts." Yet another meaning identifies technology as "technical nomenclature"—the very terminology or vernacular—*logos*—of a particular art. Only in the second half of the nineteenth century would the meaning begin to refer to the practical arts themselves, in transformational terms ("his technology consists of weaving, cutting canoes, making rude weapons"). Etymologically, "technology" comes from the Greek root *techne*, or art—not the finer arts but the useful crafts, rather carpentry and shoemaking than poetry and dance—and from *logos*, articulate speech or discursive reason. But the Greeks did not ideate the compound *techno-logos*. The closest they came to any such notion would have had the emphasis reversed: not an account about art (a *logos* of *techne*) but an art of speaking. Rhetoric, the art of persuasive speech, was indeed a *techne* of *logos*, and in the view of the sophists, a means for rationalizing political life free of the need for force (Melzer, Weinberger, and Zinman, 1993: 3).

We have inherited conceptual tools from the past, many of which are not adequate for acquiring an understanding of social transformations caused by important technological changes. And although we have seen a rise in the number of new terminologies for describing social and technological changes since the 1950s—postindustrial, post-Fordist, postcapitalist society, Information Revolution, knowledge industry, the Third Wave, the microelectronics market, the postmodern era—concepts of the sort do not, in our view, capture the essence of the changes that we have been experiencing. Thus, the best way to proceed is to characterize as accurately as possible the impact of modern information and of the communications technologies on the conceptualization of technology itself.

Technology has often been understood as "hardware": whether a weapon, a production facility, or a piece of telecommunications equipment. In order to differentiate the conceptual structure of technology, however, we should note that technology, like Janus, has two faces: the hardware face (material product), and the software face (technological knowledge). Most technology is not merely a material product or solely technological knowledge, but usually a combination of both. Hardware is useless without the knowledge of usage. Moreover, technological knowledge alone often has no utility until it is embodied in tools, instruments, or machines. The hardware face of technology is generally easier to grasp because of its tangibility, which is why we tend to think about technology in terms of "doing"—of hardware only.

Technology is "the systematic application of scientific or other organized knowledge to practical tasks by ordered systems that involve people, organizations, living things, and machines" (Pacey, 1983: 4–7). Technology has four *aspects*: machines, knowledge, organizations, and people. In this chapter, we identify four related aspects of technology, each with its very own

Figure 3.1
The Conceptual Structure of Technology (A Simile of an Iceberg)

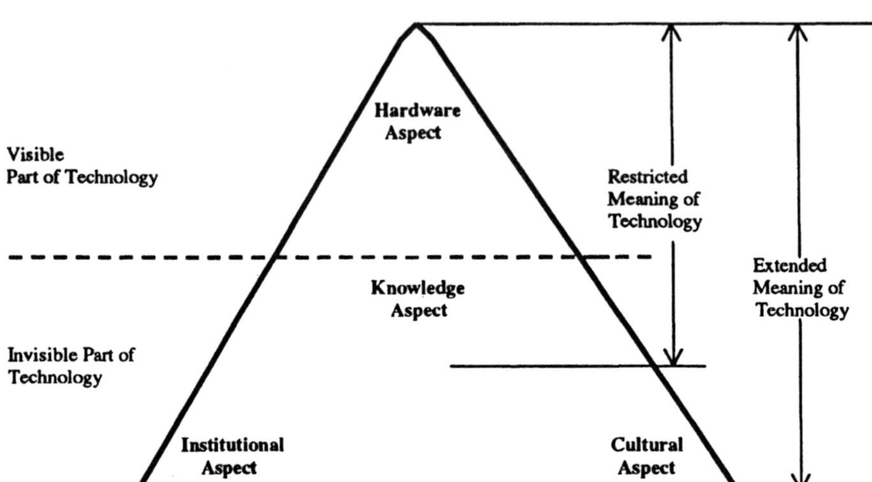

policy implications for technological development: (1) material products, (2) knowledge, (3) institutions, and (4) culture. Only the first two of these can fall within the "restricted" meaning of technology. In order to grasp the whole picture, therefore, we also need an "extended" meaning of the concept of technology, which may include all four aspects.

In the restricted meaning of technology, the adoption of new technologies is purely pragmatic in nature. It does not consider the possible impact of technology on institutions and culture. In the extended meaning of technology, technology policy is closely related to an assessment of the immediate and potential impacts of new technologies on social institutions and culture.

We know from empirical study of the process of technological adaptation and diffusion that technological change does not occur in isolation from institutional and cultural considerations; and that institutional and cultural factors have an important impact on the development and diffusion of new technologies. To a certain extent, each new technology "encodes" a set of institutional and cultural practices in itself as a conditional part of the process of its acceptability in different societies. And that is exactly why countries technologically trying to "catch up" often become involved in intense internal debates about which technologies to pursue and how to reconcile these technologies with their culture and institutions.

Figure 3.1 implies that technology is like an iceberg—with a visible part above the water line and a larger, invisible part below the surface. The visible part of technology is often embodied in hardware, whereas the invisible is embodied in supporting "software" that includes the knowledge that made the technology possible in the first place. The emphasis on the visible versus the invisible elements of technology may depend on the conceptualization of technology in a particular society or culture. For example, in the nineteenth century, China's outlook was different from Japan's: The Chinese were more hardware-oriented, focusing on the visible tips of the iceberg, uninclined to paying attention to the invisible part of technology, especially in the early stages of modernization. In contrast, the Japanese were willing to accept the invisible as well as the visible part of Western technology. This is the point from which Chinese and Japanese responses sharply diverged at the initial stages of their modernization. This divergence in conceptualizing is evident in almost every aspect of their modernization processes (Kim, 1995).

The conceptual core of technology involves the knowledge aspect—"the semi-visible part." Three characteristics of technological knowledge are noteworthy in the information age: appropriability, codifiability, and compatibility. The first of these deals with the credibility and enforceability of claims of ownership. Codifiability means the ability of people to write down in some reproducible form the essence of a given technology. And compatibility implies the possibility of transferring usage rights for a technology that has the capability of being used in a system without need for special modification to accommodate it.

Three types of appropriability of technological knowledge have been proposed (Krugman, 1987): (1) largely appropriable knowledge, such as production-process knowledge reflected in firm-specific learning curves; knowledge, assimilable within a firm and therefore broadly appropriable; (2) semi-appropriable knowledge, say, of product design, which—once generated—often can be captured by competitors through "reverse engineering"; and (3) spreadable ("footloose") but non-appropriable knowledge that can spread beyond the innovating firm, although not necessarily as easily so, beyond national or sometimes even regional boundaries. It is often embodied in people and is likely to spread through social and academic networks.

The ability of firms or nations to reverse-engineer the new technologies developed elsewhere speeds international diffusion but at some cost. True, both the speed and the expense of copying the technologies of others are lower for spreadable technologies than for appropriable technologies. For national governments, an interesting tension exists between the desire to promote the development of spreadable technologies in the public interest and to promote the development of largely appropriable technologies as a way of creating at least short-term advantages for domestic private industry and for military capability. The governments of major industrialized nations recognize this tension by splitting bureaucratic responsibility for the funding of basic and applied research among different agencies. Thus, basic research funding is generally administered by Ministries of Education and Research and usually is spent by universities and government laboratories in the form of mostly outright grants. Applied research funding is generally administered by Ministries of Commerce, Industry, and Defense and generally is spent by private firms under contract to the government. Similarly, almost all governments recognize the desire of private actors to appropriate new technologies and to exploit them for financial gain, and in the process to foster technological innovation. This recognition materializes primarily through intellectual property protection: patents, copyrights, and the like (Long, 1991). This raises the question of the extent to which a given technology can be codified in order for it to be able to qualify for intellectual property protection.

The appropriability of technological knowledge is closely related to codifiability. An uncodifiable technology is more appropriable than a codifiable one in that it is usually less transferable; a codifiable technology is less appropriable than an uncodifiable one in that it is usually more transferable. In the information age, however, codifiable technologies have become largely appropriable in both technological and legal terms. One of the more important features of this age is the very effort now being exerted on codifying by electronic hardware and software many of the previously uncodified human practices. Thus, for example, it is not unusual to find filtering programs for E-mail software that help weed out unwanted messages from untrusted sources. The software, sometimes called an intelligent agent, learns how to do this by emulating human filtering behavior. Until recently, it was a secretary's job or the boss's task to do this—the filtering of knowledge was human-embodied and not codified. After filtering agents do their job, the knowledge becomes software—embodied in computer hardware and codified.

The increasing trend toward codifying knowledge in software has raised the salience of intellectual property laws and of law enforcement in the perception of national governments. To promote the software industry as part of the larger task of promoting the computer industry, many of the governments of industrially advanced nations grant temporary monopoly privileges to the writers of new software through patent and copyright laws. Patenting/licensing fees paid to firms that make/sell software compensate the expense of developing the software in the first place. However, software is relatively easy to "pirate" (by selling illegal copies), and so software firms frequently turn to their home governments for help in enforcing intellectual property rights at home and abroad.

Often, it is not in the interest of the less industrialized countries to cooperate vigorously with the intellectual property regimes established by the industrialized countries because those regimes force them to pay a premium for new technologies, largely invented abroad. If they can use the technologies by copying them illegally and therefore enjoy much lower prices, then ordinarily they will do so. However, there are two major costs associated with this practice. First, if the country condoning piracy seeks to develop its own domestic software industry, it will be highly handicapped in doing so because of lax or nonexistent enforcement of intellectual property rights. Second, the firms that control the development of valuable intellectual property, many of which are multinational enterprises, may be less willing to sell their most advanced products in countries that do not care to enforce intellectual property laws—if only due to the low likelihood of making a reasonable profit. So the country that chooses this path may thereby be unwittingly or otherwise also cutting itself off from the benefits of the latest innovations in hardware or software.

Along the issue of intellectual property, another important matter is the issue of codifiability. In the information age, the importance of human-embodied craft knowledge is rising. This is the technological knowledge embodied in the creators or users of technology rather than in software or hardware. Sometimes, it is called tacit knowledge, or uncodifiable knowledge, and is closely related to the creation and learning processes (such as learning-by-doing or learning-by-using) usually associated with the development and diffusion of new technologies. As a general rule, the more complex the technology, the more time and effort required to train a human to use it, and hence the higher value of human-embodiment of technological knowledge. If technological knowledge is tacit or uncodifiable, technological development is likely to be more dependent on historically determined skills and search routines. Often, technology cannot be easily transferred because of its dependence on the specific competence of localized individuals. The failure of many attempts elsewhere in the world to reproduce the Silicon Valley of northern California provides a good example. None of the rare limited successes has been able to equal, let alone duplicate, the size and breadth of activity in the original site.

Uncodifiable craft knowledge still plays an important role in industrial production—in fine machining or in laying out a design for a printed circuit board, for instance—despite efforts since the beginning of the Industrial Revolution, to root out the craft elements in order to reduce managers' dependence on craft workers and on their powerful unions (Piore and Sabel, 1984). The software business is rife with practitioners of craft knowledge, to the chagrin of the Japanese and others trying to create "software factories" (Cusumano, 1991). Especially able programmers are often called "wizards" and draw higher salaries and better perquisites, even stock options, compared to their fellow software employees, mainly to prolong their professional loyalty to the firm.

Compatibility is particularly important for technologies that become more useful to humans to the extent that they are widely shared. A good example would be a telegraph or telephone network. Network infrastructures become increasingly valuable to their users as the number of people who can be reached via the network increases. Economists identify this effect as *network externality*. Languages work this way, too: The more those who share a given language, the greater the usefulness (at least in theory) for those who use that language. If a technology is hard to use, if it is priced unreasonably, or if ownership rights are difficult to guarantee, then compatibility problems might arise. A technology easily transmitted via existing transportation and telecommunications networks is potentially more shareable and compatible than one that cannot be diffused in that easy manner. The software side of information technology is highly dependent on compatibility, hence the relatively new high-speed networks of telecommunications currently being built. But such technology may prove difficult to appropriate, owing to the ease with which it can be pirated via illegal copying and transmission over the network.

Technological compatibility can serve as a useful strategic instrument for firms. "Nation-states are likely to use national and international infrastructures as instruments of competition in world affairs. There will always be some temptation to use incompatibilities in national infrastructures . . . [so as to shelter] domestic firms or workers from international competition" (Hart, 1989: 8.) In the setting or updating of technological standards for information technology industries, the politics of standards and compatibility have been remarkable in recent years. The U.S. decision to adopt a digital HDTV (high-definition television) standard incompatible with Japanese and European analogue standards, as well as the competition between two incompatible formats for home VCRs (videocassette recorders)—Beta versus VHS—provide two examples of the politics of standardization in the world at large as well as in the Japanese economy. The periodical standard updating of computer hardware and software by such major computer companies as Intel and Microsoft is also tainted by politics. The two firms are market leaders. IBM-compatible computers have Intel x86-family microprocessors and DOS/Windows operating systems. It is remarkable that, as Kenney (1996) suggests "(s)ome products such as personal computers are now on a three-month product cycle, demonstrating that even as value is being created more quickly, it is . . . destroyed more quickly. In the case of software, the quintessential product of the Information Economy, obsolescence is also extremely rapid. . . . the economy is obsolescence-based."

THE EVOLUTION OF THE CONCEPT OF TECHNOLOGY

To conceptualize the current transformation of technology, we need to understand the origin and historical evolution of the idea. What is the modern concept of technology? What are the differences between the modern and premodern technologies? Are there any midrange or microlevel changes in the concept of technology in any given era? To answer these questions, we need to explore the conceptual history of technology at three levels: (1) technology as hardware, (2) technology as knowledge, and (3) technology as an institutionally and culturally embedded entity.

Hardware invention has been developed in four stages: in the primitive, premodern, modern, and information societies, as per Figure 3.2. Three criteria help distinguish them: the intention of the invention, its linkage to specific persons, and the knowledge applied. In primitive society, invention is just a discovery with rare if any human intention for invention. In premodern society, invention is often the intentional making of tools. Invention does not yet include the invention of machines. Tools serve as an extension of the craftsman's hands and cannot be understood on their own merit. In the modern world, invention becomes designing and making a machine— of active and direct action on the object being worked, albeit still under the command of a human operator. Man is master of machine, but—unlike craftsman's tools—machines make their own demands on the operator; and the organization that buys and operates the machines (usually not the operator-worker) may impose further restrictions on the worker's behavior. In the information age, invention becomes the making of intelligent (or at least programmable) machines with far greater autonomy from their human users than modern-era machines. Intelligent machines require software as well as hardware. The intelligent machine of the information age is now a "co-worker" or "assistant" of sorts.

Technology has implications for the destructive, productive, and communicative potential of human societies. And technological innovations tend to co-evolve in three sectors, as per Figure 3.2. Of interest here is the overlap between military (destructive) and industrial (productive) technologies, and the related issues of spinoff, spin-on, and the promotion of dual-use (military and civilian) technologies (Vogel, 1992). Of similar interest are the triple-use technologies that have military, industrial, and communications dimensions and implications simultaneously. This newer tendency of technologies to overlap may be an important and possibly distinctive feature of technological knowledge in the information age, even if some overlaps did exist even earlier on.

Of the many things written on the concept of technology as knowledge, the work of José Ortega y Gasset (1972) is probably the most famous. Ortega y Gasset outlines technological evolution by dividing it into three main periods: the technics of chance, the technics of the craftsman, and the technics of the technician. The difference among the three is in the mode of discovery, and in the means of realization elected—the "technicity" of technical thinking. We extend Ortega y Gasset's categorization by adding the technics of the information worker in Figure 3.3.

The Technics of Chance

In the first period, there are no methods or technics at all. A technic must be discovered simply by chance, and technics are regarded as a part of nature. It is a revelation of nature that uncovers them. Thus, technics belong

Figure 3.2
The Evolution of Technology as Hardware

	Pre-modern Society	Modern Society				Information Society
The Meaning of Invention	tool as passive hardware	machine as active hardware				intelligent machine as assistant
Military Technology (land)	sword spear/bow	gun cannon	rifle automatic gun	tank	missile nuclear weapon	laser weapons SDI
(sea)	sail ship row ship	steamship		turbine ship submarine	nuclear ship aircraft carrier	
(air)	hot air balloon			engine plane bomber	jet plane fighter	spaceship satellite/stealth
Industrial Technology		textile	iron/steel railroad	electrical equipment automobiles chemistry	electronics aerospace nuclear power	information industries biotech
Communication Technology	writing	telegraph	telephone	wireless telephone radio	satellite communications broadcasting	computer communication

Figure 3.3
The Evolution of Technology as Knowledge

	Primitive Society	**Pre-modern Society**	**Modern Society**	**Information Society**
the subject of technological behavior	the technics of chance	the technics of craftsmen	the technics of technicians	the technics of knowledge workers
the essence of technics	nature (discovery-based)	man (human-based)	knowledge (knowledge-based)	knowledge in a broad sense
the nature of technological behavior	practice = probability	practice = plan (the principle of similitude)	practice ≠ plan (beyond similitude searching for universality)	practice = planning (allows for custom solutions to universal problems)

to the sphere of probability. In this pre-technological concept, technics are integral to the mysteries of nature.

The Technics of the Craftsman

In this second period, certain kinds of technics become conscious, and they are passed from one generation to the next by a special class of individuals—the artisans. Still, there is no systematic study of technics worthy of the label "technology." A technic of this period is simply a skill, an art, or a craft embedded in individual, not scientific or systemic (socially shared), knowledge. Also, the technics of planning are not yet separated from the technics of practice as they are to become in the modern era. A craftsman is worker as well as technician. To acquire the technics of the craftsman, a person must enter one of the exclusive communities of craftsmen, whether guilds or workshops, and accumulate experiences within that community. These technics cannot be explained by words or writings alone, only by training. The aspiring artisan must learn through a long apprenticeship. There may be no concept of progress among craftsmen that are now imbued with notions of virtuosity. Most premodern Oriental technics belong in this category, as do also most Western technics before the Industrial Revolution.

The Technics of the Technician

It is only in this third period, with the development of the analytic way of thinking associated with the rise of modern science, that the technics of technicians or engineers—"scientific" technics—"technology" in our literal sense, comes into existence. The great document of this dramatic shift from skill to technology was the *Encylopédie*, edited in the period from 1751 to 1772 by Denis Diderot and Jean D'Alembert. This famous work attempted to bring together, in an organized and systematic form, the knowledge of all crafts in such a way that the non-apprentice could learn to be a "technician." In this new period, discovering the technical means for realizing any end has in itself become a self-conscious scientific discipline. Now, the "technicity" of modern technics is radically different from that which inspired all previous technics, because it manifests itself both in technics and in scientific theory. As Ortega y Gasset puts it, now humanity has "the technology" before "a technics." People can know how to realize any project they might elect, even before actually choosing it. Technology now has become a system of knowledge, emancipated from nature, specific to human acumen.

The Technics of the Information Worker

In the continuum of the above categorization, we would like to introduce here the idea of the technics of information workers and a provisional new term, *technoledge*—compounding technology and knowledge—to communicate the new meaning of technology in the information age. It is our hypothesis that another fundamental transformation of the concept of technology is now taking place with the introduction of new information technologies, particularly of computer software and telecommunications technology, into the processes of technical innovation. The "technicity" of the current technics is radically different from that of previous technics. Now, there is knowledge of how to take a general systems approach and apply such flexibility toward solving problems for specific users of a given technology. "Technoledge" combines knowledge about machines with knowledge about humans using those machines. Thus, in the information age, technological discourse becomes much more open to participation by users of technology (often the general public) and includes many of the factors excluded in the earlier, narrower discourses among technologists. Most importantly perhaps, both diversity and universality permeate the goals of technological activity in the information age.

THE FIT BETWEEN PREEXISTING INSTITUTIONS AND NEW TECHNOLOGIES

Since the emergence of the modern concept of technology, our technologies and institutions have tended ever more to co-evolve. It has therefore become increasingly important to understand the embedding of cultural and institutional elements within the newer technologies. One issue raised by

Figure 3.4
Types of State-Societal Arrangements

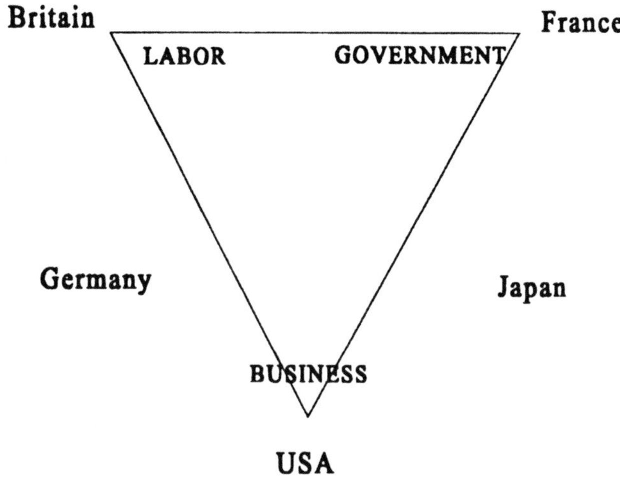

Source: Hart (1992), p. 281.

the foregoing is the ease with which new information technologies can be adapted and diffused within different societies. This is obviously important if—as we assume—power, just like international economic competitiveness, pivots on the rapid adaptation and diffusion of new technologies. Since new technologies embed cultural and institutional practices into the technology itself, there may be new types of impediments to the transfer of these technologies across national boundaries that did not exist in earlier periods.

Two approaches in the literature can provide some answers here. The first deals with the major differences in institutional arrangements among leading industrialized countries and relates those differences to important economic outcomes. The second deals with the possible institutional requisites of the new technologies. Both are useful and can be summarized on the basis of two references: Hart, 1992, and Kitschelt, 1991.

Which types of state-societal arrangements are conducive to the diffusion of new technologies? In *Rival Capitalists* (Hart, 1992), the relative power held by government, business, and labor is the crucial issue (see Figure 3.4). The five countries in Hart's study divide into two groups: (1) dominance of one factor; and (2) the sharing of power by two factors. The three factor-dominant patterns are either government-centered, business-centered, or labor-centered. France, the United States, and Britain belong in the one-factor dominance category: strong government in France, strong business in the United States, strong labor in Britain. Shared-power patterns consist of three types: government and business, government and labor, and business and labor. Japan and Germany belong to the shared-power category: coalitions of strong government and strong business in Japan, and coalitions of strong business and strong labor in Germany.

Based on his empirical study, Hart can hypothesize that in the last two decades, countries with shared-power configurations have experienced increased competitiveness relative to those with factor dominance. Shared-power arrangements are more flexible. They provide a favorable environment for the rapid introduction of technological innovations. Countries with factor dominance are relatively less flexible because the dominated factors resist technological change (see Chapter 9). The competitiveness of Britain and the United States in major industries, such as steel, automobiles, and semiconductors, has declined, whereas that of Germany and Japan in those industries has increased and the performance of France has been somewhere in between.

Can these results be generalized to all technologies? Hart raises this question in discussing variations within countries. For example, even though becoming internationally more competitive overall in the 1980s and 1990s, German industry remains markedly weaker than that of the United States and Japan in "hi-tech" electronics. Similarly, Japan seems to have had trouble catching up with the United States in microprocessor and software technology. Thus, the question: Is there a set of feasibly desirable institutional arrangements specific to a particular technology?

Kitschelt (1991) says that any technology has two important dimensions—coupling and complexity. First, we are to distinguish whether the elements of a technological system are loosely or tightly coupled. The extent of coupling refers to the requirement for spatial or temporal links between different production steps. If the steps must be executed at the same location or at the same time, they are tightly coupled. If they can be undertaken in any sequence, at any location, they are loosely coupled. In loosely coupled systems, each step or component of production is separate from every other step in space and time. Tight coupling requires close supervision, so as to contain problems that otherwise might quickly spread to other processes. Loose coupling permits less centralized control. The more tightly the technological elements are coupled, the more centralized the controls are required to be. The concept of coupling is closely related to the level of capital investment and to the size of the economy. If a technological system is tightly coupled, it generally requires a large economy with high levels of capital investment for local firms to be successful. Loosely coupled, the technological system does not require a large economy or high levels of capital investment for its local firms to be successful.

Second, we must assess the complexity of causal interactions among production stages. Complexity refers to the overall extent of interactive feedback among the production stages on which will depend the smooth run of the whole process. Linear systems that proceed from one stage to the next without feedback are uncomplex, whereas those that are iterative and inter-

Figure 3.5
Types of Technology

high	Type 2	Type 4
	Type 3	
Level of		Type 5a
Coupling		
	Type 1	Type 5b
low		
	low **Level of** **high**	
	Complexity	

Sources: Kitschelt (1991): 468–475; Golden (1994): 129.

active are, in degrees, relatively more complex. Complex systems have large information requirements to manage the intricate flow of connections across processes, but large communications flows also can overload the capacity of centralized governance structures. Consequently, complex systems favor decentralized production units coordinated through network connections. Technological processes that are more sequential, and less interactive, have fewer information requirements. They are therefore more amenable to centralized control. If the technology is not complex, its trajectories are predictable, and production advances in continuous, incremental steps. If the technology is complex, technological innovations have to be explored by trial and error. They yield fast-paced technological change with major breakthroughs followed by small incremental improvements.

Based on these two dimensions, Kitschelt distinguishes five technological clusters from Mark I to Mark V technology. In this chapter, we intend to modify his categorization slightly—by reinterpreting his Mark III category and by dividing his Mark V into two distinct technological clusters, thereby creating six types in all. Like Kitschelt, we hypothesize that each technology will require a distinct governance structure for its maximum performance. Although the combinations of coupling and complexity of a technology do not determine a uniquely optimal governance structure, they do somehow constrain the efficient possibilities (see Figure 3.5). The possible efficient governance structures, or the favored institutional arrangements, for Type 1 to Type 5b are as follows.

Type 1 Technology (1770–1840)

A loosely coupled technological system endowed with linear interaction among its components characterizes this category. Concentrated ownership is not necessary, nor are there important economies of scale. Because knowledge intensity is quite low, technological trajectories in this case are readily predictable. Thus, new technologies are incrementally innovated. Consumer goods, light machine tools, and textiles belong to this type. In the case of Type 1 technology, a decentralized, market-oriented system with weak government and strong business is the way to exploit most energetically the opportunities offered by the new technological trajectory. Innovation in these systems stems from the incremental process of "learning by doing," not by the organization of systematic research.

Type 2 Technology (1830–1890)

This is a tightly coupled technological system with linear causal complexity. Because knowledge intensity remains fairly low, the advance of products is still made incrementally along predictable trajectories. But this type of technology requires large capital investments, and economies of scale increase rapidly. The heavy industries, such as iron/steel and railroads, belong here. The efficient governance structures for Type 2 technology shift from small to large corporations, from competitive to oligopolistic markets. The domestic structures that succeed in innovations are business-oriented arrangements, which facilitate industrial centralization, but incremental innovations are propelled above all by large corporations through systematic research in private laboratories. In the late-industrializing countries, the state-societal arrangements that deeply involve government across the stages of industrial development also belong in this category.

Type 3 Technology (1880–1940)

This is a highly-to-moderately coupled technological system of low-to-moderate causal complexity. This type of technological system involves moderate knowledge intensity; the technological trajectories are readily predictable. Hence, product advancements are made incrementally. Requirements of capital are relatively high. Economies of scale are quite large. Chemical production, electrical engineering, consumer-/durable-goods, and automobiles fit into this category. Centralized institutional arrangements are required to develop Type 3 technology—and especially so, in monopolistic markets. Historically, this technology was practiced in the "Fordist" mass production of consumer goods. It permitted the rise of the large multinational corporation.

Type 4 Technology (1930–1980)

A tightly coupled technological system of high causal complexity, this type of activity requires intensive knowledge. The trajectory is quite unpredictable. The advancement of its product occurs in leaps and bounds—not incrementally. The scale of economy is very large, and investment risks are very elevated. Representatives of this type include nuclear power and aerospace. In Type 4 technology, it is appropriate and common to have highly centralized governance structures, capable of placing the burden of investment risks on public agencies, even in cases where the technologies are meant to be developed or produced in privately owned facilities. Historically, two categories of countries have excelled in these technologies: economies governed by states with well-developed, centralized capabilities, often before the new technologies even surfaced; and countries, which acquired such capabilities in connection with the military competitions of World War II and the exigencies of the Cold War that followed. Note that, while the victors of World War II all ventured into the development of these Type 4 "state technologies," the losers and small neutral countries were forced to stay on the sidelines.

Type 5a Technology (1970–)

This is a low-to-moderately coupled technological system with high-to-moderate causal complexity. Because this type of technological system involves a very considerable intensity of knowledge, the technological trajectories are not readily predictable. Product advances are made in incremental steps with some breakthroughs. The economies of scale, initially moderate, increase over time. An example is a type of integrated circuit, the Dynamic Random Access Memory (DRAM). DRAMs are used in computers and now increasingly in consumer electronics. For Type 5a technology, countries with power-sharing institutions are better able to take advantage of such conditions. Cooperative networks between state-societal actors impart flexibility into production systems and reduce investment risks for firms.

Type 5b Technology (1970–)

This is a loosely coupled technological system with high causal complexity in which problem solving is difficult and complicated. Type 5b's technological trajectories are not readily predictable. The economies of scale, moderate in the beginning, increase over time. This type of technology incorporates computer software, microprocessors, and biotechnology. Type 5b technology requires more sophisticated institutional arrangements than all other types. Here, the technologies no longer reward the organized capabilities of highly integrated private or government-run enterprises. Corresponding governance structures include mixed private and public research and development consortia as well as national and international intercorporate alliances of all sorts. Because of the high technological uncertainties, organizational decentralization has to be combined with a certain dose of public funding, to stimulate requisite private investments (Kim, 1994).

To summarize, Hart's and Kitschelt's theories together give us some insight as to which institutional arrangements are most likely to promote technological innovation for different types of technologies. A question left unanswered is whether institutional arrangements already existing in various countries can be changed as needed in order to pave the way for innovative successes. The reader needs to refer to the theory of "technological paradigms," which covers "national innovation systems"—the network of public and private institutions that affect the creation and adoption of technologies within an economy (Freeman, 1987; Dosi, 1988). This theory asserts that relatively infrequent changes in technological paradigms require changes in products, processes, and organizations. Based on the aforegoing, it is now possible to address the query of how to observe power in the information age.

OBSERVING POWER IN THE INFORMATION AGE

There are basically three different ways of empirically observing power: (1) as a resource, (2) as a relationship, and (3) as a structure (Hart, 1976). We hypothesize that as a result of the growing importance of information technologies: (1) the main locus of power as resource has been shifting from the military to the economic and now to the informational purview, and (2) the main mechanisms for exercising power have also been shifting: from relational power to structural power.

"In the power as resources approach, power is measured in terms of control over a resource (potential power) which can be converted . . . into control over others or over outcomes (actual power). These resources, also called capabilities, may be connected with measurable phenomena such as economic wealth or population" (Hart, 1989: 3). Realist theories of international relations and works on geopolitics often rely on power-as-resource approaches. Power is measured or assessed in terms of certain capabilities— functions of control over specific types of resources—land area, population, GNP, energy production, and so on.

In recent years, besides the usual set of capabilities used to measure power, technological capabilities have begun to count for power resources. In the early 1990s, world production shares of semiconductors appeared as one of the indicators monitored by the Central Intelligence Agency in its annual publication, the *Handbook of International Economic Statistics*. It is foreseeable that future issues of that publication will contain tables on the number of server computers linked to the Internet or the number of World Wide Web sites extant in major countries. As information technology grows in importance in international relations, these sorts of changes in conventional power assessment are likely.

It has been suggested that the development of information technologies shifts the basis of power from violence to wealth on to knowledge through a phenomenon described as the "powershift" (Toffler, 1990). While we do not necessarily agree with Toffler on this score, there is evidence for such a shift in the recent works of realists and students of geopolitics. A key unresolved issue for us, however, is whether it is really necessary to try to reconceive the inherited notion of national security, to seek to redefine the international power game, and to re-situate its players as a result of the rise of information technologies.

The new technologies clearly have had an impact on both power and power assessment. If a country possesses high-tech communications equipment, then it can all the more easily access information resources. If a country has developed an information superhighway system, then citizens of that country can ever more easily access important information resources, and the country thus gains an informational edge over those without such system.

The information age is producing a blurring of boundaries between power resources. In the information age, there appears to be greater concern than in previous eras about the importance of dual-use (military and civilian) technologies, the role of the media in society, the importance of having the means to project one's culture abroad, and the vulnerability of communications networks to disruptions by hostile forces. These are not entirely new concerns, of course. Iron-clad ships also combined dual-use technologies; the telegraph and telegraph cables, too, played an important role in preserving British hegemony during the nineteenth century; and there was obviously not lesser concern about the integrity of radio and telegraph communications networks in both world wars. Still, the intensity of concern has shifted in these directions to an extent that now makes it possible to assert that a noticeable qualitative change has taken place.

The information age has made intangible forms of power more important. Control over knowledge, over beliefs and ideas, is now increasingly regarded to be a complementary control over tangible resources, including military forces, raw materials, and economic productive capability. In this context, the extent to which the politics of ideas complements power politics is becoming larger than before. Thus, "whoever is able to develop or acquire and to deny the access of others to a kind of knowledge respected and sought by others; and whoever can control the channels by which it is communicated to those given access to it, will exercise a very special kind of structural power" (Strange, 1988: 30).

Information is a flexible power resource that is less constrained by time and place than any other power resource. It is in many ways more fungible—transferable from one actor to another—than other forms of power. It is much more like money and other economic resources than it is like any military power resource in that regard. This commodification of information is not new. It has simply accelerated with the growth of high-speed tele-communications technologies and following the digitalization of information. The deployment of these new technologies has made it easier to package, sell, and distribute information than ever before (Giese, 1994). However, one could never overstate the fact that information without knowledge is not very useful and that information about technology is especially difficult to transfer to others unless there exists a solid cognitive and institutional basis for doing so. An example would be the dubious utility of supplying raw digital data from a spy satellite to a friendly country that did not have the capability of turning the data into images or did not have experts capable of interpreting the images for security purposes. Another example would be the sharing of a secret microchip design with a friendly country that had no semiconductor production facilities.

In the power-as-relationship approach, power is measured or assessed in terms of interactions between pairs of social actors. A has power over B when A and B have conflicting views about the desirable outcome of a specific situation but B acts as if it had adopted the preferences of A. Relational power can result either from coercion or persuasion. In a coercive power relationship, A threatens B in order to get B to act on A's preferences. In a persuasive relationship, A communicates with B in a non-threatening manner, to convince B to adopt A's preferences. This category of power is difficult to measure because it requires knowing A's and B's preferences both before and after their interaction. Relational approaches to power are based on empiricist conceptions of power.

With the end of the Cold War, power relationships hitherto based on bipolar enmity or alliances are being redefined to take into account the absence (with the noteworthy exception of the People's Republic of China) of a communist bloc. Integral to that adjustment is an increased interest in avoiding the commitment of military resources in attempts to influence specific other actors in the international system. Thus, there is greater interest in economic sanctions as an alternative response to various forms of bad behavior. We predict that sanctions involving deprivation of access to informational resources will become a likely substitute for military threats, as the information economy develops.

Joseph S. Nye's concept of soft power may be one way of understanding power in the information age, at least from the relational perspective. Soft power is the ability to achieve a desired outcome through attraction rather than coercion. It works by convincing others to comply with norms and institutions that produce a particular desired behavior. Soft power depends on the appeal of ideas and an actor's ability to set the agenda in ways that shape the preferences of others. If a state can legitimize its power by establishing and supporting new regimes, then it may be able to economize on its expenditure of traditional military and economic resources (Nye, 1990).

More important, international actors seem to be thinking more about the larger set of norms, rules, and procedures that govern the world's political and economic systems now that the Cold War is over. They are thus more interested in exercising structural power.

Susan Strange says that

structural power . . . confers the power to decide how things shall be done, the power to shape frameworks within which states relate to each other, relate to people, or relate to corporate enterprises. The relative power of each party in a relationship is more, or less, if one party is also determining the surrounding structure of the relationship . . . What is common to all four kinds of structural power is that the possessor is able to change the range of choices open to others, without apparently putting pressure directly on them to take one decision or to make one choice rather than others. Such power is less "visible." Today the knowledge most sought after the acquisition of relational power and to reinforce other kinds of structural power (i.e. in security matters, in production and in finance) is technology. The advanced technologies of new materials, new products, new systems of changing plants and animals, new systems of collecting, storing and retrieving information—all these open doors to both structural power and relational power. (Strange, 1988: 25–31)

Later in the same work, however, she goes on to emphasize that "Structural analysis suggests that technological changes do not necessarily change power structures. They do so only if accompanied by changes in the basic belief systems which underpin or support the political and economic arrangements acceptable to society" (Strange, 1988: 123).

This emphasis is consistent with our argument about the cultural and institutional impediments to the transfer of technology in the information age. Information technologies embed institutional and cultural practices into the technology itself. A certain amount of structural power is implicit in the transfer of information technologies across national boundaries. The country which is the source of new key technologies—microprocessors, fast digital switches, operating system software, and the like—frequently gets to impose its institutional and cultural arrangements on others. For example, Microsoft now dominates the personal computer market with the Windows operating systems on computers that use Intel's microprocessors. Computer companies and users in Europe and Asia have tried unsuccessfully to compete directly with these firms and now are forced to adapt to the technological solutions that the dominant firms have imposed on them as well as on the rest of the world. This generates a certain amount of resentment, even of irritation, that sometimes percolates up to the level of national governments. Yet it is arguably an outcome of the success of both Microsoft's and Intel's ability to anticipate the demands of the marketplace, and to some extent also of their ability to extend sufficient incentives to overseas users to accept and buy products not of domestic origin.

CONCLUSIONS

Technological change clearly influences the distribution of power in the international system. If a country wields advanced technology, it can that much better produce military weapons and that much more competitively manufacture civilian products. This is why politicians and business leaders pay so much attention to acquiring new technological knowledge. Historically, and at least since Bacon, technological innovation has been seen to offer a way of making a society strong and wealthy. Success in acquiring or adapting to a new technology produces winners; lack of success produces losers. In recent years, the development of information technology has increasingly linked power of technology to power of information in a form of power that we call technoledge.

Information-based technological power is different from earlier forms of technologically based power in a number of important ways. It is connected with the successful creation or adaptation of new technologies which contain a great deal of institutional and cultural information embedded in them. As a consequence, these new technologies do not flow across national boundaries as easily as the technologies of previous eras. Also, information technologies have forced the governments of nation-states to rearticulate their internal structures in order to cope with the trend toward globalization of international business—a trend made possible by faster and cheaper computing and advanced telecommunications (Douglas, 1996: 7; Hart and Prakash, 1997).

Third, the development of information technology has greatly reduced the difficulty and expense of surveillance, and has given greater surveillance power both to states and to the citizens of contemporary nation-states (Hewson, 1994). The ability of the citizenry to use its new surveillance powers will depend on its ability to force the state to permit access to information that was previously jealously guarded. It will also depend on the creation and diffusion of new encryption technologies, which are increasingly used by commercial enterprises and individuals, and thus are no longer under the stringent control of national governments.

Finally, information technologies have created a new frontier for exploration, in ways analogous to the creation of new frontiers when wind power was harnessed and sail-ships could be launched into an age of exploration. The challenge here is that these new frontiers are more than actual (territorial or geographic)—they are virtual. It is these virtual boundaries that may yet divide an otherwise actually uniting world in unusually profound ways.

REFERENCES

Bacon, F. (1624). New Atlantis. In B. Vickers (ed.), *English Science, Bacon to Newton*. Cambridge: Cambridge University Press, 1987.

Cusumano, M. (1991). *Japan's Software Factories: A Challenge to U.S. Management*. New York: Oxford University Press.

Dosi, G. (1988). The Nature of the Innovative Process. In G. Dosi et al. (eds.), *Technological Change and Economic Theory*. London: Pinter.

Douglas, I. R. (1996). The Myth of Globali[z]ation: A Poststructural Reading of Speed and Reflexivity in the Governance of Late Modernity. Paper presented at the International Studies Association Annual Meeting, San Diego, April 16–20.

Freeman, C. (1987). *Technology Policy and Economic Performance: Lessons from Japan*. London: Pinter.

Giese, M. (1994). Taking the Scenic Route: The Internet as a Precursor to the Information Superhighway. Unpublished manuscript.

Golden, J. R. (1994). *Economic and National Strategy in the Information Age: Global Networks, Technology Policy, and Cooperative Competition*. Westport, CT: Praeger.

Hart, J. A. (1976). Three Approaches to the Measurement of Power in International Relations. *International Organization* 30, 2 (Spring): 289–305.

——— (1989). ISDN and Power. Discussion Paper 7. Center for Global Business, the Business School of Indiana University.

——— (1992). *Rival Capitalists: International Competitiveness in the United States, Japan, and Western Europe*. Ithaca, NY: Cornell University Press.

———, and A. Prakash (1997). The Decline of "Embedded Liberalism" and the Rearticulation of the Keynesian Welfare State. *New Political Economy* 2: 65–78.

Hewson, M. (1994). Surveillance and the Global Political Economy. In E. A. Comor (ed.), *The Global Political Economy of Communication: Hegemony, Telecommunication and the Information Economy*. New York: St. Martin's Press.

Kenney, M. (1996). The Role of Information, Knowledge and Value in the Late 20th Century. *Nova Economia* (December).

Kim, S. (1994). Institutions, Technology, and the Japanese Software Industry: The New Institutional Approach Reconsidered. Unpublished manuscript.

——— (1995). The Strong-Army Policy and Technological Development in 19th Century China and Japan. Unpublished manuscript.

Kitschelt, H. (1991). Industrial Governance Structure, Innovation Strategies, and the Case of Japan: Sectoral or Cross-national Comparative Analysis? *International Organization* 45, 4 (Autumn): 468–475.

Krugman, P. (1987). Strategic Sectors and International Competition. In R. M. Stern (ed.), *U.S. Trade Policies in a Changing World Economy*. Cambridge, MA: MIT Press.

Long, P. O. (1991). Invention, Authorship, "Intellectual Property," and the Origin of Patents: Notes toward a Conceptual History. *Technology and Culture* 32, 4.

Melzer, A. M., J. Weinberger, and M. R. Zinman (1993). *Technology in the Western Political Tradition*. Ithaca, NY: Cornell University Press.

Nye, J. S. (1990). *Bound to Lead: The Changing Nature of American Power*. New York: Basic Books.

Ortega y Gasset, J. (1972). Thought on Technology. In C. Mitcham and R. Machey (eds.), *Philosophy and Technology: Readings in the Philosophical Problems of Technology*. New York: The Free Press.

Pacey, A. (1983). *The Culture of Technology*. Cambridge, MA: MIT Press.

Piore, M., and C. Sabel (1984). *The Second Industrial Divide: Possibilities for Prosperity*. New York: Basic Books.

Strange, S. (1988). *State and Markets: An Introduction to International Political Economy*. New York: Basil Blackwell.

Toffler, A. (1990). *Power Shift*. New York: Bantam Books.

Vogel, S. (1992). The Power Behind "Spin-Ons": The Military Implications of Japan's Commercial Technology. In W. Sandholtz, M. Borrus, J. Zysman, K. Conca, J. Stowsky, S. Vogel, and S. Weber (eds.), *The Highest Stakes*. New York: Oxford University Press.

CHAPTER 4

The Meaning and Challenges of Economic Security

KRISTIN M. LORD

BACKGROUND

With the end of the Cold War and the rise of new economic powers in Asia and elsewhere, scholars and policymakers have become increasingly interested in the economic dimensions of national security. Despite this growing interest, economic security continues to mean very different things to different people, including:

- aspects of trade, investment, and infrastructure that directly affect a country's ability to defend itself, such as a state's ability to produce and acquire weapons and ensure reliable supplies of military equipment (Cable, 1995; Scharfen, 1995)

- economic power and competitiveness and the influence they confer (Cable, 1995; Moran, 1993a)

- the ability to maintain a stable, prosperous, just, equitable, productive, and dynamic economic system (Neu and Wolf, 1994; Thomas, 1987)

- invulnerability to economic shocks including disruptions to supplies of critical resources, currency fluctuations, price fluctuations, and the terms of trade (Cable, 1995; Moran, 1993b).

Each of these issues is important. Yet, without further guidance, we must consider drought, oil embargoes, naval quarantines, poverty, and stock market crashes, all under the same rubric. This approach treats most economic and social issues as matters of national security, turning economic security into a concept that is ambiguous, overly broad, and therefore of little use. Clearly, each of these issues can impair economic competitiveness, weaken sovereignty, debilitate power quite directly. But which are truly matters of national security? And how are they interrelated?

This chapter addresses these questions as well as the many difficulties policymakers confront in trying to fathom economic security. To that end, I shall discuss the meaning of economic security more specifically and explain its complex relationship to national security more generally. In doing so, I will examine how economic security needs evolve according to the meaning of the threats that states face. I will survey economic vulnerabilities and instruments of power in an economically interdependent world. And I will analyze the challenges of economic security, including its inherent tensions, the trade-offs that policymakers face in trying to improve it, and the strategies they pursue to such end.

THE MEANING OF ECONOMIC SECURITY

Economic security is one aspect of national security, which is defined as the ability of a state and its people successfully to protect themselves from perceived threats to their control of their sovereign affairs—including the integrity of territorial boundaries, the independence of political institutions, economic viability, and the preservation of culture—and as the absence of fear that such values will be attacked (Goldgeier, 1997; Wolfers, 1962). Hence, economic security is a state's ability to protect against perceived threats to its sovereign economic affairs and the absence of fear that such values will be attacked.

Economic security has both an active and a passive component (Knorr, 1973). The active component concerns a state's ability to advance its economic interests and to defend against threats. It includes the ability to reward, coerce, deny, threaten, or punish through recourse to both economic and non-economic means. The passive component concerns the extent to which a state's economy is open to manipulation and to harm and the likelihood that such misfortune will materialize.

In other words, economic security is a function not only of power (see Chapters 3 and 6) but of vulnerability (see Chapters 5, 7, 8, 9, and 10) as well. But what makes states economically powerful, and what makes them economically vulnerable? The question, a complex one, is at the heart of debates about economic security. The short answer is that it depends on the types and likelihood of threats. Like power, security is a relative concept and should be considered in context (Baldwin, 1989).

Two types of threats to economic security are noteworthy: short-term versus long-term; and internal versus external.

Short-Term Threats versus Long-Term Threats

In the short term, a state's economic security pivots on its vulnerability in the immediate to external pressure and its concrete ability to stop or endure such pressures. States that are heavily dependent on foreign markets for energy, raw materials, or critical inputs to defense systems, for example, are vulnerable to economic shocks. Such shocks may be "natural," as in the case of severe weather, or "intentional," as in the purposeful manipulation of currency values. To eschew such insecurities, states must either increase their autonomy or be sufficiently powerful to counter threats. Even powerful states must beware of short-term economic vulnerabilities, however, since the successful exploitation of these vulnerabilities (such as the 1973 OPEC oil embargo against the United States) can allow even significantly weaker states to harm stronger ones. And it is these types of short-term security threats that are linked most closely to national security in its traditional interpretation.

In the long term, a state's economic security hinges on its overall economic power and wealth, which allows it to fund strong militaries to protect interests, gives it leverage over allies and enemies (see Chapter 2), provides a wider variety of policy tools to achieve its objectives, and is altogether a most important component of overall power. As Klaus Knorr notes,

Economic wealth is convertible into virtually all types of power and influence . . . it is a basis of military power. It figures as one foundation of international prestige. In the conduct of international propaganda, foreign intelligence, and bribery, it is an indispensable subsidiary to skill. (Knorr, 1973: 75)

Virtually any economic condition or policy that increases economic competitiveness or macroeconomic health, therefore, promotes economic security over the long term. It is this aspect of economic security to which leaders refer when discussing the economic security implications of trade agreements or poverty (Ahmed, 1997; MacLarty, 1997).

By such distinction, the full range of the issues mentioned above—from access to materials directly necessary for national defense to equitable distributions of societal wealth—presents aspects of economic security. The relevance of these dimensions to national security is simply either "more" or "less" immediate. Whereas ensuring access to semiconductors (see Chapter 3) used in guided missile systems may become critical in times of conflict, developing a stable, well-educated, productive society (see Chapters 6 and 11) may have a strong and lasting long-term effect on national wealth and stability—two important components of security over the more distant horizon.

The distinction between short-term and long-term economic security recognizes that states routinely face trade-offs between prosperity and security—butter and guns—in both the short and the long terms. Even though prosperity is an important component of economic security, therefore, its importance in the immediate present may be secondary at times when a state's (or government's) vital security interests seem threatened. In these cases, longer-term economic security (in the form of economic prosperity and wealth) may be sacrificed in favor of the shorter-term benefits of higher control and greater ability to deny benefits to others (Grieco, 1988, 1990). States may avoid cooperation, such as free trade arrangements or lenient investment regulations, that may seem to benefit others disproportionately, even when they stand to benefit from the arrangement themselves (Grieco, 1990) Conversely, states that feel secure will be more likely to accept some loss of autonomy, or even a partner's disproportionate gain, in order to achieve increased prosperity for their own people.

Internal Threats versus External Threats

Some states (particularly in less developed countries) may face trade-offs between their internal and external security. Policies that promote economic growth and enhance external security may also produce a society of haves and have-nots characterized by class tensions and by political instability (Chapters 7, 9, and 10). The benefits of particular policies may be enjoyed unequally by particular regions, ethnic groups, political party members, or government officials (Thomas, 1987: 2). Or they may undermine the government's authority by producing new centers of power with the potential to challenge the authority of current leaders or undermine the influence of groups supporting the regime. As the economic power of lower castes in India grows, for example, these constituencies may exert greater pressure for political change. Finally, a nation may be unhappy with the potential winners and losers created by steps to enhance long-term security and even economic wealth. In Sub-Saharan Africa, for example, foreigners and multinational corporations were the most likely winners from economic liberalization in many countries. However, this outcome threatened indigenous African control over the economy—one of the main pillars of post-independence Africa (Nelson, 1989: 9).

THE CONTEXT OF SECURITY THREATS

When examining economic security, it is important to note that economic factors are both a cause and a product of a broader security environment. As a cause, they can lead nations to worry about their own vulnerability or to threaten others' weaknesses. As a product, economic security can vary dramatically, depending on a state's broader security goals, which fluctuate according to the distribution of international power, military considerations, domestic stability, and the interactive dimensions of politics.

In general, states try to achieve increasing levels of might and security in order to advance their interests and power. Economic power and security are no exception. The degree of security that states pursue depends on their understandings of safety, on the relative depth and urgency of their sense of the threats opposed to their economic security, on their current levels of power and economic development, on the resources at their disposal, and on the chances for armed conflict. Nevertheless, there is a rough hierarchy of basic security interests common to all states. The most basic of these is survival, which is threatened only rarely (Waltz, 1979). This goal is followed in importance by territorial integrity; the ability to satisfy a people's basic economic needs and wants such as food, shelter, and health care; the ability to absorb economic shocks such as currency and price fluctuations or some unexpected limits on strategic imports; the state's ability to control its destiny; the ability to exert influence so as to achieve desired economic outcomes; and the ability to achieve economic "hegemony" (a situation in which a country has unrestricted access to vital raw materials, adequate control over major sources of capital, a large market for imports, comparative advantages in services and goods with high added value, and is stronger on these dimensions taken as a whole than any other country [Keohane, 1984: 33–34]). States usually satisfy each security interest in the hierarchical sequence suggested before gaining ability to move on to the next, even though advancing to a higher level of economic security may require them to make choices. For example, states may trade some degree of autonomy to become more involved in international economic affairs and build wealth. Both Mexico and Brazil have evidenced a willingness to make this trade-off in recent years by privatizing domestic industries and reducing trade barriers.

Economic factors also play an important role in determining a state's overall security by changing the costs and benefits of conflict and the perceived need for autonomy. Although economic factors such as trade and economic growth may impede conflict, they may also heighten states' insecurity and make policies of isolationism, import substitution, mercantilism, or even conquest seemingly attractive. This view is controversial, since much of the literature on the role of economic factors in situations of conflict (with the notable exceptions of Hirschman, 1945; Liberman, 1996; and Milward, 1977) tends to view them as a force for peace.

The debate over whether economic factors do help prevent conflict is often cast as a debate between liberals and realists (Harris, 1993). The liberals view economic factors predominantly as reinforcing peaceful relations: states become wealthier when they form mutually beneficial links in trade, investment, finance, and the costs of cutting such ties is too high (Rosecrance, 1986; Keohane and Nye, 1977; Kaysen, 1990). Since states stand to lose more than they can gain from fighting, the incentive to wage wars declines (Mansfield, 1992). For the leading industrial economies, the costs of war are so great that war may altogether disappear as a policy option for these democracies (see Chapter 6).

Realists do not deny that states profit from internationally entertained economic relationships; they are just more skeptical about the extent to which these relationships deter war. This skepticism arises from the realist view that economic relations are also a source of power, a point of vulnerability, basically an instrument of influence that can be manipulated for political or even strategic advantage (Hirschman, 1945; Gowa, 1994). For example, states can use the proceeds from trade to enhance their military strength, to seize foreign investments, to cut off other states' access to vital raw materials, or even deny the economic benefits of trade to others. Since security—not prosperity—is a state's highest priority, realists say, economic interdependence is not enough to deter war. In some circumstances, it may even make war more likely by heightening insecurity and increasing the benefits of conquest (Liberman, 1996).

In a sense, both sides are right. Depending on the security environment in which states exist, economic factors can reinforce stable international relationships or exacerbate tensions. During the Cold War, in Europe, economic growth among Western powers was considered positive "for all." These states were allies against a common threat and the increased strength of one ally, the tighter economic relations with its partners, made the whole alliance that much more effective (Gowa, 1989). Note that Britain had considered Germany's economic development in the years before World War I to be extremely menacing even though economic ties between the two states were very extensive (Kennedy, 1980). Indeed, such economic interdependence and parallel growth made the relationship worse.

By enhancing wealth, a source of power that "could" be used for military purposes, economic factors exacerbated an already labile security situation, making either state overly sensitive to the relative gains in power achieved by the other. The "languaging" (see Chapter 1) used to justify the crisis did not help: "Every one of these new factory chimneys [in Germany] is a gun pointed at England" (Kennedy, 1980: 315). A comparable fear from economic power convertible into military might has also been observed in East Asia, where economic prosperity, combined with underlying security concerns, has spurred regional build-ups of armaments. By one estimate, expenditures for arms among the five members of the Association of South East Asian Nations (ASEAN), excluding Vietnam, increased over 77 percent between 1980 and 1993 (Acharya and Stubb, 1996: 103).

ECONOMIC INTERDEPENDENCE AND SECURITY

What are the implications of global economic interdependence for national security? From an economic security perspective, globalization of economic activity is both an opportunity and a threat (see Chapters 6, 7, 10, and 11). On the opportunity side, economic interdependence may improve economic security by increasing the extent and variety of policy instruments that states have at their disposal. The most common of these instruments are power over trade, power over money, and power over information. *Power over trade* employs tools that range from boycotts and sanctions to export/import licensing and even "dumping." *Power over money* includes controls over aid and loans, stable currency, and financial accounts. *Power over information* includes technology export controls and patent denial (Scharfen, 1995: 103–126). States may also use non-economic instruments of power effectively against economic targets, such as air strikes against power generators or naval quarantines aimed at preventing trade in critical materials.

States with well-developed economies, substantial wealth, and extensive international activities tend to have more of these instruments at their disposal. During the Cold War, for example, the United States was able to limit high-technology exports to the Soviet Union and to Eastern Europe, to impose a grain embargo on the Soviet Union, and to build up the economies of states that opposed the Soviet Union—all of which were policies requiring no violence (cf. Chapter 2). Less developed countries may not have this range of options, and this may lead them to use the blunter instruments of military force to achieve such objectives.

Global economic interdependence may also create threats. Since national economies are so intricately linked, states can control their economic security only partially. Economic crises in one state may rapidly spread to another. When the stock market crashes in Hong Kong, for example, the consequences may stretch from São Paulo to London. And when there is political turmoil in the Persian Gulf, oil prices may skyrocket across the globe.

But it is crucial to remember that not all events impacting national economies need be matters of economic security as such. The distinction between economic *sensitivity* and *vulnerability* is helpful in separating unpleasant economic events from hurtful and imminent economic security threats. According to Keohane and Nye (1977: 12), sensitivity measures how swiftly changes in a given country bring about costly changes in another. There occurs an initial shock, which is corrected over time by policy changes: If a supplier of aluminum brusquely enacted an export embargo, a large importer of the item would suffer some negative economic effects in the short term. But in the medium to long term, this important buyer would probably find other suppliers, develop local sources of supply, or find substitutes for aluminum at a reasonable cost.

Vulnerability, in contrast, "can be defined as an actor's liability to suffer costs imposed by external events even after policies have been altered" (Keohane and Nye, 1977: 13). A widely upheld oil embargo would probably expose vulnerabilities. With the option of finding alternative sources of supply curtailed, a country would have a hard time absorbing this type of shock. Developing domestic sources of supply is often costly or just impossible, and finding useful substitutes is a long-term process because many energy consumers, such as automobiles, may not be converted to using solar or electric power easily or quickly. The sources of economic vulnerability that have the most serious consequences for national security are extensive and diverse.

Reliance on Imported Raw Materials and Energy

One of the most widely noted economic vulnerabilities is the reliance on imported raw materials and energy. Dependence on foreign sources of raw material and energy creates the potential for suppliers to use their ability to control the trade of these materials as a political weapon. Dependence becomes all the more dangerous, when

(a) Supplies come from concentrated sources.

(b) Asymmetric status disproportionately favors the suppliers (Kapstein, 1993).

(c) Imports necessitate lengthy transport or intricate routings.

(d) There are no substitutes or alternatives (Hirschman, 1945).

In addition, when leading industries (defined as those industries at the helm of innovation that fuel economic progress) are based more on raw materials than on knowledge or skills, the cost of disruption in supplies is higher and can have as devastating effects in times of peace as in times of war (Porter, 1990; Rasler and Thompson, 1991). The latter case can be lethal.

The given fact of the world situation . . . is not peace but war and the danger of war; and, if raw material supplies are in the hands of powers with whom the state is likely to be at war, or from whose territories it may be cut off, then the preservation of national power must necessarily involve concern with securing adequate provisions. (Robbins, 1939).

Even in peacetime, states may be more secure when they are less dependent on natural raw materials. This can be true even in countries with a large base of high-technology industries, since

when a small number of foreign suppliers account for a lion's share of global output, they have the power to place conditions or restrictions on its use, thereby undermining America's [or any other dependent country's] national autonomy. Under these circumstances . . . policy intervention to secure a more competitive supply base may be warranted, even if such intervention violates free trade or market principles. (Tyson, 1993: 11)

In most cases, however, countries with a large concentration of high-technology industries may be better placed to circumvent scarce factors than less developed states (Porter, 1990: 14). The factors most important to productivity growth in the industrially advanced economies—human resources, knowledge, and capital—are created within nations (Porter, 1990: 74). And the resources that a country would need to become or remain powerful are preferably available domestically. Semiconductors, for instance, are made from cheap, ordinary, and ubiquitous raw materials.

Indeed, some scholars argue that the spread of knowledge-intensive industries has actually reduced international conflict since countries so endowed have fewer incentives to invade other states (Jervis, 1991/1992: 49–51; Kaysen, 1990; Van Evera, 1990/1991) if only because they would have less to gain from doing so and far more to lose from the international instability that would ensue. Though compelling, this notion is seldom developed and never fully tested empirically. There is considerably more evidence for the converse argument that countries with a heavy concentration of low-technology industries and dependent on scarcer raw materials are more likely to have border disputes than states with a larger pool of high-technology industries (Mandel, 1980).

A corollary of the argument that knowledge-based industries may tend to decrease the economic incentives for conflict would be that economies with large service sectors are less vulnerable than those with large manufacturing sectors—because they are far less vulnerable to supply disruptions and are less attractive as targets of invasion (Jervis, 1991/1992; Van Evera, 1990/1991). They may have a strong incentive to maintain international stability since the products of many service industries have high price elasticity. Economic downturns and the consequent decreases in demand therefore hurt these industries disproportionately.

Protectionist Trading Regimes

Another important aspect of economic security is the existence of free trade regimes that allow states to buy and sell critical materials through the market instead of securing imports or exports through strong-arm tactics or doing altogether without them (Spiegel, 1942: 16). When states sense that they must secure markets and diverse sources of supply instead of relying on open trading regimes, they will become more competitive and will be highly sensitive to other states' relative advantages. In terms of long-term security, free trade regimes promote efficiency and increased transactions, conducive to increased wealth for many states. States that avoid the free trade regime, such as the Soviet Union during the Cold War, often end up with uncompetitive economies and decreased economic power over time.

It is helpful to note that, as an input, a free trade regime reinforces a stable security environment, of which it is also a product. When free trade relationships flourish, there are strong incentives to maintain them since the costs of severing ties is very high. And because a stable security environment makes such profitable relationships possible, free trade also reinforces the commitment to uphold such stability-fostering arrangements.

High Levels of Imports and Exports

All else being equal, a lower ratio of foreign trade to gross domestic product makes states less vulnerable to international disruptions and, consequently, more secure in the short term (Waltz, 1979). The fact that the United States and Soviet Union depended little on one another economically helped to stabilize the Cold War; conflict may have been harder to avoid if the two most powerful nations in the world were also more economically vulnerable to each other (Waltz, 1979). A corollary to this is that states will feel more secure if they trade with trusted allies. Faced with a common threat, allies can check their hunger for relative gains among themselves and create secure, liberal trading agreements (Gowa, 1989) favorable to (most) all of them.

Currency Manipulation

One frequently overlooked aspect of economic insecurity is susceptibility to currency manipulation. When states are obliged to defend exchange rates, pressures on a state's currency force it to draw down its reserves. Unintentional currency depreciation may produce inflation, balance of payments crises, capital flight, and a reduction in living standards (Kirshner, 1995: 8–9).

Depreciation, while often dictated by economic fundamentals, can also be manipulative when seeking to attain political ends. An excellent example of both the power and vulnerability that such currency manipulation can create is the 1967–1970 Nigerian Civil War between the federal government and the secessionist republic of Biafra. According to Jonathon Kirshner, predatory currency manipulation was one of the most influential tactics employed by the federal government to win the war. In January of 1970, the head of the federal government announced that Nigerian currency would be changed entirely within a 19-day period. He then set a cap on the amount of money businesses and private persons could exchange before the old currency became worthless. The policy, designed specifically to prevent the secessionists from using Nigerian currency to finance their war against the government, was successful almost immediately. The announcement sent the secessionist province into "panic selling" of the old currency, causing its value to plummet and deal a "massive blow" to the rebels' financial resources (Kirshner, 1995: 192–106). Although this example is somewhat unique because it focuses on two enemies sharing the same currency, it illustrates the severe consequences that a seemingly reformative move on a stable currency can cause.

THE CHALLENGE OF ECONOMIC SECURITY

As we have seen, economic security is a very complex issue that sometimes forces policymakers to make tough decisions. One of the most important decisions is the choice between emphasizing short-term or long-term security interests, for the inherent high tensions between the two call for very different, sometimes even opposite, policy responses. Yet another puzzle arises from the so-called economic security dilemma in which both aiding and not aiding another country financially may have equally negative outcomes. Finally, economic security may prove politically most difficult to handle when security concerns are at an ebb. The absence of an overwhelming threat to unite domestic opinion can present an ironic, if trying, challenge.

BALANCING SHORT-TERM AND LONG-TERM INTERESTS

The policies required to advance long-term and short-term security interests are very different. Policymakers wishing to increase long-term security may seek to increase exports, to keep trade barriers low, and to pursue policies that increase economic competitiveness. Such policies may consist of reducing government regulation, strengthening the educational system, reversing a brain drain of talented citizens out of the country, and—quite ironically—restricting aid to domestic industries in order to force them to compete in a global market. Even if these types of arrangements are known to be effective in building prosperous, flexible, and competitive economies, states tend to pursue these strategies only when they feel secure. When they do not, they may choose to focus on short-term economic security. With this focus, maximizing autonomy and control takes precedence even if it comes at the expense of added wealth, which is necessary to meet long-term security goals. Improving short-term economic security may require governments to divert resources to support strategic domestic industries, stockpile oil, restrict imports, and develop diverse sources of supply even when such options are more costly.

Two key examples of the trade-offs required when balancing long-term and short-term economic security are the debates about strategic petroleum reserves and export controls on encryption technology. The former represents a classic "guns versus butter" dilemma (Kapstein, 1993). Policymakers must say if governments should stockpile energy resources to ensure adequate supplies and stabilize prices in the event of a crisis or if they ought to allocate funds to more useful pursuits, such as infrastructure projects likely to increase national productivity. If one is concerned with short-term security because there are immediate and convincing threats to resources, it may indeed be wise to stockpile. If one is concerned with long-term security, however, it may be wise to spend government funds productively elsewhere.

Whether to maintain strict export controls on sophisticated encryption technology presents an even more complex problem. On one hand, security and criminal justice specialists argue that not controlling access to unbreakable encryption will "allow drug lords, spies, terrorists and even violent gangs to communicate about their crimes and their conspiracies with impunity. We will lose one of the few remaining vulnerabilities of the worst criminals and terrorists upon which law enforcement depends to successfully investigate and often prevent the worst crimes" (Freeh, 1997). On the other hand, businesses argue that strong encryption technology is vital to their ability to protect sensitive information. Limitations on access to such technologies would undermine their commercial viability. The United States currently is home to many of the world's leading producers of sophisticated encryption technology. However, they are not the only producers of those products: manufacturers in Sweden, Israel, and Japan are also leaders in this industry.

Balancing these concerns is difficult and, in the United States, has brought the Clinton administration under fire from both sides (Reinsch, 1997). The issue is so difficult because both sides have legitimate concerns, and, in fact, both sides are raising important security issues. National security and law enforcement officials are focused on the short term: a terrorist or spy could encrypt messages that lead to very harmful outcomes tomorrow, next week, or next month (see Chapter 10). The position held by businesses upholds long-term security interests. Although individual firms could have their proprietary information compromised or themselves become less competitive than foreign firms that are not subject to such restrictive export controls, there are few macro-consequences for American national security in the short term. In the long term, however, restrictions (if they are not global) could theoretically undermine an entire high-technology sector of the economy and reduce profits in a number of other sectors as well. The loss of American prosperity and tax revenue has clear implications for American power. A somewhat less obvious consequence is the loss of power that would result from relying on foreign suppliers of encryption technology. If this occurred, the American government would be able to exert far less control over the activities of those firms and would lose a significant instrument of economic power.

ECONOMIC SECURITY DILEMMA

In addition to the tension between long- and short-term economic security, policymakers can face an economic security dilemma of sorts when deciding whether to help promote another state's economic growth (Harris, 1993: 37). On the one hand, that state's growth may well increase opportunities for exports and investment. And it may provide a more powerful ally in conflicts and shore up favored political groups. It can even increase that state's internal stability (see Chapter 9), which can have many positive effects: social stability, reduced immigration (see Chapter 8), and good protection of existing contracts and agreements. On the other hand, economic growth can increase a state's overall power, provide it with more tools of influence, fuel disquieting arms races, and produce an alarming level of military might. The economic security dilemma is a well-known, relatively common situation faced in deciding whether or not to provide foreign aid. It has been experienced in Europe, in the United States, and Asia, and in recent years by governments trying to decide whether or not to aid Russia and North Korea. In both cases, policymakers had to evaluate whether security risks would be greater if these countries became stronger or weaker: Should they increase that state's economic strength, knowing that it can be used as a tool of influence and a source of military might? Or should they be more concerned about its endemic weakness, which is likely to produce a host of other security problems, including emigration, crime, or an interest in provoking regional conflict to divert attention from domestic troubles?

This problem is particularly acute in the case of rising powers since, historically, rising powers have often made use of aggressive means to restructure an international economic system organized to serve a declining power's interests (Gilpin, 1981; Organski and Kugler, 1980). Contests between rising economies seeking to flex their economic muscle and declining powers that cling to their unenforceable privileges are usually settled through war (Gilpin, 1981). Examples include the Franco-Prussian War and the African wars of independence against the colonial powers.

China presents a particularly challenging dilemma. A rising power with a huge population, nuclear weapons, and the capability of destabilizing an entire region, China possesses strengths and weaknesses that are almost equally threatening:

If the PRC disintegrates, the mass social chaos and human suffering could well result in waves of refugees, rampant crime, weapons and nuclear arms proliferation, and staggering economic losses. If China remains united and strongly authoritarian, a coalition of party ideologues, state capitalists, and xenophobic People's Liberation Army (PLA) officers could gather the reins of power in Beijing while constructing a new legitimacy based on Han nationalism and an aggressive foreign policy. If China remains united and mildly authoritarian, it could well become a destabilizing force in the international system, and in any case would still be difficult to deal with. (Shinn, 1996: 5–6)

THE CHALLENGE OF DECLINING THREATS

Ironically, economic security may receive even greater attention as a state's actual security increases—because the choices involved are more complicated when there are no clear and present dangers to a state's survival, territorial integrity, or economic sovereignty. When states are in danger, leaders often experience a "rally around the flag" effect during which they are accorded an unusual degree of support in making tough decisions and in reallocating scarce resources. A leader might, for example, be free to impose market controls at the expense of domestic industries, insist on more diverse sources of supply, and divert energy supplies to the military at the expense of consumer industries. Trading guns for butter is easier. When the level of external threat is lower, however, threats to economic security interests seem much more amorphous and much less urgent. The need for costly trade-offs seems postponable, and leaders may be faced with many of the tensions described above.

These trade-offs partially explain why states may pursue seemingly "irrational" policies toward promoting their economic security. When autonomy is perceived to be more important for either internal or external security reasons, states may choose to pursue exclusionary policies (such as severe protectionism) that clearly inhibit economic growth. This was the case two decades ago when several Latin American countries pursued policies of import substitution.

Indeed, the absence of an external threat to justify foreign policy behavior may lead to policies that seem outright strange. A recent example is the American trade embargo against Sudan, intended to exert economic pressure to punish Sudan's threatening political behavior. U.S. Secretary of State Madeleine Albright, suggested that Sudan must be admonished for its continued sponsorship of terror, its effort to destabilize neighboring countries and its abysmal record on human rights, including religious persecution. To protect the revenue of its soft drink and candy companies, the United States exempted the export of gum arabic (a key ingredient in the products of these companies), which accounts for fully half of all Sudan's exports to the United States (*Washington Post*, 1997: A24). With its national security under no direct threat from Sudan, American policymakers simply could not justify the economic harm that sanctions would bring to some of its large industries. Consequently, the impact of the damage inflicted on Sudan's economic security was far less than half of what it could have been.

STRATEGIES

In the face of these various threats, vulnerabilities, and challenges, what can governments do to protect state economic security? The policies they may pursue are almost endless and depend on the importance of their various security objectives.

Depending on the severity of their economic insecurity, states are likely to adopt one of roughly five strategies to reach the proper balance of autonomy and wealth, guns and butter, and short-term and long-term security. These strategies vary in their emphasis on state intervention.

States can adopt any one of the following strategies for improving the actual and potential economic security conditions and contexts of their concern:

Autonomy/Self-Reliance

When relatively weak states worry about their vulnerability, they endeavor to decrease their reliance on other states for inputs, markets, energy, and foreign investment. This strategy is fairly costly, since it is economically less efficient than trading widely, welcoming foreign investment, and reaping the economic benefits that such openness brings. This strategy is feasible mostly for weaker states with limited or no international interests. North Korea and Albania have pursued it.

Consolidation

States that are insecure, yet powerful, are likely to focus on their short-term economic security interests, and, if the cost of using force is low, they may take aggressive approaches to increase their security. States in this situation are extremely sensitive to shifts in their own relative power and are likely to use strong-arm tactics, including forced vertical partnerships with weaker states, to ensure reliable access to markets and supplies (Hirschman, 1945). The classic example of this strategy is Nazi Germany's trade relationships with weaker Eastern European countries. Accepting losses of efficiency, Nazi Germany structured these relationships with the distinct goal of maximizing the other states' dependence on Germany and minimizing its own vulnerability (Hirschman, 1945). Imperial Japan and the Soviet Union also followed this strategy.

Mercantilism

States that are very insecure in both the short and long term compete intensely for supplies and for markets in order to limit vulnerabilities and build the economic power necessary to exert control over others. They are markedly sensitive to relative shifts in power that may disadvantage them. They will, however, behave less aggressively than states pursuing a consolidation strategy. They may try to build power resources in anticipation of conflict in the medium to long term. European trade relations in the late nineteenth century exhibited this strategy.

Controlled Economic Policy

Countries support free trade and open markets in principle, but they practice competition for supplies and markets. Economic security and limited possibilities for armed conflict make states content with the status quo, but domestic considerations intensify concerns regarding economic security. Competition will probably not escalate to the use of force over economic matters, but tariff wars, protectionism, and restrictions on investment are a real possibility. States are very concerned with the long-term distribution of international wealth and domestic issues such as employment. This scenario is common among states that have industries with internal economies of scale, which normally operate in oligopolistic markets. The newly industrializing countries in East Asia and Japan adhered to this strategy in the 1980s.

Open Market Regimes

When states are content with the economic status quo and the likelihood of war is low, states generally adhere to free trade and open market principles. Some competition and protectionism exists as states attempt to serve domestic interests. Trade among allies (especially in a bipolar system where allies rarely defect to the other side) is pursued without much concern about power and security; sensitivity to shifts in relative power is low. States are able to focus on increasing wealth so that they can meet long-term security needs. They do not view themselves as inordinately vulnerable to economic shocks. European-American trade relations in the Cold War were like that.

CONCLUSION

Based on this discussion, what are the primary economic security challenges that developed and developing states will probably encounter in the coming years? For developed states, economic security concerns should be relatively low. In addition to a general condition of international security in which no advanced industrial power seems likely to go to war with any other, strictly economic conditions reinforce economic security. States are able to access supplies and attain markets through a relatively open world trade and investment regime, and leading industries rely on inputs such as knowledge and creativity that cannot easily be attained through force. They are able to focus on their long-term security, and they try to maximize economic wealth and power. Ironically, however, economic security issues may increasingly capture the attention of policymakers if domestic calls for economic protection may achieve even greater prominence in an evolving global economy.

The ability of developed states to concentrate on long-term security does not mean that developed states will not suffer economic setbacks as a result of downturns, currency devaluations, or stock market crashes in other countries. Indeed, developed states in an interdependent global economy will continue to be sensitive to foreign and international economic and political events. Their vulnerability to those events, however, is likely to be low. Not only do developed states have all too few serious vulnerabilities under free market regimes, but they also dispose of many instruments of power that can preserve their interests.

Developing states may have to face a very different context. Although they will probably be able to meet many of their economic needs by trading on the international market, they will generally have much less influence over international currency markets and terms of trade than developed states. Their main industries may rely on domestic natural resources or energy supplies, which may make them more vulnerable to strong states inclined to perpetuate their access to these same resources as a matter of politics or policy. They may become targets of invasion by other developing countries, which may find incentive to use force to secure vital raw materials or profitable factories, and so on. They may sometimes even be forced to sacrifice economic growth in order to achieve domestic stability since rapid economic growth may, in some cases, risk creating new groups capable of challenging the ruling regime.

In addition to their high sensitivity to international economic events, developing states are likely to be more easily vulnerable to economic shocks. Although they may become no more dependent on critical raw materials than developed states, they may exert less control over the international economy and the other states. For these reasons, developing states may be forced to focus much more on short-term than long-term economic security—a regrettable likelihood since this would force them to develop even more slowly than they otherwise might have. Thus, the gap between developed and developing states may widen even faster.

This view is consistent with the predictions of scholars who perceive a shift in international relations that is likely to produce a world marked by extreme regional differences in state behavior. According to these scholars, advanced industrialized states in the core face entirely different economic and political incentives than less developed states in the periphery can only hope for (Goldgeier and McFaul, 1992). It is relatively unlikely that they will wage armed international conflicts. By contrast, some developing countries still stand to benefit from war, and this increases the likelihood of conflict in the periphery. If this assessment is accurate, states in the periphery may face increasingly worsening economic security concerns as their economic relationships turn into zero-sum games. In contrast, the economic security of developed states may grow so fast as to create an even wider gulf between states in the core and those in the periphery. This perspective argues against neocolonialist revival or domination by advanced industrial nations of less developed ones, if only because the former will have little or no incentive to do so. Instead, it envisions "zones of peace"—in which the developed states generally avoid armed international conflict and enjoy relatively harmonious relations—and "zones of conflict"—in which developing states often compete for influence and settle differences through the use of force (Snow, 1995).

The gap between developed and developing states may generate its own set of risks for advanced industrial states, however, if only because economic weakness may often create an even greater threat than economic strength. States with advanced economies may struggle to deal with such troubling economic security dilemmas as whether or not to aid rogue states like North Korea, which present risks in either case. If they become stronger, they may pursue more aggressive foreign policies. If they become weaker, they may turn into havens for international criminals, vengeful terrorists, and pirates, or may consequently produce floods of refugees.

Although there are many reasons for caution, there is still some hope for the economic security of developing countries in the years ahead. If a globalizing international political economy prompts developing nations to mind their own domestic stability and economic growth, and if developing nations structure their own economies in ways to take greater advantage of the latitudes thus created by the expansion of domestic and foreign markets (see Introduction), the traditionally disadvantaged will increase their ability to focus on their longer-term economic security (cf. Chapter 7). In so doing, they could potentially follow the path of Malaysia and Chile, which have achieved phenomenal economic success and improved their long-term economic security dramatically, recent setbacks notwithstanding.

They could also borrow the road taken by Yugoslavia or Zaire.

REFERENCES

Acharya, Amitav, and Richard Stubb (1996). The Perils of Prosperity? Security and Economic Growth in the ASEAN Region. In M. Jane Davis (ed.), *Security Issues in the Post-Cold War World*. Cheltenham, UK: Edward Elgar.

Ahmed, Moamad (1997). The Security of Small States. Lecture delivered at The George Washington University, Washington, DC, October 15.

Bakeless, John (1972). *The Economic Causes of Modern War: A Study of the Period, 1878–1918*. New York: Garland Publishing.

Baldwin, David A. (1989). *Paradoxes of Power*. New York: Basil Blackwell.

Cable, Vincent (1995). What Is International Economic Security? *International Affairs* 71, 2.

Freeh, Louis J. (1997). The Impact of Encryption on Public Safety. Statement before the Permanent Select Committee on Intelligence, United States House of Representatives, September 9.

Friedberg, Aaron L. (1991). The Changing Relationship between Economics and National Security. *Political Science Quarterly* 106, 2.

Gerschenkron, Alexander (1962). *Economic Backwardness in Historical Perspective*. Cambridge, MA: Belknap Press of Harvard University Press.

Gilpin, Robert (1981). *War and Change in World Politics*. Cambridge: Cambridge University Press.

Goldgeier, James M. (1997). The Psychological Dimension of International Security. Paper presented at the Annual Meeting of the International Studies Association, Toronto, Ontario, March 18–22.

———, and Michael McFaul (1992). A Tale of Two Worlds: Core and Periphery in the Post–Cold War Era. *International Organization* 46, 2 (Spring).

Gowa, Joanne (1989). Bipolarity, Multipolarity, and Free Trade. *American Political Science Review* 83 (December): 1245–1256.

———— (1994). *Allies, Adversaries, and International Trade*. Princeton, NJ: Princeton University Press.

Gowa, Joanne, and Edward D. Mansfield (1993). Power Politics and International Trade. *American Political Science Review* 87 (June): 408–421.

Grieco, Joseph (1988). Anarchy and the Limits of Cooperation: A Realist Critique of the Newest Liberal Institutionalism. *International Organization* 42 (Summer).

———— (1990). *Cooperation among Nations: Europe, America and Non-tariff Barriers to Trade*. Ithaca, NY: Cornell University Press.

Harris, Stuart (1993). The Economic Aspects of Security in the Asia/Pacific Region. In Richard Higgott, Richard Leaver, and John Ravehill (eds.), *Pacific Economic Relations in the 1990s: Cooperation or Conflict?* Boulder, CO: Lynne Rienner.

Headrick, Daniel R. (1981). *The Tools of Empire: Technology and European Imperialism in the Nineteenth Century*. New York: Oxford University Press.

Hirschman, Albert O. (1945). *National Power and the Structure of Foreign Trade*. Berkeley: University of California Press.

Jervis, Robert (1991/1992). The Future of World Politics: Will It Resemble the Past? *International Security* 16, 3 (Winter).

Kapstein, Ethan Barnaby (1993). *The Political Economy of National Security: A Global Perspective*. Columbia: University of South Carolina Press.

Kaysen, Carl (1990). Is War Obsolete? A Review Essay. *International Security* 14, 4 (Spring): 42–64.

Kennedy, David M. (1980). *Over Here: The First World War and American Society*. New York: Oxford University Press.

Keohane, Robert O. (1984). *After Hegemony: Cooperation and Discord in the World Political Economy*. Princeton, NJ: Princeton University Press.

————, and Joseph S. Nye (1977). *Power and Interdependence*. Boston: Little, Brown.

Kirshner, Johnathon (1995). *Currency and Coercion: The Political Economy of International Monetary Power*. Princeton, NJ: Princeton University Press.

Knorr, Klaus Eugen (1973). *Power and Wealth: The Political Economy of International Power*. New York: Basic Books.

Liberman, Peter (1996). *Does Conquest Pay? The Exploitation of Occupied Industrial Territories*. Princeton, NJ: Princeton University Press.

MacLarty, Thomas F. (1997). Lecture at Economic Strategy Institute, Washington, DC, November 5.

Mandel, Robert (1980). Roots of the Modern Interstate Border Dispute. *Journal of Conflict Resolution* 24 (September): 427–454.

Mansfield, Edward D. (1992). The Concentration of Capabilities and International Trade. *International Organization* 46 (Summer): 731–764.

Milward, Alan S. (1977). *War, Economy, Society 1939–1945*. Berkeley: University of California Press.

Moran, Theodore (1990). International Economics and National Security. *Foreign Affairs* 69, 5 (Winter).

———— (1993a). *American Economic Policy and National Security*. New York: Council on Foreign Relations Press.

———— (1993b). An Economics Agenda for Neorealists. *International Security* 18, 2 (Fall).

Nelson, Joan M. (1989). *Fragile Coalitions: The Politics of Economic Adjustment*. Washington, DC: Overseas Development Council.

Neu, C. R., and Charles Wolf, Jr. (1994). *The Economic Dimensions of National Security*. Santa Monica, CA: RAND.

Organski, A.F.K., and J. Kugler (1980). *The War Ledger*. Chicago: University of Chicago Press.

Porter, Roy (1990). *English Society in the Eighteenth Century*. Rev. ed. London and New York: Penguin Books.

Rasler, Karen, and William R. Thompson (1991). Technological Innovation, Capability Positional Shifts and Systemic War. *Journal of Conflict Resolution* 35, 3: 412–442.

Reinsch, William A. (1997). Administration Encryption Policy. Testimony before the House Subcommittee on Telecommunications, Trade and Censure Protection, Committee on Commerce, September 4.

Robbins, Lionel Charles (1939). *The Economic Causes of War*. New York: Jonathan Cape.

Romm, Joseph (1993). *Defining National Security: The Nonmilitary Aspects*. New York: Council on Foreign Relations Press.

Rosecrance, Richard (1986). *The Rise of the Trading State*. New York: Basic Books.

Sandholtz, Wayne, Michael Borrus, John Zysman, Ken Conca, Jay Stowsky, Steven Vogel, and Steve Weber (eds.) (1992). *The Highest Stakes: The Economic Foundations of the Next Security System*. New York: Oxford University Press.

Scharfen, John C. (1995). *The Dismal Battlefield: Mobilizing for Economic Conflict*. Annapolis, MD: Naval Institute Press.

Shinn, James (ed.) (1996). *Weaving the Net: Conditional Engagement with China*. New York: Council on Foreign Relations Press.

Snow, Donald M. (1995). *The Shape of the Future: The Post Cold War World*. Armonk, NY: M. E. Sharpe.

Spiegel, Henry William (1942). *The Economics of Total War*. New York: D. Appleton-Century Co.

Thomas, Caroline (1987). *In Search of Security: The Third World in International Relations*. Boulder, CO: Lynne Rienner.

Tyson, Laura D'Andrea (1993). *Who's Bashing Whom? Trade Conflict in High Tech Industries*. Washington, DC: Institute for International Economics.

Van Evera, Stephen (1990/1991). Primed for Peace: Europe After the Cold War. *International Security* 15, 3 (Winter): 7–57.

Waltz, Kenneth N. (1979). *Theory of International Politics*. New York: McGraw-Hill.

Washington Post (1997). Soda Pop Diplomacy. November 8, p. A24.

Wolfers, Arnold (1962). *Discord and Collaboration*. Baltimore, MD: Johns Hopkins University Press.

CHAPTER 5

Environmental Insecurity:
Nature as a Geopolitical Threat

SIMON DALBY

ENVIRONMENT AND THE "RETHINKING SECURITY" DEBATE

In a recent scholarly gathering, it was suggested that a medical metaphor—portraying security analysts as diagnosing and prescribing remedies to all sorts of ailments in the body politic—might best depict what practitioners of security now do as part of their normal professional activities (Bobrow, 1996). The need for a new metaphor comes because, as many commentators in the 1990s have intimated, it is now apparently necessary to broaden the ambit of security, to deal with the geopolitical difficulties of the post–Cold-War era (Buzan, Waever, and de Wilde, 1998). Adding such items as diseases, migration, economic dislocations, and the gamut of human rights issues to the security agenda also suggests that new tools and ways of thinking are needed to offer an all-encompassing approach to multitudinous threats.

Since the late 1980s, these debates about reformulating security and focusing on new "threats" have encompassed the relations between the natural environment and security as well. "Environmental security" discussions benefited from a heightened public awareness of environmental issues in the late 1980s and early 1990s. They have also taken place against a backdrop of important questions within the North-South political dialogue (Chatterjee and Finger, 1994). In 1992, the largest summit of world leaders ever assembled took place in Rio de Janeiro to deal with issues of environment and development. Five years, later the United Nations held a follow-up conference to review what, if any, progress had been made, and the issue of climate change was the focus of a major conference and international agreement in Kyoto late in 1997.

Although the level of attention does fluctuate, the global environment has become a matter of international political concern. Since 1991, it has been explicitly listed as a concern to American national security in the federal government's annual statement on the National Security Strategy of the United States. As has been made clear in numerous speeches by senior officials, the second Clinton administration has assigned foreign policy priority to environmental concerns. A number of policy-specific research projects were under way in the mid-1990s, including the Woodrow Wilson Center's project on "Environmental Change and Security," Thomas Homer-Dixon's research on environmental degradation and conflict at the University of Toronto, and NATO's advanced research workshops on the environment, conflict, and related matters (Gleditsch, 1997).

The renewed emphasis on the environment has focused scholarly and policy-making attention on the pressing need for adequate conceptualizations of both environment and security (Deudney, 1991; Gleick, 1991; Brock, 1992; Mische, 1992; Kakonen, 1994; Stern, 1995; Tennberg, 1995). Debates about what ought to be studied and in what ways concepts should be used continue apace. Especially when linked to the concern with the environment, the idea of "security" evokes a series of complex dilemmas and anything but a simple framework for evaluating policy options (Dokken and Graeger, 1995; Dabelko and Dabelko, 1996; Eckersley, 1996; also, Graeger, 1996; Dalby, 1997a). As this chapter suggests, the relations between environment and security are far from simple, despite widespread assumptions in conventional analyses and policy-making circles that they can be relatively straightforwardly linked. By drawing on cognate perspectives to take a closer look at the literature on environmental security, this chapter identifies some of the limits of the "environmental degradation-leads-to-conflict" argument and the many pitfalls of interpreting contemporary political events, or the environmental changes now being noticed, exclusively in terms of security.

Examining the "silences" in the discourse of environmental security—those issues and non-issues left out of consideration due to conceptual confusion, definitional foreclosure, or even disciplinary convention—is essential to a thorough understanding of the politics of security in the post–Cold-War era. In this chapter, I suggest that specifying the problems of environmental insecurity, as with security in general, is not a sheer technical exercise but rather a highly charged political act through which security invokes multiple discourses of danger (see Dillon, 1996; Dalby, 1997b). How threats are identified, and crucially, who has the authority to specify these threats in ways that influence policy-making, is an important and integral part of rethinking the concept of security, and its newer implications for those in "the North" as well as in "the South," in a globalizing political economy, even as we prepare to leave a tired century and enter a new millennium (Buzan, Waever, and de Wilde, 1998).

GEOPOLITICS AND ENVIRONMENTAL SECURITY

The theme of environment as threat-to-political-stability, threat-to-national-security, or threat-to-the-state has been circulating in academic and policy circles at least since the mid-1970s (Brown, 1977), even if it has not been taken seriously until much more recently. It became a major theme in the World Commission on Environment and Development's (WCED) report, *Our Common Future* (1987), in which we read that "(e)nvironmental stress is both a cause and an effect of political tension and military conflict" (WCED, 1987: 290). This widely cited report also argued that even if causative linkages are far from being simple or well understood, conflicts seen to be linked to the environment "are likely to increase as these resources become scarcer and competition for them increases" (WCED, 1987: 290). A few of these themes appeared to be alarmist Malthusian fears of rapid overpopulation or chaos induced by "collapsing states" in the poorer parts of the world (Kaplan, 1994; Dalby, 1996).

Some researchers argue that such statements are not proven and that the parameters of such linkages are not well understood even in situations where they might hold (Deudney, 1992; Levy, 1995; Homer-Dixon et al., 1996; Gleditsch, 1997). The scholarly debates have addressed empirical research and policy pursuits—both the search for linkages between conflict and environmental degradation, and the scrutiny of policies likely to take any such linkages for granted—if only because the environment is taken to represent a national security matter (Dalby, 1999). Critics have also charged that security agencies—the military in particular—play a major part in environmental damage in many parts of the world (Westing, 1997). As will be elucidated later in this chapter, a discussion of the connections between environmental change and conflict can prove difficult, if at least some of the implicit conceptual assumptions related to the debate about broadening security are not made explicit beforehand.

While leaving aside the related concern of damage caused by military activities, it can be a useful initial heuristic device to divide environmental "security" issues into three categories: existential, physical, and political; and to test these against the security backdrop of a single state (Levy, 1995). Existential threats stemming from environmental destruction, in principle, can be argued to make humanity generally insecure (Renner, 1989; Myers, 1993). It is relatively easy to argue that existential versions of the link between security and environment are so undertheorized as to be analytically almost useless: The notion of security becomes so diffuse that it loses any meaning in regard to the vital interests of states, and especially so in the case most frequently discussed in the extant literature—the one relating to the national interest of the United States (Levy, 1995). If all environmental damage were a security threat, then, so the argument goes, conventional policy formulation would be impossible, since neither the damages nor the responses would be calculable and the priorities for policy action would therefore be impossible to establish. A counter-argument often made, however, asserts that numerous facets of environmental damage have serious implications for many societies and thus demand urgent attention (Renner, 1996). But this argument is not related to the narrow sense of security—an issue for states to try to resolve. It is concerned with broader matters of human security (Commission on Global Governance, 1995). It introduces the complicating matter of governance, broadly understood, and the important point that states themselves often render their populations insecure in many ways, despite the facile rationale that they guarantee security.

As regards direct physical damage from environmental threats to any nation—and to the United States in particular—stratospheric ozone depletion, and medium-term global climate changes provide good examples. Ozone depletion is an obvious direct threat to human health. Disruptions caused by changes in climate may also cause agricultural and infrastructural damage due to storms, droughts, and flooding. A broad interpretation of "the national interest" suggests that these hazards ought to be considered under an overarching notion of security. But, ironically, the practice of dealing with environmental problems suggests that this may not be the most appropriate policy response. At least in the case of ozone depletion, the widely supported 1987 Montreal Protocol and its subsequent updates—on limiting the use of ozone-depleting substances—gained approval in the United States precisely "because" the negotiations were not treated as a matter of high politics or as a security concern (Deudney, 1992; see also Litfin, 1994). Along this logic—where flexible arrangements and customized responses were negotiated to accommodate many widely differing interests—the use of a "top-down" environmental policy framework of precise rules, strict monitoring, and true enforcement by an international security agency has little to no chance of providing the flexible responses needed to counter the longer-term dangers presented by climate change and other possible future hazards of nature.

The third danger to the West and to the United States is from indirect political disruptions caused by environmentally induced political conflict in economically poor states. Much of the empirical literature on environmental degradation and conflict has focused on the likely parameters of migration and the causal mechanisms that lead to the breakdown of societies and to violence and displacement. Environmental refugees, collapsing states, and migration issues have all been investigated in various ways in both the popular press and scholarly writings as threats to the states of the North. Political instabilities, induced by direct conflicts over resource uses and by indirect problems generated by ensuing waves of refugees and migrants, will, so the argument goes, cause spillover effects in the affluent Northern states, which will then be obligated to provide a security response. Skeptics, however, have challenged the logic of these arguments, suggesting that while these are matters of concern, the exact formulations of cause and effect and of the policy responses have thus far been adequately conceptualized (Suhrke, 1997; Wood, 1994).

EMPIRICAL RESEARCH ON ENVIRONMENT AND CONFLICT

One method of dealing with the conceptual difficulties and the great fuzziness of the term "security" has been to avoid it altogether and to focus instead on what may link environmental degradation to overt violent conflict. Although evidence obtained from such research has suggested to some analysts that there are, indeed, some clear linkages between environmental degradation and conflict (Homer-Dixon, 1994, 1996a, 1996b), most case studies are complicated and subject to multiple interpretations. Scarcity of environmental resources is definitely a factor in some conflicts; forced migrations sometimes lead to identity conflicts as refugee claims clash with those of local residents. Relative scarcities encouraging elites to seize control over environmental resources often further aggravate the marginalization of poor populations. Recent research on China and Indonesia, focusing on the state's capacity in the face of likely future environmental constraints, suggests that the links between environmental degradation and civil conflict are far from simple (Barber, 1997; Economy, 1997).

In some ways, the debates divulge much more about the prior assumptions underlying such contemporary research than about the plight of those bearing the consequences of environmental change (Levy, 1995; Homer-Dixon and Levy, 1995/1996; Homer-Dixon et al., 1996). Thus, their significance depends in part on whether or not one starts with the assumption that environmental degradation is widely understood as a problem for security, as well as on whether and why the premise needs empirical validation prior to policy initiatives. If one follows the argument held by the WECD (1987) and takes for granted that environment is a cause for political strife, then detailed research into case studies can appear less useful than research into policy options and regional responses. Environmental matters are already recognized as integral to contemporary intra-state violence (Homer-Dixon, 1994, 1996a, 1996c). And whether or not they have spillover effects, the very fact that people are being killed in some states is—in and of itself— an important matter for scholarly investigation and a security concern, when security is understood to include broad concerns beyond the mere safeguard of political order in the modern West. The basic syllogism of precisely how security ought to be conceptualized is an unavoidable issue in this discussion.

This in turn leads to the related questions as to whether a research design that explicitly focuses on the environment is to be preferred to one concentrating on regional conflict portraying the environment as a causal factor, and whether some intervening variables may not prove even more important than the environment as determinants and predictors of likely conflict (Levy, 1995). If violence is a domestic issue for states and if environmental factors contribute to it, then environmental insecurity—although of concern—may not be so directly related to regional conflict. Intervening variables may prove more helpful in predicting and in explaining the causes of violence, given the variety of political and sociological conditions that can affect the circumstances in which conflict may occur (see Chapters 4, 8, 9, and 10). The literature to date offers very poor explicit focus on the causative role that "intervening variables" might play in circumstances of environmental degradation. Missing still is the suggestion that these political, economic, and/or sociological intervening variables might be simultaneous in their effects relating to violence and environmental degradation.

If the intervening variables are a crucial part of the process, then the causes of both degradation and violence may be understood in a rather different fashion. Such analysis would suggest that the causes of environmental degradation are, indeed, more intimately connected to conflict and insecurity and that the larger concern should be with political activities engendered by the processes that are causing degradation. Such an analysis would also hint that concerns about intergroup violence, which is the traditional focus of security analysts, might be somehow occluding the significant political actions of social movements (see Chapter 7) that resist degradation, and also challenge the processes of enclosure and dispossession which are part of the development strategies of many states. Emphasizing this dimension of the environment-conflict nexus leads to a very different problematique, one that latches on to larger questions of political economy. In contrast to a conventional "degradation leads to conflict" approach, such a research agenda would address the processes of globalization and the various specifically local conflicts over changing resource ownership and use, among others.

Such matters do not even appear in most of the security and conflict debates over the appropriate methods and priorities for the empirical research of the connections between environmental degradation and conflict. Insight into what such a revised agenda might reveal can be gained by looking at cognate fields, and more specifically at political ecology, anthropology, and sociology. In these fields, the dilemmas inherent in the current debates about rethinking security are illuminated by a critical stance, which argues that conventional state-centric formulations of security, in fact, conceal important causal relationships (Dalby, 1997b).

SOURCES OF INSECURITY: DEVELOPMENT AND ENVIRONMENTAL DEGRADATION

Where states are seen not to be acting in the interests of their populations, the assumption usually is that they will do so when their level of economic development rises high enough. This may await the building of nonexisting infrastructure and the long conversion of a subsistence economy into a modern social system. In the process, from the Amazon to the Narmada Dam project in India, large numbers of people may find themselves displaced and in direct conflict with state forces and corporations. As Chapters 6, 9, and 10 quite explicitly suggest, modernization comprises a process that often involves conflict. Development itself can be understood as a violent process by which people are uprooted and homelands are flooded for dams, invaded by roads and pipelines, or converted to commercial ends while waterways bear the brunt of pollution from mines and agricultural chemicals (Gadgil and Guha, 1995; Rich, 1994).

Where states are the direct providers of insecurity, as is often the case with the largest of these infrastructure projects, the provision of security cannot be separated from the political questions of who is being thereby made insecure. Environmental displacements leading to conflicts of identity are one possible cause of violence (Homer-Dixon, 1994). But possibly more serious is the insecurity caused by state-supported or state-imposed "developments" that engender resistance and opposition from those who find themselves banished while environmental resources are appropriated and access to them is withdrawn via the commercial-industrial arrangements of cattle ranches, clear-cut logging, or agricultural plantations (Gedicks, 1993; Johnston, 1994).

While broadened definitions of security may be much too unwieldy to provide clear criteria for policy action, narrowed formulations of state-centered security would preclude arguments about the practical everyday struggles for livelihood in specific places. It is precisely because these are not directly about the state's vital interests that these remain excluded from security debates, regardless of the fact that food, human rights, access to clean water, absence of arbitrary violence, and other human necessities are integral to any discussion on security broadly understood (Renner, 1996). When these dilemmas of who is secure and who is not are worked into the discussion, the whole matter of environmental degradation as a cause of insecurity becomes suddenly much more complex (Dalby, 1999)—even urgent.

The failure to incorporate these considerations may simply be a result of disciplinary overspecialization. Many political scientists, most of those involved in research or engaged in policy debates on environmental security, are not very familiar with much of the work being conducted in sociology, anthropology, and development, let alone in geography or ecological sciences. Many specialists of international security are often also not experts in land tenure systems, the complexities of ethnic political mobilizations, plantation agriculture, commodity pricing, structural adjustment policies, migrant labor, or gender-divided rural political economies. And the centralized importance and attention that security experts direct to state institutions presupposes their universal efficacy. This is often an ethnocentric mistake in international relations, one that feeds discussions of "failed states"—especially African politics (Grovogui, 1996)—but that is otherwise inappropriate in many places. Yet it is also a result of the neat divisions extant between the disciplines of social science: Social scientists not familiar with the language (see Chapter 1) used in political science to reflect that discipline's central concerns also fail to grasp implicit aspects of national and international security. Yet this does not counter the argument submitted below.

POLITICAL ECOLOGY: LOCAL AND GLOBAL

The concern with environmental degradation is quite often imprecisely attributed to population pressures and to pollution—both of which are understood as an inevitable part of development. Concerns with the specific causation of environmental degradation require that the Malthusian dimensions of the scarcity debate be a little more deeply reexamined. While population increase is obviously an important factor in some locations, it is not that obvious a cause of either environmental degradation or acute conflict in many places—not excluding Rwanda—where simplistic and hasty generalizations point at population increases as a major cause of degradation and conflict (Ford, 1995).

Investigating specific locations to uncover relationships between social conflict in particular places and global economic processes, as the "political ecology" framework does, suggests that expeditive preconceptions about processes of environmental degradation are inadequate (Blaikie and Brookfield, 1987; Bryant and Bailey, 1997; Peet and Watts, 1996). The same research also reveals that gender plays a crucial role in environment-specific and resource-related issues of access (Rocheleau, Thomas-Slayter, and Wangari, 1996). The physical and environmental conditions characterizing a given locality need to be incorporated in an analysis that links ecological factors to conflict. Degradation comprises a complex interactive set of processes, many of which are reversible, some of which are permanent.

Some environment-and-conflict analytical frameworks do adopt facets of such an approach in the search for causal factors when investigating the increasing relative scarcity of environmental resources or the difficulties of capturing resources at the cost of ecologically marginalizing those thereby being dispossessed of them (Homer-Dixon, 1996a, 1996b). Also understood in terms of the political ecology framework is that conflicts from rivalries for direct control over resources are about matters only indirectly involving environmental degradation and, even then, not in ways that would make such degradation the driving cause of those very conflicts. In political ecology, larger-scale global economic forces and commodity markets are integral to the processes that drive modernization and commercialization, both of which, in turn, occasion displacements (Peluso, 1993).

So interpreted, environment might itself now turn into an "intervening" variable in the political processes that lead from capture of resources to conflicts precipitated by the actions of the marginalized simply resisting dispossession or expropriation (Rubin, 1997; Swift, 1996). If processes of resource-capture are explained in their larger political economic context, along a perspective of changing resource ownership, then understandings of conflict, environmental change, and policy issues are likely to become much more insightful. But they do not fit easily into the environmental-degradation-leading-to-conflict framework. And the policy implications also are very different.

DISASTERS, VULNERABILITIES, AND (IN)SECURITY

A similar argument can be made by drawing from the scholarly literature on disasters and on their "management." While "natural phenomena" may or may not be gaining in frequency or severity, their impacts by way of storms, floods, tornadoes, droughts, and volcanic eruptions have been swifter in coming and exceptionally damaging during the last few decades. Impacts are increasing in part because many people are living in more vulnerable locations, such as on lowlands or steep slopes. While human activities—from deforestation to dam building—do affect the parameters of floods and droughts and may therefore indirectly induce increased vulnerabilities, many casualties are simply a product of physical insecurity engendered by the poverty and dispossession that force people to live in dangerous locations (Blaikie et al., 1994) to begin with.

The processes of marginalization are often compounded by ethnic rivalries and state inaction (see Chapters 8 and 9). But vulnerabilities need to be understood as cumulative social processes. The specific links between the components of the very poverty that produces vulnerability are important considerations in the analysis of disasters and of the responses to them. Besides, the suggestion that disasters are political events should not be overlooked. As an analysis of Central America makes very clear, the political dimensions of disasters are related in a number of ways to the more traditional considerations of national security (Pettiford, 1995).

Disasters can offer myriad possibilities for social change. Disruptions offer occasion for the direction of emergency and reconstruction aid to the dominant groups of the damaged society and thus to the further marginalization of its poor. This can occur simply during such processes as the designation of aid for housing reconstruction. In such cases, renters and squatters do not qualify for aid, whereas the wealthy holders of title to lands and buildings get additional advantages in the processes of reconstruction. The diversion of aid to elites has been a matter of political contention after many a disaster in Central America. The collapse of the Somoza regime in Nicaragua in the 1970s is a clear example, as outrage over the diversion of aid swelled the ranks of the regime's opponents. Similarly, the failure to deal with famine in the early 1970s by Haile Selassie's administration in Ethiopia undoubtedly hastened its demise (Molvoer, 1991).

CRITICAL ANTHROPOLOGY AND INSECURITY

Another extension of this line of argument can be made in terms of the destruction of livelihoods and lands by development projects, such as mining, logging, or damming on the territory of indigenous peoples. Postcolonial states have often continued to practice many of the once-maligned policies of their colonial predecessors whose paths to "development" they now try to emulate (Jewitt, 1995). Those indigenous to the "jungles" of the tropical world are considered to be primitive peoples, whether in Malaysia or in Brazil. Modernity deems their traditional ways of life not worth taking seriously (Kuehls, 1996). Their tribal cultures and experiences are dismissed as devoid of science and hence not very useful beyond providing pharmaceutical companies with the sources of traditional remedies that can be "developed" to provide drugs for the medical establishments of a few global industrial powers.

Not surprisingly, the defining language here is politically loaded. The terms "jungle" or "rainforest" connote biologically similar but politically different entities. Not many people worry about "jungles," but once "rainforests" are turned into a cause by the environmentalists of the North, "the Amazons" become a treasure to be "protected" against "the state" claiming lawful sovereignty over it (Pinheiro and Cesar, 1994). The anthropologists' convergence on the human rights of "local" peoples, on their struggles against encroachment, adequately clarify the question of exactly what is being rendered secure (Johnston, 1994; Gedicks, 1993). In most cases, what ends up being secured is neither the integrity of indigenous societies nor the natural benevolence of the settings that support their ways of life.

Violence on the frontier is nothing new in the history of colonization. It is a very old pattern that has little to do with Malthusian interpretations of poverty driven by overpopulation (Dalby, 1996). In some cases, resistance to exploitation of indigenous resources has the classic makings of the struggles of independence that replay the history of decolonization conflicts (Boge, 1992; Rangan, 1996). In an interesting inversion of the conventional assumptions about state security and territorial sovereignty, Bernard Nietschmann (1994) takes this theme to its logical conclusion and argues that through much of this century, in effect, the industrialized world has been involved in a war of destruction waged against indigenous cultures, sometimes better known as the "fourth world."

RISK SOCIETY AND GLOBAL THREATS

If geographers have concerns about ecological degradation from development, and anthropologists worry about the destruction of indigenous cultures, sociologists afford theoretical visions of postmodernity that add another interdisciplinary critique to the discussions of environmental security (Redclift and Benton, 1994). One line of argument that is especially germane here is the discussion of "risk society."

This critique starts from the argument that conventional dualisms between nature and society are not useful starting points for sociological analyses in the period after industrial modernity (Beck, 1992). Instead, threats and fears are defined in terms of "fabricated uncertainties" that civilization produces: "risk, danger, side-effects, insurability, individualization, . . . globalization" (Beck, 1996: 1). Basically, technical matters now become politicized in context of a "world risk society" (Beck, 1992; Lash, Szerszynski, and Wynne, 1996). This typology of global threats distinguishes between wealth-driven ecological damage (or destruction related to industrial wastes and to phenomena such as "holes" in the ozone layer) and poverty-driven destruction (which refers to peasants who annihilate their milieu in their desperate fight to escape economic marginalization). A third global danger, the potential of nuclear, biological, and chemical weapons can be added to those of ecological destruction. In combination, these risks are eroding the logic of conventional technological risk, if only for producing situations in which "hard to manage dangers prevail instead of quantifiable risks" (Beck, 1996: 15).

Understanding the question of threats and insecurities in this framework complicates even more the conventional assumptions that environmental degradation presents a threat to the security of Western states. First of all, risks and threats are not purely objective phenomena but socially mediated political constructs. This is where identity latches on to security and endangerment. Here, what can be credibly articulated as being threatened is an identity in need of being "secured" (Buzan, Waever, and de Wilde, 1998). But the identity of modernity is simply taken for granted in nearly all of the literature on security. If security is not sustainable without ever-growing efforts to expand state control, or ever-increasing abuses of local resources toward supplying an ever-expanding production system, then the resulting disruptions and displacements render numerous constituencies insecure. This is especially the case where military establishments take part in the resource extraction process, thereby escalating the potential for direct violence against opposition to displacement (Wolpin, 1992).

Second, such disruption affects trans-state politics by way of an emergent sphere of political activity linking human rights, environment, gender, and development issues. Discussions of global security are premised on the modern assumptions that the state is the provider of security, that legal systems uphold individual human rights, that the latter have been universalized to provide a benchmark for political conduct globally, and that—as is implicit to much of the conventional security discourse—modernity has to be extended to the poor and backward parts of the world, for the greater benefit of all. There remain grounds for dismissing such formulations as ethnocentric, despite the semblance of inclusivity conveyed by numerous appeals to global governance (Commission on Global Governance, 1995; Baxi, 1996). But if impoverishment and disruption are the unintended consequences for certain localities in the global economic system necessary for worldwide modernity, the contradictions become palpably painful.

Third, in such a domain of global concern, the legitimacy of technical expertise offered is of crucial importance if trust is to prevail. Should environmental risks be perceived as being contingent on larger political processes and beyond technical preoccupations with localized impacts, technical expertise itself may lose its claim to legitimacy in irreversible ways. The theory of "world risk society" investigates the emergence of discourse communities (see Chapter 1) capable of arguing that the long-neglected side effects of industrial production must from now on be understood to entail risks that can deprive the system of its legitimacy and its "rational" technocratic controls. In many places, environmental degradation goes hand in hand with intense political criticisms of imperialistic politics, and even with nationalist identity politics bent on protecting the homeland—an important, if often overlooked, process that contributed a political angle to the demise of the Soviet Union and the Warsaw Treaty bloc in the late 1980s.

Also relevant to our argument here is the fact that "world risk society" pushes politics beyond the conventional parameters, drawing political constituencies together for joint boycotts and protests around telegenically mediated "tableaux" of corporate perfidy and telling snapshots of ecological destruction (Wapner, 1996). These emergent discursive political communities are questioning the technical procedures of expert regulatory agencies and corporations on the grounds that the ultimate effects of their habitual practices may lead to unforeseen ecological consequences. In the process, the very legitimacy of the state's environmental experts is becoming highly politicized, while the administration of ecological regulations is being politically contested.

This also relates to the politics of trans-state movements and to global regimes where interstate treaties may provide at least a loose framework suited to constrain state activities (Vogler, 1995). Claims to expertise in environmental disputes are mobilized by both environmentalists and policymakers during the political bargaining processes of international regime formation (Litfin, 1994). State development experts, pollution experts, medical science, and planning procedures are now all in doubt; the politics of technical expertise can no longer be obfuscated under an unquestioned acceptance of the writ of science. "Security experts" are not immune to these developments. The presentation of environment as a threat is a complex political process, not simply an issue "security experts" can paraphrase to elicit a conveniently adequate policy response.

INSECURITY, RESOURCES, AND "THE TERRITORIAL TRAP"

The difficulties with the emergence of "global" arguments about environmental threats and with the politics of specifying the nature and geography of the threat are even reinforced when the geographical assumptions of the "territorial trap" in the domain of international relations are added to the discussion (Agnew and Corbridge, 1995; Agnew, 1998). This "trap" reifies the practice by sovereign states of assuming that they are autonomous permanent entities rather than understanding that they are really convenient and changing arrangements. This often obscures the importance of crucial flows of resources across state borders.

The way "the territorial trap" operates becomes very clear in a recent scholarly volume on "environmental aid." Although this work is not specifically about environmental insecurity, its premises are similar to some of the key arguments advanced in the environmental-degradation-leads-to-conflict literature, as is its concern with transboundary environmental security threats. The investigation focuses on the institutions that are most suitable for channeling expertise and finances to poorer states in order to alleviate their environmental problems. On the very first page of the introduction to the volume, the readership is invited to imagine two maps of the world—the text does not actually provide maps, so one has to imagine. One imaginary map is meant to convey the "relative severity of environmental problems," and the other, to portray the distribution of "the capabilities of governments [that] have to cope with these problems" (Keohane, 1996: 3).

The territorial trap functions in the suggestion that the variation in problems and capabilities is derived from indigenous factors within autonomous entities. As submitted in my discussion of political ecology, these assumptions about autonomous states obscure a crucial third map—the map divulging the various flows of resources, which are the very sources of wealth that provide governmental capabilities, and the very cause behind some crucial aspects of environmental degradation. Only this third "imaginary" geopolitical map, which identifies the transboundary flows of resources, can emphasize the essential role of the interconnections between the first two maps, and their value in fostering an understanding of environmental insecurity and of the causes of both degradation and government capability.

The flows of resources shown in the third map are obviously not the whole story. But they ought to provide insight to states in the North—best able to make policies for dealing with global problems—precisely because they provide that part of the global puzzle, which the geopolitical theorists of security in the North could possibly help transform in the immediate (Dalby, 1997a).

The larger picture of global insecurities is cut through by an overarching irony that needs to be kept in mind. The wealthy of this world have by far the largest environmental impact on the planet. They are also those who usually have the means to avoid and to remedy the impacts of their actions (Redclift, 1996).

Past emphases on common vulnerabilities are unlikely to hold as points of departure in future international fora. Political negotiations of "global" issues have helped to expose the severe limitations of conventional strategies of regime formation in the face of—among other things—the power of global corporations and other transnational actors (Vogler, 1995). Ever more important to any discussions of security and international politics is the fast-emerging "South" and its new breed of policymakers who now insist on discussing issues of future "global" dangers that the nomenclature of the "North" either downplays or ignores. In the discourses of environmental threats, of "chaos" following state "failings," of threats from migration or fears of disease, there is little recognition of the flows across borders that perhaps are in part responsible for the phenomena that are now feared. Given a certain tendency to blame the poor and the "South" for most (if not all) of the globe's calamities, any political dialogue or "grand bargains" over issues of justice, development and economic arrangements seem in advance doomed to fail (Chatterjee and Finger, 1994; Chubin, 1996; Dalby, 1998 and 1999).

GEOPOLITICS AND ENVIRONMENTAL INSECURITY

All of this suggests that a substantial challenge to modern territorial modes of governance is implicit in the wider debates on environmental security and in related issues of "ecopolitics" (Kuehls, 1996). In particular, assumptions about state capacity have to be reexamined much more closely, because contemporary arguments from both anthropology and political ecology, as well as from sociology, continue to suggest that many of the social processes that matter in contemporary politics and that relate directly to the environment are missed when the focus of inquiry is placed squarely on the state and only on its capabilities. Surely politics is about much more than the struggle to control specific states or the struggles perpetuated between states.

The dangers from traditional geopolitical formulations of security, including the militarization of relations between rich and poor, persist in many of the formulations of environmental insecurity: where the poor are portrayed as constituting a threat to the global order of the affluent; where migrants and refugees are vilified as cultural others; and where the excluded are subjected to threats of violence in a polarizing world. All of this may well come true in a geopolitically specified world, where postmodern affluence in technologically rich enclaves is pitted against hopeless impoverishment in zones of penury and dispossession. Reduced to servicing the livelihood of those in the enclaves of affluence and subjected to exclusionary measures by the self-satisfied, "the South" lacks the "certainties" that the "North" derives from advanced modernity. If knowledge is not now shared toward altering the specifications of geopolitical danger, the ensuing insecurities can only increase the likelihood for conflict, as a simple matter of self-fulfilling prophecies.

The conventional definitions of the vital interests of the United States itself may not hold, once the longer-term prospects are reconsidered and the complex interconnections between cross-frontier phenomena are also comprehensively reexamined. If the makings of instability in the poorer parts of the planet are understood to be, in part, a consequence of the affluence in other parts of the world, global security will have to become attainable in ways that would not hold the peripheral providers of resources hostage to the accumulative predispositions of consumers at the center (Gadgil and Guha, 1995; Athanasiou, 1996; Redclift, 1996). For many states, both in the North and in the South, the current patterns of resource flows render national security environmentally unsustainable. If this dilemma is clearly understood, there may be considerable room left to rethink policy actions and to attend to some of the deleterious consequences of globalization.

CONCLUSION

The complex debates about environmental security seem to suggest that traditional ideas about security cannot be simply extended to cover environmental issues. Talks of broadening the definition of security to encompass new threats reveal that many presumptions are taken for granted in conventional reasoning. When examined using insights from cognate disciplines, approaches in international security studies appear to be constrained by assumptions—of the efficacy of states and of the nature of threats—which tend to ignore many of the significant causative mechanisms that make people insecure as a result of environmental change. This is leading to a recognition of the need for some fundamental rethinking of security in the face of contemporary global environmental problems, a few of which command a certain urgency.

The geopolitical question of "who is securing what where" impinges directly on scholarship as well as on the policy debate about new threats. The question of "scholarship for/by whom" is not easily avoided in these debates, as some of the critical questions raised in this chapter have sought to suggest. Scholarly formulations of national security in terms of the need for both the non-industrialized and postindustrialized to ensure the vital interests of their "state" are no longer that easy to take for granted. The emphasis on global issues often acts to obscure the specific interests involved. On the other hand, the focus on the "global" does succeed in shifting attention to interconnections and to downplay the importance of single states. Critical scholars have a role to play in challenging what can be taken for granted through facile assumptions in matters regarding security and environment.

All this suggests that geopolitical specifications of danger and classical notions of state governance are no longer adequate for the design and pursuit of tomorrow's policies of "global" security. It points to the sense of urgency with which the very makings of security and the conceptual foundations of their basic theories need to be reviewed.

This is not about broadening the mandates of security agencies, but rather about understanding the meaning of the term "security" in ways that supersede the practices of violence and exclusion, founded on yesteryear's intellectual premises (Dalby, 1998, 1999; Dillion, 1996).

The broader worldviews and interdisciplinary approaches to insecurity examined in this chapter propose different ways of conceiving the complex notions of environment and security. In particular, they reveal that notions of direct causality do not provide solid grounds on which to base a study of environmentally induced conflict, much less a lookout for identifying tomorrow's threats, fears, or foes.

REFERENCES

Agnew, J. (1998). *Geopolitics: Re-Visioning World Politics.* London: Routledge.

————, and S. Corbridge (1995). *Mastering Space: Hegemony, Territory and International Political Economy.* London: Routledge.

Athanasiou, T. (1996). *Divided Planet: The Ecology of Rich and Poor.* Boston: Little, Brown.

Barber, C. V. (1997). *Environmental Scarcities, State Capacity, Civil Violence: The Case of Indonesia.* Cambridge, MA: American Academy of Arts and Sciences.

Baxi, U. (1996). "Global Neighbourhood" and the "Universal" Otherhood: Notes on the Report of the Commission on Global Governance. *Alternatives* 21: 525–549.

Beck, U. (1992). *Risk Society: Towards a New Modernity.* London: Sage.

———— (1996). World Risk Society as Cosmopolitan Society? Ecological Questions in a Framework of Manufactured Uncertainties. *Theory, Culture and Society* 13: 1–32.

Blaikie, P., and H. Brookfield (1987). *Land Degradation and Society.* London: Methuen.

————, T. Cannon, I. Davis, and B. Wisner (1994). *At Risk: Natural Hazards, People's Vulnerability and Disasters.* London: Routledge.

Bobrow, D. B. (1996). Complex Insecurity: Implications of a Sobering Metaphor. *International Studies Quarterly* 40: 435–450.

Boge, V. (1992). *Bougainville: A "Classical" Environmental Conflict?* Swiss Peace Foundation in Berne, ENCOP Occasional Paper No. 3.

Brock, L. (1992). Security Through Defending the Environment: An Illusion? Pp. 79–102 in E. Boulding (ed)., *New Agendas for Peace Research: Conflict and Security Reexamined.* Boulder, CO: Lynne Rienner.

Brown, L. (1977). *Redefining National Security.* Washington, DC: Worldwatch Institute.

Bryant, R., and S. Bailey (1997). *Third World Political Ecology.* London: Routledge.

Buzan, B., O. Waever, and J. de Wilde (1998). *Security: A New Framework for Analysis.* Boulder, CO: Lynne Rienner.

Chatterjee, P., and M. Finger (1994). *The Earth Brokers: Power, Politics and World Development.* London: Routledge.

Chubin, S. (1996). The South and the New World Order. Pp. 429–449 in Brad Roberts (ed.), *Order and Disorder after the Cold War.* Cambridge, MA: MIT Press.

Commission on Global Governance (1995). *Our Global Neighbourhood.* Oxford: Oxford University Press.

Dabelko, G. D., and D. Dabelko (1996). Environmental Security: Issues of Conflict and Redefinitions. *Environment and Security* 1: 23–49.

Dalby, S. (1996). The Environment as Geopolitical Threat: Reading Robert Kaplan's Coming Anarchy. *Ecumene* 3: 472–496.

——— (1997a). Canadian National Security and Global Environmental Change. Pp. 19–40 in Jim Hanson and Susan McNish (eds.), *Canadian Strategic Forecast 1997—Canada and the World; Non-Traditional Security Threats.* Toronto: Canadian Institute for Strategic Studies.

——— (1997b). Contesting an Essential Concept: Reading the Dilemmas in Contemporary Security Discourse. Pp. 3–31 in Keith Krause and Michael Williams (eds.), *Critical Security Studies: Concepts and Cases.* Minneapolis: University of Minnesota Press and London: Pinter.

——— (1998). Ecological Metaphors of Security: World Politics in the Biosphere. *Alternatives: Social Transformation and Humane Governance* 23, 3: 291–319.

——— (1999). Threats from the South? Geopolitics, Equity, and Environmental Security. In Daniel Deudney and Richard Matthew (eds.), *Contested Grounds: Security and Conflict in the New Environmental Politics.* Albany: State University of New York Press.

Deudney, D. (1991). Environment and Security: Muddled Thinking. *Bulletin of the Atomic Scientists* 47, 3: 22–28.

——— (1992). The Mirage of Ecowar: The Weak Relationship among Global Environmental Change, National Security and Interstate Violence. Pp. 169–191 in I. H. Rowlands and M. Greene (eds.), *Global Environmental Change and International Relations.* London: Macmillan.

Dillon, M. (1996). *Politics of Security: Towards a Political Philosophy of Continental Thought.* London: Routledge.

Dokken, K., and N. Graeger (1995). *The Concept of Environmental Security—Political Slogan or Analytical Tool?* Oslo: Peace Research Institute Oslo.

Eckersley, R. (1996). Environmental Security Dilemmas. *Environmental Politics* 5: 140–146.

Economy, E. (1997). *Environmental Scarcities, State Capacity, Civil Violence: The Case of Indonesia*. Cambridge, MA: American Academy of Arts and Sciences.

Ford, R. (1995). The Population-Environment Nexus and Vulnerability Assessment in Africa. *GeoJournal* 35: 207–216.

Gadgil, M., and R. Guha (1995). *Ecology and Equity: The Use and Abuse of Nature in Contemporary India*. London: Routledge.

Gedicks, A. (1993). *The New Resource Wars: Nature and Environmental Struggles Against Multinational Companies*. Boston: South End Press.

Gleditsch, N. P. (ed.) (1997). *Conflict and the Environment*. Dordrecht: Kluwer Academic Publishers.

Gleick, P. H. (1991). Environment and Security: The Clear Connections. *Bulletin of the Atomic Scientists* 47, 3: 16–21.

Graeger, N. (1996). Environmental Security. *Journal of Peace Research* 33: 109–116.

Grovogui, S. N. (1996). *Sovereigns, Quasi Sovereigns and Africans: Race and Self Determination in International Law*. Minneapolis: University of Minnesota Press.

Homer-Dixon, T. (1994). Environmental Scarcities and Violent Conflict: Evidence from Cases. *International Security* 19: 5–40.

——— (1996a). Environmental Scarcity, Mass Violence, and the Limits to Ingenuity. *Current History* (November): 359–365.

——— (1996b). The Project on Environment, Population and Security: Key Findings of Research. *Environmental Change and Security Project Report No. 2*, pp. 45–48. Washington, DC: Woodrow Wilson Center.

——— (1996c). Strategies for Studying Causation in Complex Ecological-Political Systems. *Journal of Environment and Development* 5: 132–148.

——— and M. Levy (1995/1996). Correspondence: Environment and Security. *International Security* 20: 189–198.

———, M. Levy, G. Porter, and J. Goldstone (1996). Debate. In *Environmental Change and Security Project Report No. 2*, pp. 49–71. Washington, DC: Woodrow Wilson Center.

Jewitt, S. (1995). Europe's "Others"? Forestry Policy and Practices in Colonial and Postcolonial India. *Environment and Planning D: Society and Space* 13: 67–90.

Johnston, B. R. (ed.) (1994). *Who Pays the Price? The Sociocultural Context of Environmental Crisis*. Washington, DC: Island Press.

Kakonen, J. (ed.) (1994). *Green Security or Militarized Environment*. Aldershot, UK: Dartmouth.

Kaplan, R. (1994). The Coming Anarchy. *Atlantic Monthly* 273, 2: 4–76.

Keohane, R. O. (1996). Analyzing the Effectiveness of International Environmental Institutions. Pp. 3–27 in Robert O. Keohane and Marc A. Levy (eds.), *Institutions for Environmental Aid: Pitfalls and Promise*. Cambridge, MA: MIT Press.

Kuehls, T. (1996). *Beyond Sovereign Territory: The Space of Ecopolitics*. Minneapolis: University of Minnesota Press.

Lash, S., B. Szerszynski, and B. Wynne (1996). *Risk, Environment and Modernity: Towards a New Ecology*. London: Sage.

Levy, M. (1995). Is the Environment a National Security Issue? *International Security* 20: 35–62.

Litfin, K. (1994). *Ozone Discourses: Science and Politics in Global Environmental Cooperation*. New York: Columbia University Press.

Mische, P. (1992). Security Through Defending the Environment: Citizens Say Yes. Pp. 103–119 in E. Boulding (ed.), *New Agendas for Peace Research: Conflict and Security Reexamined*. Boulder, CO: Lynne Rienner.

Molvoer, R. K. (1991). Environmentally Induced Conflicts? *Bulletin of Peace Proposals* 22: 175–188.

Myers, N. (1993). *Ultimate Security: The Environmental Basis of Political Stability*. New York: Norton.

Nietschmann, B. (1994). The Fourth World: Nations versus States. Pp. 225–242 in G. Demko and W. Wood (eds.), *Reordering the World: Geopolitical Perspectives on the 21st Century*. Boulder, CO: Westview Press.

Peet, R., and M. Watts (eds.) (1996). *Liberation Ecologies: Environment, Development, Social Movements*. New York: Routledge.

Peluso, N. L. (1993). Coercing Conservation: The Politics of State Resource Control. Pp. 46–70 in R. D. Lipschutz and K. Conca (eds.), *The State and Social Power in Global Environmental Politics*. New York: Columbia University Press.

Pettiford, L. (1995). Towards a Redefinition of Security in Central America: The Case of Natural Disasters. *Disasters* 19: 148–155.

Pinheiro, A., and P. Cesar (1994). A Vision of the Brazilian National Security Policy on the Amazon. *Low Intensity Conflict and Law Enforcement* 3: 387–409.

Rangan, H. (1996). From Chipko to Uttaranchal: Development, Environment and Social Protest in the Garhwal Himalayas, India. Pp. 205–226 in R. Peet and M. Watts (eds.), *Liberation Ecologies*. New York: Routledge.

Redclift, M. (1996). *Wasted: Counting the Costs of Global Consumption*. London: Earthscan.

———, and T. Benton (eds.) (1994). *Social Theory and the Global Environment*. London: Routledge.

Renner, M. (1989). *National Security: The Economic and Environmental Dimensions*. Washington, DC: Worldwatch Institute.

——— (1996). *Fighting for Survival: Environmental Decline, Social Conflict and the New Age of Insecurity*. New York: Norton.

Rich, B. (1994). *Mortgaging the Earth: The World Bank, Environmental Impoverishment and the Crisis of Development*. London: Earthscan.

Rocheleau, D., B. Thomas-Slayter, and E. Wangari (eds.) (1996). *Feminist Political Ecology: Global Issues and Local Experiences*. New York: Routledge.

Rubin, E. (1997). An Army of One's Own. *Harper's Magazine* (February): 44–55.

Stern, E. K. (1995). Bringing the Environment In: The Case for Comprehensive Security. *Cooperation and Conflict* 30: 211–237.

Suhrke, A. (1997). Environmental Degradation, Migration, and the Potential for Violent Conflict. Pp. 255–272 in N. P. Gleditsch (ed.), *Conflict and the Environment*. Dordrecht: Kluwer Academic Publishers.

Swift, J. (ed.) (1996). War and Rural Development in Africa. Special Issue of *Institute of Development Studies Bulletin* 27, 3.

Tennberg, M. (1995). Risky Business: Defining the Concept of Environmental Security. *Cooperation and Conflict* 30, 3: 239–258.

Vogler, J. (1995). *The Global Commons: A Regime Analysis.* London: John Wiley.

Wapner, P. (1996). *Environmental Activism and World Civic Politics.* Albany: State University of New York Press.

Westing, A. (ed.). (1997). Armed Forces and the Environment. Special Issue of *Environment and Security* 1, 2.

Wolpin, M. D. (1992). Third World Military Roles and Environmental Security. *New Political Science* 23: 91–120.

Wood, W. (1994). Forced Migration: Local Conflicts and International Dilemmas. *Annals of the Association of American Geographers* 84, 4: 607–634.

World Commission on Environment and Development (WCED) (1987). *Our Common Future.* Oxford: Oxford University Press.

Development, Modernization, Democracy, and Conflict

HENRY TEUNE

BACKDROP

Development is a long-term process by which human societies become more complex. Today it is the major driving force for social change. Modernization is but one historical manifestation of that process. For the past three centuries, development—as modernization—took place in differentiating hierarchical organizations of production, politics, and social life. First, it created the European world. Then from the middle of the eighteenth century onward, it expanded through population and economic market growth, establishing the conditions that gave rise to strong nation-states and representative democracy in the nineteenth century and that also provided the organizational capacity to fight large-scale wars in the twentieth century. The "strong" democracies are now entering a new stage of democratic development which will move them from representation of interests in partisan elections to more directly accountable democracy—judged by what a polity is and does rather than how it selects authorities and how they make decisions. Democratic nation-states have destroyed all of the empires of this century. They are now engaged in developmental processes that are global. Hierarchies have been weakened by their multiplication and diversification, as well as through the increase of localities and regions which can be constituted democratically, as "new localisms," to provide more extensive choices for individuals. Conflict and competition among states is being replaced by exchange and cooperation among entities within them. Large-scale wars are becoming obsolete as human social development, which defines the future, becomes global.

This chapter examines each of the four dimensions given in the title as well as the past makings and implications of their complex interactive relationships, with an eye to the future of human societies.

RATIONALE

Macro theories of social change tell why relationships among systems of variables change. But because we see the world and what it might become from particular theoretical perspectives, we can lose sight of the historically circumscribed validity of those views. A most remarkable historical fact is the development of human societies on an unprecedented scale. Development taking place at an accelerating rate was not always the case. There have been periods of regression, stagnation, and disintegration. And so, we seek to know why they happened: Why did the Roman empire degenerate into a Babel of languages and warring manors? Why did the Inca empire disappear? Why did China, promising so much a few centuries ago, end up in a corrupt and impoverished place? Our obsession with the question of development, especially with the failures of the past, also expresses a common fear that they might happen again. And so, we remain attracted to fantasies of a new plague, of invasions by aliens or of rocks from outer space, and the collapse of fragile governments through knave conspiracies.

But something did change a few hundred years ago that seems to be new and also permanent in human history. Its most accepted name is modernization. Neither a bifurcation in the flow of human history nor a departure from some "golden age" of old, the story of modernization is the thrust of human adventures toward what is better (Stent, 1969). Its path is called progress, and its goal is nothing short of human betterment.

Starting around 1750 and to this day, the world's real per capita income has crept at a compounding increase of about 1 percent or less per year. As economics gradually began to dominate politics and religion, the causes of war, too, started to be interpreted as embedded in economics—not merely as grounded in an instinct of survival. In 1848, the Communist Manifesto would assert that abundance for all should lead to societies without conflict and to unlimited opportunities for all—in spite of increases in the population. That simple notion of a sufficing material existence, accepted today without utopian views about harmony and happiness, constitutes a repudiation of the early "modern" quantitative social science analyses, which—based on scientized projections of population growth—would conclude that the poor would always be there, forever doomed to a miserable way of life.

Simple economic growth, no matter how inaccurately expressed, has provided the developmental base for an inversion of this 150-year-old paradigm of change, from fate of nature to feat of human purpose—whereby collectivities and individuals now have a choice among alternative futures. Founded on common assessments of basic reality, the first principle of democracy is freedom. Grounded on freedom, secular democratic politics determines not only the very nature and course of improvements in material prosperity but also the very principles of governance for justice. Free individuals and free collectivities continue to change the conditions of war, for having altered their society's capacity to mobilize for it.

Today, developmental change has become an ongoing, purposive human endeavor. It has reached such a high stage that its rate is accelerating, its reach extending worldwide, beyond specificity to human niches. But hierarchy, deemed indispensable to stability and economic growth, remains antithetical to democratic political development. As a process, which creates political, social, and economic hierarchies that have been studied in the contemporary social sciences, modernization also occasions the proliferation of new localities and human communities, which dilute hierachy, even as modernization expands individual choices globally in a world-system (see Chapter 7).

The practice of democracy today is undergoing a change—from institutional representations of conflicting interests to direct engagements in the politics of justice. This is creating two separate worlds of democratic governance—one still geared to the old politics of conflict, and the other producing newer forms of participation and accountability. Liberation from the hierarchy of the singular sovereignty of a state is now making it possible for democracy to be based on communal choices. But when based on the preferences and choices of communities, and governed by the principle of accountability to the electorate, the practice of democracy also weakens human organizational dispositions for war even as it strengthens incentives for cooperation at all levels. A better understanding of the complex interdimensional linkages between current changes and future conflicts should be helpful.

UNDERSTANDING HOW WE GOT WHERE WE ARE

The origins of modernization and democracy are related. They can be traced to the liberation of societies from the harness of agricultural production, from the whims of absolute authority, and from individual hatreds sustaining intergroup conflicts. These new freedoms contributed to the conditions necessary for several temporally bounded revolutions in the nineteenth century—among them, the rise of industries; the growth of big cities; and the advent of ideologies of constitutional governance based on the consent of the governed. Factories and public schooling would provide the leading institutional forces of modernization; constitutions would provide the very foundations for social and political pluralism in society.

A major by-product of modernization in the second half of the nineteenth century was the professional organization of the meaning of great social changes in secular terms. Social scientists and analysts recognized for their qualifications began to gain modest legitimacy as interpreters and prognosticators of change. They were joined by the chroniclers of human experiences now pursuing veracity, not flattery, as their standard. This enlightenment was built on the careful combination of theory and observation in an evolutionary theory of living systems found useful in explaining the more obvious macro changes in the European social universe. The two attractive theories of social change in those days were the ones proposed by the evolutionist Herbert Spencer and by the neo-evolutionist Karl Marx. Spencer purported to explain the modern nation-state and Marx to reveal large-scale capitalism. Both were grounded on visions of a level of human development superior to what had proved achievable in traditional societies through feudalism. Sadly, these theories would be used to serve questionable designs, and less than 50 years would go by before more limited secular theories of change could begin to gain greater authoritative status—and governments could begin to assert their ability to will their way out of economic difficulty and, in that pursuit, to achieve sustained economic growth as well.

Killing and pillaging, stealing and running, subduing and dominating for sustained taking through tribute or taxes are as much a part of recorded human history as seeking shelter (Keeley, 1996). In the earlier days, even if a society did not seek to exploit or damage other societies, it could not but observe, or hear of, the different habits of such and consequently organize its defenses depending on the importance and proximity of threat, whether imagined or real. Only recently and barely after the wars of the first half of the twentieth century has there finally emerged an understanding of sorts among the erstwhile belligerents that peaceful coexistence with one another need not be interpreted as a deprivation, abandonment, or abdication of one kind or another. But even today, evident as it has become for most that killing, pillaging, or dominating others is neither helpful nor prudent, we remain uncertain as to whether wars have enhanced or impeded human social development (Nef, 1950).

The main developmental thrust in human history is the scale of human organization, most of which took place in the twentieth century within an international system of competitive and often warring states. A political science of the state achieved substantive standing no earlier than 1900. Thereafter and in short order would enter the scene, a science of the management of production; the assertive exertion of knowledge to improve the lot of the poor and unfortunate; and almost concomitantly, the systematic intervention by the state so as to guide economic growth and ascertain its equitable distribution. These means and ways and precepts were exported to dozens among the newly independent states, following the abandonment of colonial lands after the end of World War II as a result of learned prudence, hard-earned enlightenment, shared values of human freedom, and, not least, international necessities arising under the related pressures. Many of these sociopolitical panaceas to induce and control change would prove disastrous. Here and there, they would be revised and reintroduced, and their success remains debatable.

Until a few decades ago, empires were deemed to be the most successful type of political system. They could bring together and control many different societies—by creed and force. They were polyethnic systems, comprising diverse societies, languages, and religions, rarely asserting more control than required for tranquility, extraction of taxes, and recruitment of soldiers. By attempting to gain absolute and total control over everyone and everything, Soviet Russia and Nazi Germany—the last of the empires of any significance—bloodied history with genocide and folly. After World War II, those independent nation-states in the European mold, which had shed their colonies, became even more developed and effective political systems—surpassing by far the ideals pursued to that effect by any empire past or present.

At the beginning of the twentieth century, independent nation-states were able to attract and to mobilize investments for economic development and trade; to organize and supply armies of millions; and to nurture innovation in science and in the arts. Those few nations that mutated into violent entities in the first half of this century killed millions of their neighbors' populations and even more of their own (Rummel, 1997). Almost all of the major wars among nation-states were instigated by empires, which encroached on other states militarily or attempted to subordinate them to their own administration. States mimicking totalitarian empires by taking action on behalf of a single interest, against their neighbors or against their own "minority" populations, were authoritarian systems aspiring to, and pretending, total control. Today nearly all successful states have become democratic, wield limited authority, and are relatively tranquil, choosing to foster what it takes to achieve material prosperity for their populace and in the process continuing to develop and become more complex.

What can be celebrated now is the discovery that freedom is not just a public good with a private cost but a shared asset; that problems can be addressed within institutions that welcome self-improvement and therefore change; and that human development is about futures that can be shared by all in their lifetime. But development, modernization, democracy, and conflict deserve closer scrutiny, on their own merit as well as in their joint dynamics.

DEVELOPMENT

Complexity is the integration of a diversity of systems (Teune and Mlinar, 1978). Development is an increase in complexity. All systems can be characterized by their complexity but not by their development. Based on what they can do and become, three types of systems can be defined: artificial machines, living systems, and human societies. Machines do almost what they are designed to do and run down; living systems may evolve through reproduction and mutation into more complex systems; human societies can develop autonomously, become something different, and thereby go through a transformation. Predesigned machines do not "develop"; only those concocted in science fiction may mysteriously come to life as a "Harold" or "Helen." And only very few known living systems have evolved continuously—bacteria and viruses, among them. Not many social systems have survived either—even fewer of them lasting longer than a relatively ephemeral span. Most have either faded away or dissipated somewhere, as have nearly all the machines not in service anymore. Over the past 50 years or so, our knowledge of living systems has advanced so much that the next century may be known as the era of biology, taking over from physics. It is a fact that much remains to be learned about human systems.

The relationships among these three kinds of systems are of utmost importance to humanity (see Chapters 3, 5, and 11 in this volume): how machines affect living systems and individual humans as biological entities; how societies treat (sustain or destroy) their living, ecological environments; how societies impact the genetic heritage of the human race—all help shape the course of a civilization. They also touch on how social systems develop and become more complex. And they also raise some moral questions as to what kinds of developments are good or bad.

Only human systems are developmental in that they can act to become more developed. In modern societies, development occurs through purpose and design. Societies can develop by emulating, or by importing from developed systems—depending on preferences and choices made through human decisions. Exchange and imitation are critical to social development. Development through import does not make a society developmental, however. A society can develop or be developed without thereby becoming a developmental social system. What is distinctive in all developmental social systems is that they develop "autonomously" as they become more complex—precisely owing to the soaring interactions among their own components. So far, this has occurred in a few societies only. And only recently has even the idea that societies can and should develop to their full potential become less grudgingly accepted.

A major question for our time is, Which societies are developmental? (See Chapter 9 in this volume.) In the past, economic development was assumed to be a matter for nations and countries, as memorably expressed in the title of Adam Smith's *The Wealth of Nations.* Development today has become global rather than a singly distinguishing characteristic of any specific society or country.

When societies, organizations, or sectors of related human activities attain a high enough level of development permitting them to develop further, successfully so and at will, they become "innovation-driven" entities. They penetrate a new stage of human development, quite different from those systems organized around reproduction though repetitive actions so commonplace in farming and manufacture. This novel stage can be best understood in terms of evolutionary ecological theories of living systems capable of the marginal adaptations on which, even today, most macro social theories find their basis. But not all adaptive social systems are developmental systems. The abyss between the innovation-led national economies and those driven by manufacture must be part of the explanation of the expanding differences among the United States, Western Europe, and Japan, and their overall performance in the 1990s. Once it was appropriate to speak of developed and underdeveloped countries; today the important distinction for understanding change is the stark difference between developing and growing systems, which may or may not coincide with the exact boundaries of a given society or country. The "growing" economies are measured by the increases and decreases in GNP. They do not, as of yet, provide the mainsprings of the innovations essential for triggering and sustaining development.

Innovations diffuse quickly, via communication and exchange, becoming global—by violating the boundaries of territory and of function and by trampling on the exclusive categorizations necessary for hierarchical control. The development of human societies is likely to continue on an exponential path, driven only by a few controlling macro dynamics such as growth, adaptation, and dialectics—and possibly a few more that are yet to be discovered. Among these dynamics, some are useful in illustrating why modernization is a special form of social complexity with hierarchy, and how—when it reaches a certain point—development pushes toward even more complexity, thereby necessitating not only different structures but also further diminutions of hierarchical control.

One such dynamic is the growth/distribution relationship. Growth is the production or reproduction of the same things—more rabbits, people, potatoes, and automobiles. That growth compounds is perhaps the most important law of economic systems. Any system dominated by growth confronts limits in the niches, families and places, or organizations in which it takes place (Teune, 1988). The logic of such growth systems is that they must either grow or die. But unless all components of the system grow proportionally within the system's overall fixed structure, faster growth by any component or sector can and will eventually crash the system (see Chapter 7). To continue to grow, systems dependent on growth eventually will collide and conflict with other systems of growth which they must absorb, lest they be absorbed or otherwise collapse. In this sense, all growth systems contain the "seeds of their own destruction." That "insight" of Karl Marx about capitalist economies was reformulated by Joseph Schumpeter as "creative destruction"—a force necessary for the continuation of growth and the survival of capitalist systems (Schumpeter, 1942). Such are the facts of life that relationships must change: old elements recede and disappear as new ones arise.

The key to any developing system is that both its components and their relationships continue to change—with the components becoming more diverse, and their relationships, more integrated. Hence, mere quantitative increases are not sufficient to trigger developmental change. Thus, a fundamental dynamic of development is that the greater the variety of a system, the greater the probability that any new variety will yield yet more variety. A major corollary of that law holds that the greater the variety of any system, the less the likelihood that any new item of variety will "disturb" that system. Indeed, the greater the variety of a system, the more receptive it is likely to be to more variety and the less it can find cause to fear or exclude the unprecedented.

Variety is only one of two dimensions of complexity. To be engaged in the development of a system, it must be integrated. Thus, a more highly integrated system that contains exactly the same variety as another system is more complex and has a greater capacity to develop more quickly. As systems become even more integrated, the probability increases that anything new will be that much more easily absorbed.

Two general propositions follow from the aforegoing. First, more complex developmental systems are better able to develop more rapidly relative to less complex ones. Second, as any developed system becomes more complex, its rate of development is also likely to increase. These propositions can be corroborated by comparing the levels and rates of innovations among countries as well as among sectors of economic activity on a global scale.

But there are limits to the level of integrated diversity of any system, including human ones. One aspect of that limit is how much variety any component—indeed, any human being—can absorb, assimilate, and manage. At certain points in the accumulation of variety, a person or household simply must shift some of it to a more encompassing systemic level, thereby electing henceforth to "access" that shedded variety instead of "owning" or "possessing" it at the expense of even better and newer things to hold on to.

Still another dynamic law, implicit from the above, is the attractiveness of variety. Variety attracts variety. Thus, better educated, higher skilled people, more advanced art forms, and more fashionable entertainment either move or are moved to centers of variety in countries, cities, and special places where variety commands greater "value" precisely because it enriches existing variety and whets the appetites for even more. Novel variety is less "disturbing" to the "system" at this level of aggregation if only because it is likely to be better appreciated and that much more easily assimilated there as one more item of welcome change.

Two kinds of innovation are of relevance to development. First is the obvious combinatorial fusion of variety as novelty: Two different things or areas of knowledge create a qualitatively different third—often making a very powerful difference that may be reminiscent of the times when the combustion engine and the four-wheel cart inspired the production of an automobile, and biochemistry in turn became a field that produced new medicines and materials. Second are the innovations that integrate different things and bits of knowledge across time and space. These include faster, cheaper, and more reliable systems of transportation, more easily accessible inventories, and the magic of integrating functions in computer software programs. Have not the telegraph, telephone, telephoto, and the Internet accelerated the rate of human development on a global scale? Of course, both types of innovation are wholly integral to the process of development rather than mere causes or consequences of it.

When the advantages of development become highly valued in advanced societies, certain organizations and domains of science and engineering become leading sectors of change and development. Companies that innovate succeed—whether in medicines, computers, or air transport. In the past few decades, world leadership has shifted its focus from manufacture and industrial growth to more innovation-driven political economies. And just as yesterday's industrialized societies replaced farming as a way of life for almost all of their population, so today are highly developed societies busy retiring manufacturing as the mainstay of their productive life and moving to innovation, design, and control. It is also this new rush of ideas and experiences, of science and art, of patents and "intellectual properties" that helps digitize our weapons and computerize our armies. (See the Introduction to this volume.)

MODERNIZATION

Whether modernization has come to an end and we are entering a stage of "postmodernity" is a question that comparisons with the "Great Transformation" at the end of the nineteenth century might help answer. At that time, industrialized cities were far more productive than scattered factories. Urbanization was proceeding at rates previously unknown in cities of sizes unimaginable until then. And nation-states were being consolidated by strengthening national governments and expanding their revenues. But they would soon turn their attention to the First World War. A period of 50 years from the 1870s to the 1920s endowed European nation-states with cities, roads, capitals, and harbors that have not changed very much since. What did happen is that European-style governance and production spread, sometimes through force, though often in quick spurts of adoption, throughout the world.

Government, factories, trade unions; labor, capital, land; businessmen, farmers, and workers provided the core of the macro analyses of the wealthy countries of the world. Human societies were divided between traditional and modern; populations, between peasants and city dwellers. National accounting systems reckoned and ranked the labor force as primary (mining/farming), secondary (manufacturing), tertiary (administration and services), and quaternary (science and engineering), in valid descriptions of how people were productively engaged in their countries. Setting aside the wars and the other economic shocks, the faded relevance today of these accounting systems speaks a great deal to what in fact happened during the twentieth century. The end of the Cold War left the wealthy states with nearly three-fourths of their work force ambiguously categorized in "services"; art and culture now resembled industries; agricultural output increased incrementally, as did industrial production; nationalism and the nation-state no longer were assumed to be the leading forces for the liberation of people or the best sources of hope for individual betterment. The assertive nationalisms that followed the dismemberment of the Soviet empire often appeared to embody the last gasps of peoples long suppressed, demeaned, or ignored, and now intent on achieving recognition in adverse circumstances, by any means, at any cost.

Modernization is a historical process of rationalization, standardization, and ordering along hierarchical organizational lines designed to control the environment. Its main consequence was the improvement of conditions of everyday life and the generation of unprecedented wealth for the vast majority in heated houses with running water, automobiles, telephones, and prolonged schooling. But that process of structuring societies required people to give up, mostly willingly, their sense of belongingness and identity. Modernization did yield substantial increments in complexity, but it also loosened the links of identities with localities, ethnic groups, and religion bestowed at birth (see Chapter 9). Irreparably torn, these attachments became partially replaced by those of hierarchy in modern organizations and those of identity through nation and state.

As even higher levels of development were approached during the latter part of the twentieth century, states reached their limits of control. New categories of groups, organizations, and local communities sprang up—for individuals to choose to join or to identify with—even as old identities continued to survive with updated symbols. Alternative identities and organizations diminish the exclusivity that any one of them can claim over individuals, families, or groups of individuals, however. The trend toward multiple and temporary affiliations ends up weakening the hold of all of them while continuing to strengthen individual autonomy.

In economics, modernization targets the division of labor; in sociology, it focuses on the differentiation of roles; and in government, it dwells on specialized hierarchical agencies. The bedrock indicators of modernization are seen in the complexity of individuals who once used to be identified simply as the son or daughter of somebody; later, by place of birth and occupation; and today, only on the basis of the details of their education, along with their hobbies, special skills, and preferences.

Modernization's modality of integration is organization. Organization requires rationalization, the foundation of which is grounded in temporal and spatial cognitive mappings of things, people, and their characteristics and activities. The decisive step in national rationalization for production and fighting was the modern census. In the industrializing countries of the 1850s, the census acquired its first institutional form, to be followed by even more extensive figures on trade, manufactures, cropland, education, transportation, mineral inventories, and other data and information necessary for coordination and control—and taxation. Monetization—the symbolic valuation in a standardized language of just about everything that matters—was indispensable for the expansion of trade from local to national markets and for the national governments to mobilize resources. At the beginning of this century, social scientists invented the two pillars for modernization through rationalization: the random sample and the social index number, the most well known of which is the gross national product. Together, they provided massive quantities of inexpensive information useful for prediction and control.

Government acted as the main integrator for modernization—through bureaucracies, both public and private. Transportation systems were integrated through standardization of roads, rail, vehicle size, and rights of way. That was accomplished through the national transportation authorities. Education had to be rendered common and standardized, so that greater numbers of people could be employed in organizations and willingly perform as citizens. Despite governmental controls, however, economies broke down and societies were threatened by disintegration.

National norms, including those of weights and measures, were established by both governments and large corporations. But modernization demanded more—more variety and integration than could be attained within nationally defined boundaries of all but the largest countries. By the turn of the twentieth century, world trade standards in manufactures and in the production of manufactured goods were at the brink of internationalization under the assertion of the global importance of American and German standards. By then, world trade among the producers and consumers in different countries had reached levels not to be attained until the end of the century.

In the last three decades of the nineteenth century, science-based technologies became systematically applied to production and to transportation. This offered societies the potential for plenty. The miracles of electricity and chemistry soon enabled large industrial cities to emerge and grow in Europe and North America.

In the first decade of this century, a popular controversial book, *The New Basis of Civilization* (Patten, 1907), asserted that economic sufficiency would be available to all. Whatever the term "modernization" meant for the newly emerging urban elites of the nineteenth century, the mere possibility of mass economic wealth from scientifically based industrial production was something new and controversial. Up until then, and as echoed to this day, a world of scarcity was believed to be the destiny of the human race and the moral basis for social order and economic inequality.

As the modernization stage of development matures, prospects for choice improve. A more complex society will have many more competing and complementary hierarchies, among which individuals can choose. What can individuals or groups do when they are dissatisfied with a political community or organization to which they belong? An individual could remain quietly loyal or could complain, and even suggest alternatives. Failing that, those dissatisfied could exit and go someplace else (Hirschman, 1970). Alternatives depend on the level of societal development and on information available. If one resides in a fishing village, one goes out with the boats or does not eat; if one lives in a city, participation in public decisions might be possible. Only when there is a relatively high level of development and individuals possess enough knowledge as to the when and where of alternatives does exit become a usable option. In highly advanced countries, individuals can change jobs and residences, avoid trade unions and political parties, and indeed, even add a national citizenship or two.

Why do hierarchies multiply and weaken with development? All systems have limits as to the amount of variety that they can integrate. These limits are at the theoretical core of arguments about gains and losses from the integration and diversification of economic corporations. Why are big organizations slow in their responses to competition? Why is innovation in highly developed societies concentrated in small outfits? The nature of hierarchy suggests some answers. Big organizations with preset goals can pursue them by reducing uncertainty through hierarchy. But small organizations without hierarchy can absorb variety without facing resistance from the limits of hierarchy to variety. And central governments begin to decentralize and devolve functions when the complexity of an economy reaches a certain threshold. This began to happen in almost all of the highly developed countries of the world in the 1970s. At about the same time, economic activities were floating outward into a "global political economy," reducing the relative control capacities of national capitals. In absolute terms, the developed controlled more—even if proportionally less of everything that began to be transacted throughout the planet. As new options arose through global transport and communication, localities began to bypass their national capitals and to deal directly with global entities and localities in other countries.

In countries where modernization has penetrated thoroughly, conditions have been set for the structures of the interactions of macro theoretical variables to change. Rather than development simply leading to multiple hierarchies and individual autonomy, democracy could influence the course of societal development in the future. During most of the nineteenth and twentieth centuries, liberation meant the attachment of small groups and localities to ascendant paths of national and central governments. Today, small units can become communities in larger, global contexts where contact with a national government is merely one choice among many latitudes. Now, ethnic groups can be freed from the suppression of central governments; small states once considered too small to be viable economic entities can thrive in a global context, as several already are doing; individuals can choose their communities from a range wider than before, associate with affinity groups ranked by "lifestyles," and establish durably satisfying social links with professional associations. Whereas national citizenship once was the supreme focus of all the loyalties of individuals, now people can be citizens of a locality, a region, a transnational region (Europe or North America), as well as a country or two.

DEMOCRACY

The development of democracy, grounded on the principle of individual freedom for all members of a society, is rather recent. The hallmark of mass democracy based on the principle of equality was defined in a few Western countries during the nineteenth century by extending the franchise also to non-property holders.

The principle of equality of citizenship was strengthened by the emergence of modern political parties whose main goal was to win competitive elections. Representative democracy with recurrent elections, political parties, and civil liberties, within a legal "constitutional" framework, followed from social differentiation and industrialization of the economy. Until recently, the routine sequence of this macro relationship was, first, the formation of the socioeconomic base and only thereafter the establishment of democratic institutions focusing on the social and economic interests of different groups of citizens, as articulated by the political parties (Lipset, 1960). Conflicting economic interests would be integrated through partisan politics within a framework of legally accepted rules, which would restrain the winners from destroying or weakening the losers while assuring all losers yet another chance of becoming winners.

The development of representational democracy founded on legitimate interests took several contentious steps. First came the question of including different peoples through the right to vote. Democratic politics imparted an inclusionary bias to the motives of political parties: they coveted electoral dominance by recruiting as many sympathizers as possible. Disputes over who should be included would become intense and on occasion bloody. Second came the question of economic distribution—the allocation of the new wealth generated by modernization and economic growth. Each voter had to have some independence. Wealth also became an incentive to participate, even if only symbolically so, in the elections and in the rites of political integration. Inclusionary processes easily yield to practices of promoting equality. Once the conditions for sustained economic growth were secured, most democratic states established welfare policies and programs. Third came the issue of participation in institutions that affect individuals. The politics of participatory processes gained much momentum in the second half of the twentieth century. This question generated written specifications of the rights of individuals in public and private organizations, and also of the easy access to information about decision processes within and over which all of those that are affected can have some say.

The fourth question, or step, in democratic development—now only beginning to take substance—is the politics of substantive justice. Polities should be in line with, and no less responsive to, individual conceptions of what constitutes a just and good society. Unlike the democratic politics of distribution over "who gets what, when and how" (Lasswell, 1936), a politics of justice is not apportionable. Either a society is just, or it is not.

The developmental processes responding to the new democratic politics are manifest only in a few countries, and, even there, only among a few select individuals and groups. For a substantive rather than a participatory democracy to prevail, two conditions must obtain: first, individual "citizens" must have a right to "exit" and to join an increasing number of available political communities; and, second, public authority must be accountable for its actions to the citizens, and not merely "represent" them. Both of the conditions become possible at a relatively high level of societal development, which permits a variety of communities to flourish and facilitates access to information about them.

It is still an open question whether the nations and regions that have long suffered the tyranny of totalitarian governments under dictatorships or Communist Party rule have a socioeconomic base, sufficient for traditional political partisanship and necessary for interest-group competition within a representative governmental framework. After all, freely contested elections have been the practice for a mere 10 to 20 years in those countries and regions, even if traditional political partisanship and voting seem to have taken hold in the former communist countries and in the former Latin dictatorships, where now a left, a center, and a right can identifiably compete. In very poor countries, however, the politics of ethnicity and nationalism still dominate economic issues (see Chapter 9). In the very highly developed countries, economic issues continue to recede in favor of worries about social order, education, lifestyles, the environment, and even the aesthetic, civic, and ethical dimensions of not merely a tolerable but a good society. Yet, from a global perspective, political differences among world regions remain as substantial as the stark economic inequalities that alienate them.

Unlike civil rights that limit government and are essential for the development of representative democracy in nation-states, human rights are universal, not particular to specific political venues. Human rights principles and their affirmative documents are acceded to by most states or held to be operative by default. They contain assertions about one's right to choose the language, religion, schooling, occupation, and political views of one's own preference. They are consonant with the development of democratic freedom and accountability. Because they express what individuals are entitled to by virtue of their being human, they also limit government implicitly. And by reducing the criteria of exclusion, especially those based on lineage and on affiliation with language and religious groups, human rights offer individuals a choice among polities as well.

That markets are a precondition of democracy has been much argued. What is necessary for substantive rather than procedural democracy is choice among and within democratic polities. Insofar as this obtains and governing entities, organizations, voluntary associations, and localities are free to seek success and to fail on their own, the move toward a market democracy—where all people can achieve some justice somewhere—can be said to go on.

The development of a politics of substantive justice is a step forward in the complex evolution of political systems (see Chapter 11). One must understand, however, that democratic politics can alter the nature of societies and economies of which it is a joint product. Development in general is a strong condition for this stage of democratic development because by now there are more alternatives to choose from. Not only are the constraints of economic necessities relaxed but now they can be met in many more ways, consistent with the changing packages of public amenities and patterns of civic life. Commercialization of government services can be deplored as excessive reliance on the market, but in fact it does help to expand choices for local polities, if nothing else.

Democratic politics becomes an independent force for social and economic change because localities, in choosing among their options, must bear the costs of their decisions. There are also alternatives for companies, organizations, and individuals residing in a locality. Information on alternatives are expanding on a global scale. A non-preferred activity taxed out of business in one country might survive and even thrive in others. Leaving a collectivity perceived to be unjust or harmful is a peaceful form of protest. In the absence of such alternatives, courses of action include annoying protest, corruption, or violent resistance (see Chapter 10). In accountable forms of governance, no collective decision can be final for anyone—if only because there are other democracies in which to relocate. When the pressures from perceptions or threats of loss abate, democratic politics can acquire an even greater integrity of discourse.

As these changes in democratic governance become instituted, they open new avenues for individual development. In the past, the human need to belong would produce ambivalent responses that could vacillate between repressed anger and enthusiastic loyalty, depending on what was at stake—identity, exclusion, or inclusion. In the future, an even greater choice among communities is likely to carry with it the possibility of "human dignity":

individuals will be free to reserve their allegiance for the community that best reflects what they believe is right and good and beautiful and that therefore merits their adhesion and their fully voluntary and loyal participation in its sustenance and progress.

CONFLICT AND WAR

A lot has been learned about conflict situations with two or more parties, wherein one party is convinced that it will not be better off and could be worse off unless it incapacitates or even destroys the other (Boulding, 1962). On a hypothetical continuum between conflict and integration, there is a zone of cooperation, an interval over which a range of positive relationships—from mutually rewarding amity to synergistic communal production and to symbiotic bonding—is possible, and where the many can accomplish together efficiently and effectively what no one single-handedly ever can. On the conflict side of the continuum are situations in which one party wants something that the other has but will not exchange, share, or grant access to. Here, the threat and use of force to elicit compliance may escalate to levels of violence that can culminate in pyrrhic victories. Permutations of these situations—involving multiple parties with or without alliances; sequential "games" in conflictual and cooperative situations; and compound recalculations of time-staggered payoffs or losses—can affect whether and how something benign or nasty will ensue.

Why conflict triggers violent behavior remains one of the many weak theoretical links between situations and action. The probability of a violent "event" is partially determined by past hostility, perception of success, cost of attack, and many other variables that lead to stories about the "causes" of war and the "conditions" of peace. Also to be considered are the purposes and passions of wars—whether to deflect focus; to obtain profit; to repay insult; to act out uncontrollable rage and consuming hate.

Despite arguments to the contrary, over the last 150 years, development has been a major force in reducing the share of human activities given to the preparation for, and the conduct of, war. True, war efforts have become exponentially more efficient, as has the speed in deploying the weapons and soldiers of war. Giant steel cannons; guided missiles; smart nuclear bombs; fast, large ships; long-range bombers refueled in the air; and plans for the digitized armies of the future (see Introduction in this volume) tell much about that story, as do also the growing importance of surveillance and information in far-flung command operations.

A major question for the students of peace and development is why development and its new unfolding product, democracy, does reduce the likelihood of war. It appears that those who are most capable of starting and waging wars are also those who are most inclined to avoid them. A rekindling of the old debate about the democratic "peace" after the end of the

"Cold War" between the forces of democracy and those of the last great empire is not useful here. We know enough to say that democracies generally neither go to war with other democracies nor are inclined to do so. The evidence is also clear that democracies do not systematically kill their own populations (Rummel, 1997). What seems to have been learned about modern war is that the best defense would be to promote democracy inside potential adversaries rather than to organize a credible military deterrent that only aggravates differences at great cost.

Yet wars do occur, and we hear the clamors of fighting. Do these wars imperil development? Almost certainly not, in the ever faster-approaching long run. To support this conclusion, we would have to show that as developmental processes accelerate and expand globally, conflict situations tend to become less likely; that the possible gains from impairing or destroying others also diminish. Fighting that does erupt can be localized and contained, although even those conflicts can be negotiated with far greater flexibility toward solutions made possible through development.

As democratic development spreads and the range of choices also expands through the process of global development, it is rather unlikely that an organization or country may not be able to obtain from a globalizing world economy something that it may need or want for its survival or prosperity. The dimensions of international "respect" have long outgrown war-making, to include cultural, economic, and political achievements that bring honor and prestige. In a world where everything becomes available at a price, a premature show of muscle may prove less efficacious than a "just-in-time" acquisition and conclusive delivery of an armed response, where absolutely necessary. The novelties generated by the developed and desired by the developing can be obtained at a cost, through persuasion or exchange rather than through brute force. The problem with the new, cutting-edge variety in complex machinery and electronics is not one of acquisition as it is one of proper use and maintenance over shrinking product life cycles that will continue to require intensive outlays. And transfers of know-how require trust, patience, knowledge, skills, and cooperation among producers and users that cannot afford enmities. What is new in ideas, forms of expressions, and entertainment is sooner or later diffused. Development, by generating alternatives, by spreading the novel, and by providing access to anything and everything, cannot but reduce the "value" of what exists as the value of what is yet to come soars to even newer heights.

In addition, serious war requires serious mobilization. Populations are asked to give up almost everything, including their lives. The war efforts of developed democracies with multiple democratic communities are likely to prove difficult, especially if launched at a scale reminiscent of the last "world war." Unable to benefit from a hierarchized control of information, the mobilization and propaganda machines, which require the absence of conflicting or contradictory messages, are unlikely to last long where mass communications may hinder their operations in democracies used to settling scores by shifting their gaze. Even the most intense of issues—life and death—to which democracies attach the practice of abortion and suicide, can be avoided in developed settings by localizing and privatizing these practices, thus circumscribing the need for public action for or against such practises. In sum, in the absence of a direct threat to the values or the survival of everyone, mobilization for killing becomes difficult—even the demonization of an enemy becomes nearly impossible in environments affording cross-verification, contrapropaganda, or downright disinformation.

From a developmental perspective, there are societies in which old group loyalties and the politics of "we and they" continue to be played out. Today, the conflicts that conduce to mass killings take place in the least developed regions of the world: Central Africa, the Caucasus, the Indus Valley, and the least modernized areas of the underdeveloped Balkans. Violent rioting, of course, is a different matter, but new and weak democracies are learning to respond to it with moderate force. Thus, the organization of violence to destroy or harm another group, though found in many places, remains localized—reflecting the past in motives carved in tribal identities and conduct, none of which has a future.

Would human development have taken place without war? In an agonizing reappraisal of World War II, a British military officer can only give an equivocal answer on this question (Nef, 1950). Although gunpowder and armor are among the technoscientific advances marked as a "necessity of war," it is difficult from a developmental viewpoint to imagine that the pace of human development would have been as rapid without the destruction of hierarchies gone bad, and even without some modernized societies forgetting their values. Human development did not occur because all "good men" intended it that way. Many even intended something quite different. Human progress would seem impossible without hierarchies. But some of the great human hierarchies, including those built during periods of rapid modernization during the past two hundred years, became pathological forces—constituting a threat not only to development but surely to democracy as well.

Whether the U.S. Civil War or the war against Nazi Germany, during the recent past, was any one war indispensable for human development? At a certain point, in either of those cases, war probably became unavoidable. But people learn. And the depths of the organizational perversion of the Nazi period may be lesson enough for most of us. The Second World War certainly was not the worst of all wars, even if surely it was the worst of the modern era, and the question remains as to whether any new war on the scale of our current high technological know-how will do anyone any good.

CONCLUDING COMMENTS

The most salient historical phenomena of relevance to our future are the dramatic developmental experiences of the twentieth century. Whatever the beginnings of modernization in the Western world of the sixteenth century—and surely there were many—they were restricted to a small set of religious and political leaders and to expressive elites in Western Europe. The great changes of the nineteenth century and their psychological impact on the millions who were freed from physical labor and from darkness thanks to the changes brought by carbon-based power and electricity pale by comparison with the scale of organization achieved in the twentieth century— enabling mass production and consumption, launching state-administered welfare, transmitting sounds and pictures, providing ample and healthy water, controlling temperatures, and mastering all the other amenities and possibilities that have defined development in everyday human terms.

The dark side of the twentieth century comprises the massacres in its first half and the threats of the unthinkable during most of its second half. The obsession was with war—abhorred after the First World War, despised after the Second. Soon, the world would find itself once again divided into collectivities of friends and foes, and in the last two decades of the century, half of the world's population would be born in a country and region whose political organization would radically change more than once in their lifetime. With the "second democratic revolution" at the end of the twentieth century, the lines dividing friends and foes would become blurred almost everywhere.

Whatever political system they may now find themselves in, people are acquiring a new potential for being helpful to others placed inside and outside their political borders. This new quest for what is good portends a rapid decline in those conditions that give rise to conflict. That alone is good news for human development. For however long the world remains in the commons of global development, a most remarkable period in human history is only just beginning.

REFERENCES

Boulding, K. (1962). *Conflict and Defense*. New York: Harper.

Hirschman, A. (1970). *Exit, Voice, Loyalty*. Cambridge, MA: Harvard University Press.

Keeley, B. (1996). *War Before Civilization*. New York: Oxford University Press.

Lasswell, H. (1936). *Politics: Who Gets What, When, and How*. New York: McGraw-Hill.

Lipset, S. (1960). *Political Man*. Garden City, NY: Doubleday.

Nef, J. (1950). *War and Human Progress*. Cambridge, MA: Harvard University Press.

Patten, S. (1907). *New Basis of Civilization*. Cambridge, MA: John Harvard Library.
Rummel, R. (1997). *Power Kills*. New Brunswick, NJ: Transaction Books.
Schumpeter, J. (1942). *Capitalism, Socialism, and Democracy*. New York: Harper.
Stent, G. (1969). *The Coming of the Golden Age*. Garden City, NY: Natural History Press.
Teune, H. (1988). *Growth*. Newbury Park, CA: Sage.
———, and Z. Mlinar (1978). *The Developmental Logic of Social Systems*. Beverly Hills, CA: Sage.

CHAPTER 7

Globalization: A World-Systems Perspective

CHRISTOPHER K. CHASE-DUNN

THE WORLD-SYSTEMS PERSPECTIVE

Today, the terms "world economy," "world market," and "globalization" are commonplace. They appear in the sound-bites of politicians, media commentators, and unemployed workers alike. But few know that the most important source for these phrases lies with work started by sociologists in the early 1970s. At a time when the everyday mainstream assumptions of social, political, and economic science held that the "wealth of nations" reflected mainly on the cultural developments within those nations, a widening group of social scientists recognized that national "development" was best understood (Shannon, 1996) as the complex outcome of local interactions with an aggressively expanding Europe-centered "world-system" (Wallerstein, 1974; Frank, 1978). Not only did these scientists sense the global nature of economic networks 20 years before they entered popular discourse, but they also perceived that many of these networks extend back at least 600 years—over which period the peoples of the globe became linked into one integrated unit: the modern world-system.

Now, 20 years later, social scientists working in the area are trying to fathom the history and evolution of the *whole system*, as well as how local, national, and regional entities have been integrated into it. This current research has required broadening our perspective to include deeper temporal and larger spatial frameworks. For example, some recent research has compared the modern Europe-centered world-system of the last 500 years with earlier, smaller intersocietal networks that have existed for millennia (Frank and Gills, 1993; Chase-Dunn and Hall, 1997). Other work uses the knowledge of cycles and trends that has grown out of world-systems research to anticipate likely future events with a precision impossible before the advent of the theory. This is still a new field and much remains to be done, but enough has already been achieved to provide a valuable understanding of the phenomenon of globalization.

The discourse about globalization has emerged mainly in the last decade. The term means many different things, and there are numerous reasons for its emergence as a popular concept. The use of this term generally implies that a recent change (within the last decade or two) has occurred in technology and in the size of the arena of economic competition. The general conception is that information technology has created a context in which the global market, rather than separate national markets, is the relevant arena for economic competition. It then follows that economic competitiveness needs to be assessed in the global, rather than in a national or local, context. These notions have been used to justify the adoption of new practices by firms and governments all over the world. The resultant developments have altered the political balances among states, firms, unions, and other interest groups.

The first task is, of course, to put this development into historical context. The world-systems perspective has shown that intersocietal geopolitics and geoeconomics have been the relevant arena of competition for nation-states, firms, and classes for hundreds of years. The degree of international connectedness among the economic and political/military networks was already important in the fourteenth and fifteenth centuries. The first transnational corporations (TNCs) were the great chartered companies of the seventeenth century. They organized production and exchange on an intercontinental scale. The rise and fall of hegemonic core powers, continuing today with the relative decline of the hegemony of the United States, were already in full play during the rise and fall of Dutch hegemony in the seventeenth century (Arrighi, 1994; Modelski and Thompson, 1996; Taylor, 1996).

The capitalist world-economy has experienced cyclical processes for hundreds of years (Chase-Dunn, 1989: ch. 2). These have comprised the rise (A-phase), as well as stagnation and fall (B-phase) of hegemons, along a 40-to-60-year business cycle—the Kondratieff (K-) wave; a cyclical process of warfare among core states (Goldstein, 1988); and cycles of colonization as well as decolonization (Bergesen and Schoenberg, 1980). The world-system has also experienced several secular trends, including a long-term proletarianization of the world workforce; a growing concentration of capital into ever-larger firms; an increasing internationalization of capital investment and of trade; and an accelerating internationalization of political structures.

In this outlook, globalization is a long-term upward trend of political and economic change that is affected by cyclical processes. Thus, the most recent technological changes, and the expansions of international trade and investment, are part of these long-run changes. One question is, exactly how do the most recent changes compare with the long-run trends? Another is, what are the important continuities and qualitative differences that accompany these changes? These very questions are explored in this chapter.

TYPES OF GLOBALIZATION

At least five dimensions of globalization need to be distinguished. In addition, a few misunderstandings and misinterpretations must be clarified. To begin with, let us evaluate five different meanings of globalization:

Common Ecological Constraints

This aspect of globalization involves global threats, due to our fragile ecosystem (see Chapter 5) and the globalization of ecological risks. Anthropogenic causes of ecological degradation have long operated, and these in turn have affected human social evolution. But ecological degradation has only recently begun to operate on a global scale. This fact creates a set of systemic constraints that require global collective action.

Cultural Globalization

This aspect of globalization relates to the diffusion of two sets of cultural phenomena:

1. The proliferation of individualized values, originally of Western origin, to ever larger parts of the world population. These values are propagated via theory-building (see Chapter 1), but are also expressed in social constitutions, which recognize individual rights and identities (cf. Chapter 8), as well as in transnational (see Chapter 10) and international (see Chapter 11) efforts to protect "human rights."
2. The adoption (cf. Chapter 9) of originally Western institutional practices. Bureaucratic organization, rationality, and belief in a law-like natural universe and in the values of economic efficiency and political democracy have been spreading throughout the world since first propagated in the European Enlightenment (Meyer, 1996; Markoff, 1996).

Whereas some of the discussions of the world polity assume that cultural components have been a central aspect of the modern world-system from the start (e.g., Meyer, 1989; Mann, 1986), I would emphasize the comparatively non-normative nature of the modern world-system (Chase-Dunn, 1989: ch. 5). But I would certainly acknowledge the growing salience of cultural consensus in the last 100 years. Whereas the modern world-system has always been, and is still, multicultural, the growing influence and acceptance of Western values of rationality, individualism, equality, and efficiency was an important trend of the twentieth century.

Globalization of Communication

Another meaning of globalization is connected with the new era of telematics (see Chapter 3). In fact, what does "technological" globalization mean? For the communication media, another aspect of globalization seems relevant—one on which Anthony Giddens (1996) insists. Social space comes to acquire new qualities with telematics, albeit only in the networked parts of the social world. Hence, in terms of accessibility, cost, and velocity, the political and geographic parameters hitherto known to structure social relationships now become much less relevant.

One may well argue that time-space compression (Harvey, 1989) by new information technologies is simply an extension and an acceleration of the long-term trend toward technological development over the last ten millennia (Chase-Dunn, 1994). Yet, the rapid decrease in the cost of communications may have also qualitatively altered the relationship between states and social consciousness. Global communication facilities have the power to move things visible and invisible (see Chapter 10) from one part of the globe to another, whether or not any nation-state likes it. This does not solely apply to economically relevant exchange, but also to ideas and to gathering support for issues worldwide—indeed, to forming lines of opposition. How, and to what extent, this undermines the power of the state to structure social relationships is a critical issue.

Economic Globalization

Economic globalization means nothing less than globe-spanning economic relationships. The interrelationships of world markets—namely, finance, goods, and services—and the networks created by transnational corporations are the most important manifestations of economic globalization. Although the capitalist world-system (see Chapter 4) has been international in essence for centuries, the extent and degree of globalization in trade and investment has increased greatly in recent decades. Economic globalization has also been accelerated by what telematics has done to the movement of money. It is commonly claimed that the market's ability to shift money from one part of the globe to another at the push of a button has changed the rules of policy-making, putting economic decisions much more at the mercy of market forces than before.

Political Globalization

Political globalization consists of the institutionalization of international political structures (see Chapter 6). The Europe-centered world-system has been primarily constituted as an interstate system—a system of conflicting and allying states and empires (see Chapter 2). Earlier world-systems in which accumulation was achieved mainly by means of institutionalized coercive power came to experience an oscillation between multicentric interstate systems and core-wide world empires in which a single "universal" state conquered all or most of the core states in a region. The Europe-centered system experienced a cyclical alternation between political centralization and decentralization, but this emerged in the form of the rise and fall of hegemonic core states that do not conquer the other core states. Hence the modern world-system has remained multicentric in the core. This is due mainly to the shift toward a form of accumulation—based more on the production and profitable sale of commodities—named capitalism. The hegemons have been the most thoroughly capitalist states. They prefer to follow a strategy of controlling trade and access to raw material imports from the periphery instead of conquering other core states to extract tribute or taxes.

Power competition in an interstate system does not require much in the way of cross-state cultural consensus in order to operate systemically. But since the early nineteenth century, the European interstate system has been developing an increasingly consensual international normative order as well as a set of international political structures that regulate all sorts of interaction. This phenomenon has been termed "global governance" by Craig Murphy (1994) and others. It refers to the growth of both specialized and general international organizations. The general organizations that have emerged comprise the Concert of Europe, the League of Nations, and the United Nations. The sequence of these "proto-world-states" constitutes a process (see Chapter 11) of institution-building. But unlike earlier "universal states," this one is gradually emerging by means of condominium among core states rather than by conquest. This is the very trend of political globalization. It is yet a weak, if persistent, concentration of sovereignty in international institutions. If it continues, it will eventuate in a single global state that could effectively outlaw warfare and enforce its illegality.

MEASURING ECONOMIC GLOBALIZATION

This brief discussion has portrayed economic globalization as a long-run upward trend. The idea is that both international economic competition and geopolitical competition were already important in the fourteenth century and that they became more and more important with growing international trade and investment. In its simplest form, this would posit a linear upward trend of economic globalization. An extreme alternative hypothesis about economic globalization would posit a completely unintegrated world composed of autarchic national economies, until at some point—perhaps in the last few decades or so—a completely global market for commodities and for capital suddenly emerged.

Figure 7.1
Economic Globalization: Trade and Investment

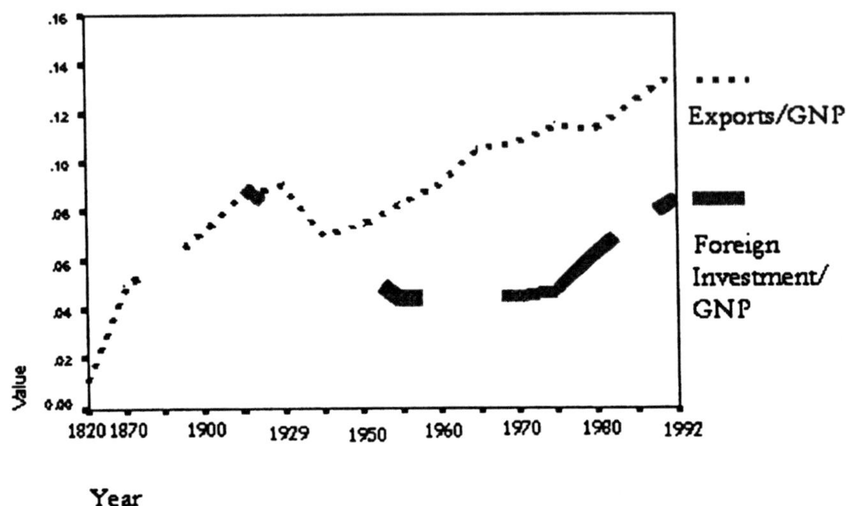

Sources: Maddison (1995): 227, 239; United Nations (1994): 130; Bairoch (1996).

Let us examine data that can tell us more about the temporal emergence of economic globalization: Potentially a large number of different indicators of economic globalization may or may not exhibit similar patterns with respect to change over time. Trade globalization can be operationalized as the share of all world production that crosses international boundaries. And investment globalization would be the proportion of all invested capital in the world, owned by non-nationals ("foreigners"). One could also study the degree of economic integration of countries by determining the extent to which national economic growth rates are correlated across countries. We could even examine changes in the degree of multilateralization of trade by examining the mean averages of export partner concentration across all nation-states over time—export partner concentration being the ratio of "the value of the exports to the largest trade partner" to "the total exports of a country." A related indicator (the degree of average national specialization) could be measured by using "commodity concentration"—the proportion of national exports composed of the single largest export commodity item—if one had the figures.

It would be ideal to materialize these measures over several centuries. But comparable figures are available only as far back as the nineteenth century, and even they are sparse and probably unrepresentative of the whole system until well into the current century. Nonetheless, we can learn important things by examining whatever comparable data become available.

Figure 7.1 shows trade and investment globalization. Trade globalization is the ratio of estimated total world exports (the sum of the value of exports of all countries) divided by an estimate of total world product (the sum of all the national GDPs). Investment globalization is the total book value of all foreign direct investment divided by the total world product. The trade globalization figures show the hypothesized upward trend as well as a downturn that occurred between 1929 and 1950.

Note that the time scale in Figure 7.1 is distorted by the paucity of datum points before 1950. It is quite possible that important changes in trade globalization are not visible in this series because of the wide temporal gaps in the data. Figure 7.1 also shows that the trade indicator differs in some ways from the investment indicator. Investment globalization was higher (or as high) in 1913 compared to what it was in 1991. By contrast, trade globalization was considerably lower in 1913 than it was in 1992. We have fewer time-points for the investment data, so we cannot say much with any certainty about the shape of the changes that took place. But these two series imply that different indicators of economic globalization may well show distinctive trajectories.

A third indicator of economic globalization resides in the correlation of national GDP growth rates (Grimes, 1993). It shows the extent to which periods of national economic expansion and stagnation have been synchronized across countries. In a fully integrated global economy, growth and stagnation periods would be expected to be synchronized across countries— there would thus be a high correlation of national growth rates. Grimes shows that, contrary to the hypothesis of a secular upward trend toward increasing global integration, the correlation among national growth rates has fluctuated cyclically over the past two centuries. In a data series from 1860 to 1988, Grimes found two periods in which national economic growth-and-decline sequences are highly correlated across countries: during 1913–1927 and after 1970. Before and in between these peaks are periods of very low concomitance.

Further research needs to be done to determine the temporal patterns of different sorts of economic globalization. At this point, we can say that the step-function version of a sudden recent leap to globalization can be rejected. The evidence we have indicates that there are both long-term secular trends and huge cyclical oscillations. Trade globalization shows a long-term trend with a big dip during the depression of the 1930s. But the investment globalization indicates a cycle with at least two peaks, one before World War I and one after 1980. And Grimes's indicator of synchronous economic growth divulges a cyclical fluctuation, with one peak in the 1920s and another since 1970.

These results, especially those that imply cycles, indicate that change occurs relatively quickly and that the most recent period of globalization shares important features with earlier periods of intense international economic interaction. Here, the similarities and differences between the most recent wave and the earlier waves of globalization are of notable significance.

SYSTEMIC CYCLES OF ACCUMULATION

Giovanni Arrighi (1994) has shown how hegemony in the modern world-system has been evolving in a series of systemic cycles of accumulation (SCAs), across which finance capital has employed different forms of organization and different relationships with organized state power. These qualitative organizational changes have accompanied the secular increase in the power of money and markets as regulatory forces in the modern world-system. In the Europe-centered world-system, the SCAs have been occurring since at least the fourteenth century.

Arrighi's model sheds light on both the similarities and differences in the relationships that obtain between financial capital and states within the different systemic cycles of accumulation. The British SCA and the American SCA featured both similarities and important differences. The main differences that Arrighi emphasizes are the internalization of transaction costs (represented by the vertical integration of transnational corporations) and the extent to which the United States tried to create organized capitalism on a global scale. The British SCA had fewer global firms and pushed hard for international free trade. The U.S. SCA is characterized by a much heavier focus on global firms and by a more structured approach to "global governance"—possibly intended to produce economic growth in other core regions, especially in those deemed to be geopolitically strategic.

Arrighi argues that President Roosevelt used the power of the hegemonic state in an attempt to create a balanced world of capitalist growth (cf. Chapter 2). This sometimes would mean going against the preferences of finance capital and U.S. corporations. For example, the Japanese miracle was made possible because the U.S. government prevented U.S. corporations from turning Japan (and South Korea) into just one more dependent and peripheralized country. This U.S. policy of enlightened global Keynesianism was continued in a somewhat constrained form under later presidents, albeit in the guise of domestic "military Keynesianism" (see the Introduction) justified by the Soviet threat.

In this interpretation, the big companies and the finance capitalists returned to power with the U.S. economy's decline in competitiveness. The rise of the Eurodollar market forced Nixon to abandon the Bretton Woods financial structure, and this was followed by Reaganism-Thatcherism, International Monetary Fund structural adjustment, streamlining, deregulation, and delegitimation of anything that constrained the desires of global capital investment. The idea that we are all subject to the forces of a global marketplace, that any constraint on the freedom to invest will result in a deficit of "competitiveness," thus provides a most powerful justification for destroying the very institutions (labor unions, welfare, agricultural subsidies, etc.) of the "Second Wave"—a concept coined by Alvin Toffler to mean "industrialism" and espoused by Newt Gingrich when he was the Majority Speaker of the House in the United States.

Under conditions of increased economic globalization, the ability of national states to protect their citizens from world market forces decreases. This results in increasing inequalities within countries and increasing levels of dissatisfaction, when compared to the relative harmony of national integration achieved under the Keynesian regimes. It also produces political reactions especially in the form of national-populist movements.[1] Indeed, some (McMichael, 1996) have even attributed the anti-government movements now emerging in the U.S. West and Midwest, including the bombing of the Federal Building in Oklahoma City, to the frustrations caused by the deregulation of U.S. agriculture.

It would also be useful to investigate the temporal patterns of the other types of globalization that I listed: cultural,[2] political, technological, and ecological. Of interest, too, should be the relationships between these and economic globalization. Much empirical work also needs to be done to operationalize these concepts and to assemble the relevant information. Here, for now, I will hypothesize that all these types exhibit both long-run secular and cyclical features. I will also surmise that *cultural and political globalization are lagging behind the secular upward trend of economic globalization.*

THE POLITICS OF GLOBALIZATION

This last hypothesis bears on the question of adjusting political and social institutions to increases in economic and technological globalization. I would submit that the current period of economic globalization has occurred in part because of technological changes that are linked to Kondratieff waves and in part because of the profit squeezes and declining hegemony of the U.S. economy in the larger world market.[3]

The financial aspects of the current period of economic globalization began when President Nixon canceled the Bretton Woods agreement—in response to pressures on the value of the U.S. dollar coming from the rapidly growing Eurodollar market (Harvey, 1995). This occurred in 1967, a date that many use to mark the beginning of a K-wave downturn.

The saturation of the world market demand for the products of the post–World War II upswing, as well as the constraints on capital accumulation posed by business unionism and by the political entitlements of the welfare states in core countries, caused a profit squeeze that motivated large firms and investors, together with their political helpers, to try to break out of these constraints. The latitudes for global investment opened up by new communications and information technology also created a new maneuverability for capital. The demise of the Soviet Union added legitimacy to the revitalized ideology of the free market, and this ideology swept the Earth.

Not only Reagan and Thatcher, but also Eurocommunists and labor governments in both the core and the periphery, adopted the ideology of the "lean state"—deregulation, privatization, and the notion that everything needs to be evaluated in terms of global efficiency and competitiveness.

Cultural globalization has been a very long-term upward trend since the emergence of the world religions in which any person could become a member of the moral community by confessing faith in the "universal" god (cf. Chapters 6 and 9). But moral and political cosmography has usually spanned a smaller realm than the real dimensions of the objective, trade-centered, and political-military networks in which people were involved. What did occur toward the end of the 1990s is a near-convergence between subjective cosmography and objective networks. The main cause of this may be the practical limitation of human habitation to the planet Earth. The long-run declining costs of transport and communications also may be an important element. Whatever the causes, the emergent reality is one in which consciousness either espouses or surpasses the real systemic networks of interaction. This geographical feature of the global system is one of its idiosyncrasies, and it makes possible in the future a level of normative order that has not existed since human societies were very small and egalitarian (Chase-Dunn and Hall, 1997).

Notwithstanding the fact that the ideology of globalization has undercut the support and rationale behind all sorts of "Second Wave" institutions— labor unions, socialist parties, welfare programs, and communist states— these institutions have not been fully destroyed everywhere. The world-systems literature on the reintegration of state communism in the capitalist world-economy (Chase-Dunn, 1980; Boswell and Peters, 1990; Frank, 1980) is substantial. The very technologies that made capitalist economic globalization possible now also have the potential to allow those who do not benefit from the free reign of capital to organize new forms of resistance or to revitalize old forms.

It is now widely agreed, even by many in the world financial community, that the honeymoon of neo-liberalism will eventually end; that the rough edges of global capitalism will need to be buffed. Patrick Buchanan, a conservative candidate for the U.S. presidency in 1996, tried to capitalize on popular resentment of corporate downsizing. The *Wall Street Journal* has reported that U.S. stock analysts worry about such a "lean and mean" philosophy becoming a fad with the potential to delegitimate the business system and even to create political backlashes. This concern was expressed in a discussion of the announcement of huge bonuses for AT&T executives promptly after yet another round of downsizing.

As to the difficulties that states are having in controlling communications on the Internet, I do not believe the warnings of those who predict a massive disruption of civilization by hordes of sociopaths waging "cyberwar," despite the large and growing "netwar" literature. These terms were minted by Rand Corporation analyst David Ronfeldt and David Arquilla of the U.S. Naval Postgraduate School in Monterey, California, in a 1993 article titled "CyberWar Is Coming!" Ronfeldt was thinking of a potential threat from an updated version of the Mongol hordes that would upset the established hierarchy of institutions. He predicted that communication would be increasingly organizing into cross-border networks and coalitions, identifying more with the development of civil society than with nation-states, and using advanced communications technologies to strengthen their activities. By 1995, Ronfeldt was characterizing the Zapatista activists as highly successful in limiting the government's maneuverability, and warning that the country that produced the prototype social revolution of the twentieth century may now be giving rise to the prototype social netwar of the twenty-first century.

But I do agree that the new communications technologies also provide new opportunities (see Chapters 3 and 6) for the less powerful to organize themselves to respond, should global capitalism run them over (see Chapter 4) or leave them out.

The important question here is, what are the most justified organizational forms for resistance? What we already see are all sorts of nutty localisms, nationalisms, and a proliferation of identity politics (see Chapters 9 and 10). The militias of the U.S. West and Midwest are ordering large amounts of fertilizer with which to resist the coming of the "Blue Helmets"—a fantasized world state that is going to take away their pistols and deer rifles. Is it not ironic that the same solid citizens of the U.S. West who were quite willing to grant the experts in Washington the benefit of the doubt on Vietnam are, 25 years later, doubting the moral and ethical foundations of the U.S. federal government?

Localisms and specialized identities are the postmodern political forms that are supposedly produced by infomatics, by flexible specialization, and by global capitalism (Harvey, 1989). However, at least some of this trend is a result of desperation over the demise of plausible alternatives in the face of the ideological hegemony of neo-liberalism and the much-touted triumph of efficiency over justice. In any case, a historical perspective on the latest phase of globalization allows us to see the long-run patterns of interaction between capitalist expansion and the movements of opposition that have tried to protect people from the negative aspects of market forces and exploitation. This perspective (Boswell and Chase-Dunn, 2000) has distinct implications for going beyond the impasse of the present to build a more cooperative and humane global system.

THE SPIRAL OF CAPITALISM AND SOCIALISM

The close interaction between expansive commodification and resistance movements can be denoted as "the spiral of capitalism and socialism." The world-systems perspective provides a view of the long-term interaction between the expansion and deepening of capitalism and the efforts of people to protect themselves from exploitation and domination. The historical development of the communist states is explained as part of a long-run spiraling interaction between expanding capitalism and socialist counter-responses. The history and developmental trajectory of the communist states can be explained as socialist movements in the semiperiphery, which attempted to transform the basic logic of capitalism but ended up using socialist ideology to mobilize industrialization in an effort to catch up with core capitalism.

The spiraling interaction between capitalist development and socialist movements is evident in the history of labor movements, socialist parties, and communist states over the last 200 years. This long-run comparative perspective provides a framework for recent events in China, Russia, and Eastern Europe, which has implications for the future of social democracy. The metaphor of the spiral means that capitalism and socialism affect each other's growth and organizational forms. Capitalism spurs socialist responses by exploiting and dominating peoples, whereas socialism spurs capitalism to expand its scale of production, to extend its market integration, and to revolutionize technology.

Defined broadly, socialist movements are those political and organizational means by which people try to protect themselves from market forces, exploitation, and domination, and to build more cooperative institutions. The sequence of industrial revolutions, by which capitalism has restructured production and taken control of labor, has stimulated a series of political organizations and institutions created by workers to protect their livelihoods. This has happened differently under different political and economic conditions, in different parts of the world-system. Skilled workers created guilds and craft unions. Less skilled workers created industrial unions. Sometimes these guilds and unions coalesced into labor parties that played important roles in supporting the development of political democracy, mass education, and welfare states (Rueschemeyer, Stephens, and Stephens, 1992). In regions where they were less politically successful, some workers managed to protect access to rural areas and to subsistence plots for a fallback or hedge against the insecurities of employment in capitalist enterprises. Today, to some extent, the burgeoning contemporary "informal sector" provides just such a fall-back in both core and peripheral societies.

The mixed success of workers' organizations also had an impact on the further development of capitalism. In some areas, workers or communities were successful in raising the wage bill or protecting the environment in ways that raised the costs of production for capital. When this happened, capitalists either displaced workers by automating them out of jobs or capital migrated to areas where fewer constraints allowed cheaper production. The process of capital flight is not a new feature of the world-system. For centuries it has been a hefty force behind the uneven development of capitalism and the spreading scale of market integration. Labor unions and socialist parties were able to obtain some power in certain states, but capitalism became all the more international. Firm size increased. International markets became more and more important to success in capitalist competition. Fordism, the employment of large numbers of easily organizable workers in centralized production locations, was supplanted by "flexible accumulation" (a system whereby small firms produced small customized products) and by global sourcing (the use of substitutable components from broadly dispersed competing producers). Both of these new production strategies lessened labor's traditional organizing power.

COMMUNIST STATES IN THE WORLD-SYSTEM

Socialists able to gain state power in some semiperipheral states used this power to create political mechanisms protective from competition with core capital. This was not a wholly new phenomenon. As discussed later in this chapter, capitalist semiperipheral states had done and were doing similar things. But the communist states claimed a fundamentally oppositional ideology in which socialism was allegedly a superior system that would eventually replace capitalism. Ideological opposition is a phenomenon that is not new to the capitalist world-economy. The geopolitical and economic battles of the Thirty Years' War were fought in the name of Protestantism against Catholicism. The content of the ideology may make some difference for the internal organization of states and parties, but every contender must be able to legitimate itself in the eyes and hearts of its cadre. The claim to represent a qualitatively different and superior socioeconomic system is not evidence that, in reality, the communist states were structurally autonomous from world capitalism.

The communist states severely restricted the access of core capitalist firms to their internal markets and raw materials. This constraint on the mobility of capital was an important force behind both the post–World War II upsurge in the spatial scale of market integration and a new revolution of technology. In certain areas, capitalism was driven to revolutionize technology further or to improve living conditions for workers and peasants because of the demonstration effect of propinquity to a communist state. U.S. support for state-led industrialization in Japan and Korea (in contrast to U.S. policy in Latin America) is only explicable as a geopolitical response to the Chinese revolution. The rivalry between "two superpowers"—one capitalist and one communist—in the period after World War II provided a fertile context for the success of international liberalism within the capitalist bloc. This formed the political/military basis for the rapid growth of transnational corporations and the latest revolutionary "time-space compression" (Harvey, 1989). This technological revolution has once again restructured the international division of labor and created a new regime of labor regu-

lation called *flexible accumulation*. The process by which the communist
states have become reintegrated into the capitalist world-system has been
long, but the final phase of reintegration was provoked by the inability to
be competitive with the new form of capitalist regulation. Thus, capitalism
spurs socialism, which spurs capitalism, which spurs socialism again—in a
wheel that gets ever larger as it turns and turns.

The economic reincorporation of the communist states into the capitalist
world-economy did not occur recently and suddenly. It began with the mobilization toward autarchic industrialization using socialist ideology, an effort that was quite successful in terms of standard measures of economic
development. Until the 1980s, most of the communist states were increasing
their share of world product and energy consumption.

The economic reincorporation of the communist states moved to a new
stage of integration with the world market and foreign firms in the 1970s
(Frank, 1980: ch. 4). Through this trend, the communist states increased
their exports for sale on the world market, expanded their imports from the
avowedly capitalist countries, and made deals with transnational firms for
investments within their borders. The economic crisis in Eastern Europe
and the Soviet Union was not much worse than the economic crisis in the
rest of the world during the global economic downturn that began in the
late 1960s (see Boswell and Peters, 1990: Table 1). Data presented by
World Bank analysts indicate that until 1989 or 1990 GDP growth rates
were positive in most of the "historically planned economies" in Europe
(Marer et al., 1991: Table 7a).

Put simply, the big transformations that occurred in the Soviet Union and
China after 1989 were part of a process that had been under way since the
1970s. The sociopolitical changes were a matter of the superstructure catching up with the economic base. The democratization of these societies is a
welcome trend, but democratic political forms do not automatically lead to
a society without exploitation or domination. Thus, the outcomes of current
political struggles are rather uncertain in most of the ex-communist countries. New types of authoritarian regimes seem at least as likely as real democratization.

As trends in the last two decades have shown, austerity regimes, deregulation, and marketization occured within nearly all of the communist states
during the same periods that they affected the non-communist states. The
simultaneity and broad similarities of the Reagan/Thatcher deregulations
and attacks on the welfare state, austerity socialism in most of the rest of
the world, and increasing pressures for marketization in the Soviet Union
and in China are all related to the B-phase downturn of the Kondratieff
wave, as are the current moves toward austerity and privatization in many
semiperipheral and peripheral states. The trend toward privatization, deregulation, and market-based solutions among parties of the left in almost every
country has been thoroughly documented (Lipset, 1991). Nearly all social-

ists with access to political power have abandoned the idea of doing much more than buffing off the rough edges of capitalism. The way in which the pressures of a stagnating world economy impact national policies certainly varies from country to country, but the ability of any single national society to construct collective rationality is limited by its interaction within the larger system. The most recent expansion of capitalist integration, termed *globalization of the economy*, has made autarchic national economic planning seem anachronistic. Yet, a political reaction against economic globalization is now under way in a variety of forms—by revived ex-communist parties, economic nationalism (be they the form advocated by Pat Buchanan or that of the Brazilian military), and even a coalition of oppositional forces now critiquing the ideological hegemony of neo-liberalism (Ralph Nader, environmentalists, populists of the right among them in the United States).

POLITICAL IMPLICATIONS OF THE WORLD-SYSTEM PERSPECTIVE

The age of U.S. hegemonic decline and the rise of postmodernist philosophy have cast the liberal ideology of the European Enlightenment (science, progress, rationality, liberty, democracy, and equality) into the dust bin of totalizing universalisms. It is alleged that these values have been the basis of imperialism, domination, and exploitation—that they should be cast out in favor of each group asserting its own set of values. Note that self-determination and a considerable dose of multiculturalism (especially regarding religion) were already central elements in Enlightenment liberalism.

The structuralist and historical materialist world-systems approach poses this problem of values in a different way. The problem with the capitalist world-system has not been with its values. The philosophy of liberalism is fine. Quite often, it has been an embarrassment to the pragmatics of imperial power and has frequently provided justifications for resistance to domination and exploitation. The philosophy of the Enlightenment has never been a major cause of exploitation and domination. Rather, it was the military and economic power generated by capitalism that made European hegemony possible.

To humanize the world-system, we may need to construct a new philosophy of democratic and egalitarian liberation. Remarkably, many of the principal ideals at the core of the left's critique of capitalism are shared by non-European philosophies. Democracy, in the sense of popular control over collective decision making, was not invented in Greece. It was a characteristic of all non-hierarchical human societies on every continent, long before the emergence of complex chiefdoms and states. My point is that a new egalitarian universalism can usefully incorporate quite a lot from the old universalisms. It is not liberal ideology that caused so much exploitation and domination. It was the failure of real capitalism to live up to its own ideals (liberty, equality) in most of the world. That is the problem that progressives must solve.

A central question for any strategy of transformation is the question of agency. Who are the actors who may want vigorously and effectively to resist capitalism and to construct democratic socialism? What is the most favorable terrain on which concerted action could bear the most edible fruit? Samir Amin (1992) contends that the agents of socialism have been most heavily concentrated in the periphery. It is there that the capitalist world-system is most oppressive. Thus, it is also there that peripheral workers and peasants, the vast majority of the world proletariat, have the most to win and the least to lose.

Yet, Marx and many contemporary Marxists have argued that socialism will be most effectively built by the action of core proletarians; that since core areas have already attained a high level of technological development, establishing socialized production and distribution should be easiest in the core, where organized workers have had the longest experience with industrial capitalism and the widest latitudes to build socialist relations.

While these "workerist" and "Third Worldist" positions have important elements of truth, the structural theory of the world-system suggests yet another alternative: the semiperiphery as the most appropriate context.

Although core workers may have experience and opportunity, a sizable segment of the core working classes lacks motivation, owing to their having benefited from a non-confrontational relationship with core capital. The extant labor aristocracy has divided the working class in the core and, in combination with large middle strata, undermined political challenges to capitalism. In addition, the "long experience," wherein business unionism and social democracy have been the outcome of a series of struggles between radical workers and the labor aristocracy, has created a residue of trade union practices, party structures, legal and even governmental institutions, and ideological heritages, which act as barriers to purer socialist pursuits. During the last two decades these conditions have changed to some extent, as hypermobile capital has attacked organized labor, dismantled welfare states, and starkly downsized middle-class workforces. They create new prospects for popular movements within the core. Thus, one can expect more confrontational popular movements to emerge as workers devise new (or revitalize old) forms of organization. Economic globalization makes labor internationalism a necessity, and so one can expect to see an old idea assume new forms and to become organizationally more real. Even small achievements in the core can have important effects on peripheral and semiperipheral areas for their example but also for mitigating the choking power wielded by core states.

The main problem with "Third Worldism" is not motivation but opportunity. Democratic socialist movements that assume state power in the periphery are soon beset by powerful external forces that either overthrow them or force them to abandon most of their socialist program. Popular movements in the periphery are usually anti-imperialist class alliances, which succeed in establishing the trappings of national sovereignty but not socialism. The low level of development of the productive forces there makes it far harder to establish socialist forms of accumulation, even though this is not impossible in principle. It is simply more difficult to share power and wealth when there is so very little of either around. But the emergence of democratic regimes in the periphery is most likely to facilitate new forms of mutual aid, cooperative development, and popular movements—once the current ideological hegemony of neoliberalism is attenuated.

SEMIPERIPHERAL DEMOCRATIC SOCIALISM

In the semiperiphery, both motivation and opportunity exist. Semiperipheral areas, especially those in which the territorial state is large, have sufficient resources to be able to stave off core attempts at overthrow and to provide some protection to socialist institutions if the political conditions for their emergence should arise. Semiperipheral regions (e.g., Russia and China) have experienced more militant class-based socialist revolutions and movements because of their intermediate position in the core/periphery hierarchy. Although core exploitation of the periphery creates and sustains alliances among classes in both the core and the periphery, in the semiperiphery an intermediate world-system position undermines class alliances and provides a fertile terrain for strong challenges to capitalism. Yet, semiperipheral revolutions and movements are not always socialist in character, as we have seen in Iran. When socialist intentions are strong, however, there are more possibilities for real transformation than in the core or the periphery. Thus, the semiperiphery is the weak link in the capitalist world-system. It is the terrain on which the strongest efforts to establish socialism have been made, and this is likely to be true for future endeavors as well.

On the other hand, the results of the efforts so far—while they have been undoubtedly important experiments with the logic of socialism—have left much to be desired. The propensity for authoritarian regimes to emerge in the communist states betrayed Marx's idea of a freely formed association of direct producers.

The Russians' imperial control of Eastern Europe was an insult to the idea of proletarian internationalism. Democracy within and between nations must be a constituent element of true socialism.

It does not follow that efforts to build socialism in the semiperiphery will always be so constrained and thwarted. The revolutions in the Soviet Union and the People's Republic of China have increased collective knowledge about how to build socialism despite their only partial successes and their obvious failures. It is important for all those who want to build a more humane and peaceful world-system to understand the lessons of socialist movements in the semiperiphery, as well as the potential for future, imaginably more successful, forms of socialism there.

Once again the core has developed new lead industries—computers and biotechnology. Much of large-scale heavy industry, the classical terrain of strong labor movements and socialist parties, has been moved to the semiperiphery. This means that new socialist bids for state power in the semiperiphery (in South Africa, Brazil, Mexico, and perhaps Korea) will be based much more on an urbanized and organized proletariat in large-scale industry than the earlier semiperipheral socialist revolutions were. This should have positive consequences for the nature of new socialist states in the semiperiphery, especially since the relationship between city and countryside within this semiperiphery should be less antagonistic. Less internal conflict is likely to make more democratic socialist regimes possible, and thus also to lessen the need for core interference. The global expanse of communications has increased the salience of events in the semiperiphery for audiences in the core. This may serve to dampen even further any need for core state intervention into the affairs of democratic socialist semiperipheral states.

Some critics of the world-system perspective have argued that emphasis on the structural importance of global relations leads to political do-nothingism while waiting for socialism to emerge at the world level. Indeed, the world-system perspective does encourage the examination of global-level constraints and opportunities and the allocation of political energies in ways that are potentially most productive when these structural constraints are taken into account. It does not follow that building socialism at the local or national level is futile but that resources *must* be spent on transorganizational, transnational, and international socialist relations. The environmental and feminist movements are already in the lead. Labor needs only to follow their example.

A simple domino theory of transformation to democratic socialism is misleading and inadequate. Suppose that all firms or all nation-states adopted socialist relations internally but continued to relate to one another through competitive commodity production and political/military conflict. Such a hypothetical world-system would still be dominated by the logic of capitalism, and that logic would be likely to repenetrate the "socialist" firms and states. This is why the cautionary rationale would be to invest political resources in the construction of multilevel (transorganizational, transnational, and international) socialist relations lest the process once again drive capitalism to perform an end run by operating on a yet larger scale.

A DEMOCRATIC SOCIALIST WORLD-SYSTEM

The emergence of democratic collective rationality—namely, socialism—at the world-system level is likely to be a slow process. What might such a world-system look like, and how might it emerge? At a bare minimum, such a system would necessitate a democratically controlled world federation (see Chapter 11) that can effectively adjudicate disputes among nation-states and eliminate warfare (Goldstein, 1988). There are many problems that badly need to be coordinated at the global level: ecologically sustainable development, a more balanced and egalitarian approach to economic growth, and lower population growth rates.

The idea of global democracy is important for this effort. There is need to push toward a popular democracy that will go beyond the election of representatives and include popular participation in decision making at every level. Global democracy can be real only if it is composed of civil societies and national states that are themselves truly democratic (Robinson, 1996). Global democracy is probably the best way to lower the probability of another way among core states. For that reason alone, it is in everyone's interest.

How might such a global social democracy come into being? The process of the growth of international organizations which has been ongoing for at least 200 years will eventually result in a world state, if the planet is not blown up first. Everyone, including international capitalists, have some uses for worldwide regulation, as is attested by the International Monetary Fund and the World Bank. Capitalists do not want the massive economic and political upheavals that would likely accompany a collapse of the world monetary system. Some of these same capitalists also fear nuclear holocaust: They may even support a global government that can effectively adjudicate conflicts among nation-states.

Of course, capitalists know as well as others that effective adjudication means the establishment of a global monopoly of legitimate violence. The process of state formation has a long history; the king's army needs to be bigger than any combination of private armies that might be brought against him.

While the idea of a world state may be a frightening specter to some, we can be optimistic about it for several reasons. First, a world state is probably the most direct and stable way to prevent nuclear holocaust, a desideratum that must remain at the top of everyone's list. Second, the creation of a global state that can peacefully adjudicate disputes among nations will transform the existing interstate system. The interstate system is the political structure that stands behind the maneuverability of capital and its ability to escape organized workers and other social constraints on profitable accumulation. While, at first, a world state may be dominated by capitalists, the very existence of such a state would provide a single focus for efforts socially to regulate investment decisions and thus to create an ecologically more balanced, egalitarian form of production and distribution.

Democratic socialists should be wary of strategies that focus only on economic nationalism and national autarchy as a response to economic globalization. Socialism in one country has never worked in the past, and most certainly it will not work in a world that is more interlinked than ever before. The old forms of progressive internationalism were somewhat premature. But today internationalism has become not only desirable but indispensable. This does not mean that local, regional, and national-level efforts are irrelevant. They are just as relevant as they always have been, but they need to have both a global strategy, and global-level cooperation, lest they be once again isolated and defeated.

W. Warren Wagar (1996) has proposed the formation of a "World Party" as an instrument of "mundialization"—that is, the creation of a global socialist commonwealth. Although his proposal has been critiqued from many angles—for example, as a throwback to the Third International—Wagar's idea is a good one: that such a party will emerge, and that it will contribute a great deal to creating a more humane world-system. Self-doubt or postmodern reticence may make such a direct approach appear Kantian or Napoleonic. But while it is certainly necessary to learn from past mistakes, one should not be prevented from debating the pros and cons of positive action.

The international segment of the world capitalist class is, indeed, moving slowly toward global state formation. The World Trade Organization is only the latest element in this process. Rather than simply oppose this move with a return to nationalism, progressives should make every effort to organize social and political globalization and to democratize the emerging global state. The operation of the interstate system must be prevented from creating future hegemonic rivalry—from causing another war among core powers (Wagar, 1992; Chase-Dunn and Bornschier, 1998). The emerging world society needs to be configured into a global democratic commonwealth based on collective rationality, liberty, and equality. This possibility is present in extant and evolving structures. The agents comprise all those who are tired of wars and hatred and who desire a humane, sustainable, and fair world-system. This is certainly a majority of the people of the earth.

CONCLUSION

The discourse on globalization has become a flood. What are the trends and processes that allegedly constitute globalization? How do they correspond with actual recent and long-term changes in the world-economy and the world-polity? What are the interests of different groups in the political programs implied by the notions of globalization? And what should be the response of those peoples who are likely to be left out of the grand project of world economic deregulation and the free reign of global capital?

These questions were addressed here from the world-systems perspective—an historically oriented analysis of cycles, trends, and long-run structural features of the world-economy. The recent explosion of awareness of transnational, international, and global processes was set in the historical perspective of the last 600 years of the emergence of a capitalist intersocietal system in Europe and its expansion to the whole globe.

International economic integration has been a long-term trend since the great chartered companies of the seventeenth century. This trend reveals a cycle in the rise and fall of the proportion of all economic exchange crossing state boundaries. Political globalization, too, has a long history in the emergence of international organizations over the last 200 years. Most of the many fashionable versions of the globalization discourse focus on a recent qualitative transformation. They emphasize the unique qualities of the new stage, while the longer view perceives recent changes as part of a much older process of capitalist development and expansion in which there are both important continuities and remarkable changes.

The trends and cycles reveal noteworthy continuities and imply that future struggles for economic justice and democracy need to base themselves on an analysis of how earlier struggles changed both the scale and nature of development in the world-system. Although some populists have gone on to suggest that progressive movements should employ the tools of economic nationalism to counter world market forces (e.g., Moore 1995), on the contrary, it is the political globalization of popular movements that will be required in order to create a democratic and collectively rational global system.

NOTES

1. See the ongoing debate on WSN (World-System Network) over nationalist versus internationalist popular responses with regard to globalization/downsizing—by consulting the address hereunder: gopher://csf.Colorado.EDU:70/00/wsystems/praxis/globprax.

2. One long-run indicator of cultural globalization would be linguistic diversity, a distributional measure of the proportions of the world's population that speak the various languages. It is obvious that linguistic diversity has decreased greatly over the past centuries, but it would be interesting to see the temporal shape of this trend. Have recent movements to revitalize and legitimate indigenous cultures slowed the long-term decrease in linguistic diversity?

3. For past evidence of relative U.S. economic decline, see Chase-Dunn, 1989: 266, where Table 12.3 shows that the U.S. share of world GNP did decline from 32.1 percent in 1960 to 26.9 percent in 1980. See also Bergesen and Fernandez (1998) for more recent data.

REFERENCES

Amin, Samir (1990). *Transforming the Revolution: Social Movements and the World System*. New York: Monthly Review Press.

———— (1992). *Empire of Chaos* (W. H. Loche Anderson, trans.). New York: Monthly Review Press.

Arrighi, Giovanni (1994). *The Long Twentieth Century*. New York: Verso.

Bairoch, Paul (1996). Globalization Myths and Realities: One Century of External Trade and Foreign Investment. In Robert Boyer and Daniel Drache (eds.), *States Against Markets: The Limits of Globalization*. London and New York: Routledge.

Bergesen, Albert, and Roberto Fernandez (1998). Who Has the Most Fortune 500 Firms? A Network Analysis of Global Economic Competition, 1956–1989. In Christopher Chase-Dunn and Volker Bornschier (eds.), *The Future of Hegemonic Rivalry*. London: Sage.

————, and Ronald Schoenberg (1980). Long Waves of Colonial Expansion and Contraction, 1415–1969. Pp. 231–278 in Albert J. Bergesen (ed.), *Studies of the Modern World-System*. New York: Academic Press.

Boli, John, and George M. Thomas (1997). World Culture in the World Polity. *American Sociological Review* 62, 2: 171–190.

Boswell, Terry, and Christopher Chase-Dunn (2000). *The Spiral of Capitalism and Socialism*. Boulder, CO: Lynne Rienner.

————, and Ralph Peters (1990). State Socialism and the Industrial Divide in the World-Economy: A Comparative Essay on the Rebellions in Poland and China. *Critical Sociology* 17, 1: 3–35.

Chase-Dunn, Christopher (ed.) (1980). *Socialist States in the World-System*. Beverly Hills, CA: Sage.

———— (1989). *Global Formation: Structures of the World-Economy*. Cambridge, MA: Blackwell.

———— (1994). Technology and the Changing Logic of World-Systems. Pp. 85–106 in Ronen Palan and Barry Gills (eds.), *The State-Global Divide: A Neostructural Agenda in International Relations*. Boulder, CO: Lynne Rienner.

————, and Volker Bornschier (eds.) (1998). *The Future of Hegemonic Rivalry*. London: Sage.

————, and Thomas D. Hall (1997). *Rise and Demise: The Comparative Study of World-Systems*. Boulder, CO: Westview Press.

Frank, Andre Gunder (1978). *World Accumulation 1492–1789*. New York: Monthly Review Press.

———— (1980). *Crisis in the World Economy*. New York: Holmes and Meier.

————, and Barry Gills (eds.) (1993). *The World System: Five Hundred Years or Five Thousand?* London: Routledge.

Giddens, Anthony (1996). *Introduction to Sociology*. New York: Norton.

Goldstein, Joshua (1988). *Long Cycles: Prosperity and War in the Modern Age*. New Haven, CT: Yale University Press

Grimes, Peter (1993). Harmonic Convergence? Frequency of Economic Cycles and Global Integration, 1790–1990. Paper presented at the annual meeting of the Social Science History Association, Baltimore, November 4.

Harvey, David (1989). *The Condition of Postmodernity*. Cambridge, MA: Blackwell.

———— (1995). Globalization in Question. *Rethinking Marxism* 8, 4: 1–17.

Lipset, Seymour M. (1991). No Third Way: A Comparative Perspective on the Left. Pp. 183–232 in Daniel Chirot (ed.), *The Crisis of Leninism and the Decline of the Left*. Seattle: University of Washington Press.

Maddison, Angus (1995). *Monitoring the World Economy, 1820–1992*. Paris: OECD.

Mann, Michael (1986). *Sources of Social Power*, Vol. 1. Cambridge: Cambridge University Press.

Marer, Paul, Janos Arvay, John O'Connor, and Dan Swenson (1991). Historically Planned Economies: A Guide to the Data. I.B.R.D. (World Bank), Socio-economic Data Division and Socialist Economies Reform Unit.

Markoff, John (1996). *Waves of Democracy: Social Movements and Political Change.* Thousand Oaks, CA: Pine Forge Press.

McMichael, Philip (1996). *Development and Social Change: A Global Perspective.* Thousand Oaks, CA: Pine Forge Press.

Meyer, John W. (1989). Conceptions of Christendom: Notes on the Distinctivenes of the West. Pp. 395–413 in Melvin L. Kohn (ed.), *Cross-national Research in Sociology.* Newbury Park, CA: Sage.

——— (1996). The Changing Cultural Content of the Nation-State: A World Society Perspective. In George Steinmetz (ed.), *New Approaches to the State in the Social Sciences.* Ithaca, NY: Cornell University Press.

Modelski, George, and William R. Thompson (1996). *Leading Sectors and World Powers: The Coevolution of Global Politics and Economics.* Columbia: University of South Carolina Press.

Moore, Richard K. (1995). On Saving Democracy: A Contribution to a Conversation about Global Praxis on the World-Systems Network (WSN). gopher:// csf.Colorado.EDU:70/00/wsystems/praxis/globprax.

Murphy, Craig (1994). *International Organization and Industrial Change: Global Governance since 1850.* New York: Oxford University Press.

Robinson, William (1996). *Promoting Polyarchy.* Cambridge: Cambridge University Press.

Rueschemeyer, Dietrich, Evelyne Huber Stephens, and John Stephens (1992). *Capitalist Development and Democracy.* Chicago: University of Chicago Press.

Shannon, Thomas R. (1996). *An Introduction to the World-System Perspective.* 2nd ed. Boulder, CO: Westview Press.

Taylor, Peter J. (1996). *The Way the Modern World Works: World Hegemony to World Impasse.* New York: John Wiley.

Toffler, Alvin (1980). *The Third Wave.* New York: Morrow.

United Nations (1994). *World Investment Report 1994: Transnational Corporations, Employment and the Workplace.* New York: United Nations.

Wagar, W. Warren (1992). *A Short History of the Future.* Chicago: University of Chicago Press.

——— (1996). Toward a Praxis of World Integration. *Journal of World-Systems Research* 2, 2. http://csf.colorado.edu/wsystems/jwsr.html.

Wallerstein, Immanuel (1974). *The Modern World-System.* Vol. 1. New York: Academic Press.

CHAPTER 8

Migrants, Refugees, and Insecurity in International Relations

REINHARD LOHRMANN
AND STEFANO GUERRA

INTRODUCTION

Since the 1980s, there has been mounting worldwide concern over the security implications of international migration for countries sending, receiving, and transiting migrants, and over the relations among them. Civil wars in Central America, northern Iraq, former Yugoslavia, Somalia, Liberia, Chechnya, Rwanda, and Zaire uprooted millions of people, with tragic consequences for the civilians caught in the middle of the fighting and complex effects on national and international security. Massive labor migration, too, has created serious security concerns for many countries of origin and destination. In reality, "the implications of migration on international security come in many forms: military, political, economic, environmental and social . . . [and] can contribute to internal or international tensions . . . [also impacting] regional security."[1]

Movements of people across borders have affected security in international relations at three significant levels. First, they have become a major issue in the national security agendas of both industrialized and developing countries; the receiving communities and their governments see them as a threat to their economic well-being, social order and culture, religious values, and political stability. Second, as movements of people created tensions within and between countries, they also burdened bilateral relations, impacting on regional and international stability. Third, irregular migration flows and involuntary population displacements have entailed significant implications for the individual security and human dignity of the migrants and refugees themselves.

QUESTIONING THE MIGRATION-SECURITY NEXUS

Since the early 1980s, preoccupations with international migration have moved beyond concerns over humanitarian issues, labor market effects, and societal integration, raising complex interactive security implications not only for governments in industrialized and developing countries but for multilateral bodies in authority as well. The complex nexus between forced population displacement and security acquired a new dimension when the Cold War ended. As of the early 1990s, the resolutions adopted by the U.N. Security Council regarding northern Iraq, former Yugoslavia, Rwanda, and Zaire, among others, explicitly admit forced population movements to be a destabilizing factor for regional and international security.

The number of refugees and asylum seekers in the world has grown dramatically since the mid-1970s. But over the last two decades, increasing perceptions of international migration as a security issue have been especially related to the quantitative and qualitative evolution of transnational migration as well as to the changing configuration of international relations since the end of the Cold War. Now that international migration has become a worldwide phenomenon affecting an ever larger number of countries, governments worry about what they perceive to be a global migration crisis. In the early 1990s, already 120 million individuals lived outside their countries of origin. Today, at least 50 million human beings can be considered to be victims of forced displacement.[2] The meager aggregate fall from the 1992 levels should not conceal the growing importance of yet another type of forced migration—internal displacement. According to the U.S. Committee for Refugees, at the end of 1996, there were 14.5 million refugees and asylum seekers in the world but over 20 million "internally displaced" persons.[3]

The end of superpower rivalry paved the way for a thorough reassessment of national interests and international security. In the heat of the Cold War, international security would focus on military issues (see Introduction to this volume), including the balance of power, the risk of nuclear and conventional war, and the need for arms reduction. The passing of the bipolar world gave rise to growing concerns for the international community over non-military sources of instability—for example, environmental degradation (see Chapter 5), population growth, ethnic tensions (see Chapter 9), human rights violations (see Chapters 1, 2, 6, 7, and 11), transnational terrorism (see Chapter 10)—not least, international migration. Thus, scholars and governments, but also multilateral bodies and non-governmental organizations (NGOs), all began to speak of security along non-military dimensions as well. And "environmental security," "food security," "common security," and "human security" came to enrich an already fecund vocabulary now used to identify the challenges awaiting the international community at the end of the twentieth century. It has even been advocated that, henceforth, security cannot be limited to a uniquely state-centric perspective—involving only the defense of national territory from external or internal aggression—but that it should be rearticulated to encompass the individual, societal, and global levels of analysis as well.

Issues related to international migration have acquired great political sensitivity in recent years in both industrialized and developing countries. Dealing with them along a security dimension is such a delicate task that we need to ask ourselves whether international migration can be studied honestly through a security lens. Behind the best intentions may lurk the danger of unwittingly facilitating the scientization of xenophobic and racist discourses, of unsuspectingly buttressing the extremist ideologies of those seeking to rationalize and legitimize their propaganda against immigration and asylum. In this regard, some general remarks would seem appropriate.

First, the connection between migration and security ought not be mistaken for a given beyond suspicion: Any association of the two concepts must be understood as a social construct—the mixed result of discourses and practices by specific social groups and institutions in particular cultural, socioeconomic, and political contexts. This would require an investigation of the social practices and political motivations at interplay in every attempt to "securize" migration—as such, an overlengthy exercise well beyond the scope assigned to us for this chapter.

Second, the concept of security now finds itself cheated of the precision of meaning that so unambiguously characterized it during the Cold War. Thus, while acknowledging the need to account for the wide range of complex interactive dimensions encompassed by the somewhat elusive term "security," it is also important to avoid simplistic uses of it, which can lead to misleading generalizations and interpretations. To avoid such risk, this chapter dwells on two levels of analysis—national and regional/international. It deals more especially with both irregular migration and refugee movements—the two categories of population flows of greatest relevant impact on national and regional/international security. It disaggregates the concept of "security" into that term's economic, societal, political, environmental, and military aspects. It places variable emphasis on these dimensions of security, depending on the geographical context in which the security implications of international migration are considered. It does not view "migration" as a monolithic construct, since different modes of migration can pose—or not pose at all—different threats to security. It discovers a continuing need to formulate discerning questions about the impact of certain categories of migration flows on national, international, and human security: Which kinds of migration flows impact security? What categories of security problems do they create? And for whom? Why are they perceived as security problems? In what kind of cultural, socioeconomic, and political context do these perceptions arise and flourish?

Third, extant and perceived threats must be distinguished. Fears about immigration are often exaggerated, and perceptions do affect policies seeking to constrain migration. Therefore, these elements must be accounted for in any analysis of the impacts of international migration on national and international security. In this respect, it is important to distinguish clearly between "threat" (as probable) and "risk" (as possible) danger.

Fourth, speaking of international migration as a security issue does not justify overlooking its positive aspects. People leaving their birthplace may succeed in finding safer or better living conditions in a receiving country, where they may bring their families. In addition to participating in the economy of their new country, economic migrants and refugees also largely contribute to the development of their country of birth by making hard-currency remittances and alleviating the burdens on its labor market. Countries of destination benefit from the economic performances of migrants, as well as from their inputs toward intercultural enrichment. Moreover, migration draws the sending and receiving countries into an international dialogue, closer bilateral relations, and multilateral cooperation.

Fifth, the most important security implications of certain kinds of population flows fall on the refugees and migrants themselves. Somehow, we tend to overlook the fact that voluntary and involuntary displacements involve millions of people in search of security. The concept of "human security," developed by the United Nations Development Program (UNDP), helps to underline the significance of individual-level analyses in any discussion of the international migration–security nexus. Until recently, the concept of security "has been related more to nation-states than to people"; therefore, a "profound transition in thinking" is needed, if the threats that could disrupt ordinary people's lives are to be addressed, since "[human security] means, first, safety from such chronic threats as hunger, disease and repression . . . [and then, also] . . . protection from sudden and hurtful disruptions in the patterns of daily life—whether in homes, in jobs or in communities."[4] In fact, the United Nations High Commissioner for Refugees (UNHCR) regards refugee movements and other forms of forced population displacements as the very product of human insecurity endured by millions of people around the world.[5]

ECONOMIC MIGRANTS, REFUGEES, AND INSECURITY IN THE INDUSTRIALLY ADVANCED COUNTRIES

Since the 1950s, the important labor shortages that have accompanied the rapid economic expansion of Western European countries have involved the recruitment of guestworkers from Southern Europe, as well as from Yugoslavia, Turkey, and, later, also from the Maghreb countries and other developing countries. Confronted with an almost similar situation, the United States admitted low-skilled workers from the Caribbean, Mexico, and Central America. As of the 1970s, the oil-producing states in the Middle East experienced a massive intake of temporary labor migrants from various Arab and Asian countries as well.

The oil crisis of 1973 provided a watershed for migration toward industrialized countries—especially Western Europe—where governments began to implement increasingly restrictive immigration policies. As of late 1973, economic recession and rising rates of unemployment pushed these states to impose a virtual ban on the recruitment of foreign workers. But the number of immigrants continued to rise in Europe's receiving countries during the 1970s and 1980s, primarily by virtue of natural increase, family reunification, and asylum solicitation. Waves of asylum seekers coming from developing countries began to appear at the end of the 1970s. This situation created an "asylum crisis" in Western European countries, many of which began to see in these newer migration flows a destabilizing role for their economic, cultural, social, and political structures.

IMMIGRATION AND ECONOMIC SECURITY

Often accused of exerting excessive strains on welfare provisions and public services (education, health, housing) in receiving countries, immigrants are also shunned as competitors in local labor markets, blamed for depressing wages, denigrated for provoking an expansion of the informal sector and impeding the development of a modern capital-intensive economy. In times of severe economic downturn, recession, shrinking public budgets, and high unemployment, native populations tend to resent the few support services given to immigrants, asylum seekers, or refugees. Regular and irregular immigrants provide a flexible labor force at low cost, often in jobs vacated by the local population. Many of them find employment at the margins of the formal economy, if not fully inside the informal sector. Irregular immigrants often work and live in precarious conditions, below minimum wage, without social security or protective labor union representation.

General conclusions regarding the economic implications of immigration for receiving countries are difficult to reach, since these depend on the specificity of the local or national contexts in which worker immigration takes place and on the character of the migration flows themselves. However, scholars seem to agree that, at a general level, the overall impact of legal and illegal immigration on a receiving country's economy is neutral at worst. In most cases, the positive economic implications of immigration for the receiving countries exceed the negative considerations.[6]

In recent years, owing to the rising number of clandestine immigrants, the political debate over complementarity/competition between irregular immigrants and native workers in local labor markets has raised its tone in Western Europe. Apparently, direct competition between local labor and immigrants has abated in the countries of Europe, as also in the new lands of destination in Southern Europe (Italy, Spain, Portugal, and Greece), because of the highly segmented nature of their labor markets.[7] Nonetheless, immigrants are increasingly portrayed as a threat to the economic well-being of recipients, both by the public and by some of the political parties in Western Europe. In the United States, in recent years strong emphasis was placed on the strain that the irregular immigrants supposedly exerted on such welfare-state provisions and public services as education and health. In times of deepening budgetary deficits and of cuts in federal subsidies to each state, the latter find it ever more difficult to cope with the costs associated with a large number of regular and irregular migrants. Voices have been heard in some states about the need sharply to reduce, eventually to suppress, the access of the children of irregular immigrants to schooling and health care.

IMMIGRATION AND CRIME

In industrialized countries, uncontrolled migration is seen to represent a growing threat to public order. Immigration and crime are highly sensitive political issues in the United States and in Western Europe, where they have been politically used to justify strict measures against immigration and asylum. Irregular migrants and asylum seekers are often impulsively associated with various criminal activities, such as drug trafficking, thefts, armed aggressions, or even terrorist acts against the receiving country (see Chapters 10 and 11). Such perceptions have strengthened in recent years, notably after the World Trade Center bombing by members of an Islamist group and the highly mediatized wave of terrorist attacks perpetrated in 1995 by some Algerian extremists on French soil. Such terrorist actions have illustrated the possible disruptive spillover effects of domestic conflicts in the sending countries on the public order and on the internal security of the receiving ones (see Chapter 9).

Although certain members of some immigrant communities engage in a variety of criminal activities, the overall impact of immigration on the crime rate and on the internal security of receiving countries tends to be misjudged and overestimated. Public debates on this issue are often biased by hasty stereotypings of the proneness of immigrants to crime and deviant behavior. According to these deep-rooted beliefs—often pushed and capitalized upon by various groups and institutions (including extremist groups, right-wing political parties, members of the media, certain police officials, and even researchers)—irregular migrants and asylum seekers are actually deviant and potentially threatening subjects. However, as a recent study shows, "bias, disparities, and disparate impact policy dilemmas are not uniquely the characteristics and problems of any particular minority groups or countries but are endemic to heterogeneous developed countries in which some groups are substantially less successful economically and socially than the majority population."[8]

IMMIGRATION, "SOCIETAL SECURITY," AND POLITICAL STABILITY: THE CASE OF WESTERN EUROPE

Western European fears of being swamped by waves of lowly immigrants with different cultural lifestyles are rooted in the age-old process of creation and evolution of the nation-state and its emphasis on cultural homogeneity. According to some scholars, issues of immigration and identity top the European security agenda of the late twentieth century: The very concept of "societal security" was developed to identify "situations when societies perceive a threat in identity terms," such as influxes of immigrants or asylum seekers: "Societal security concerns the ability of a society to persist in its essential character under changing conditions and possible or actual threats. More specifically, it is about the sustainability, within acceptable conditions for evolution, of traditional patterns of language, culture, association, and religious and national identity and custom."[9] This argument articulates (see Chapter 1) traditionalist and objectivist conceptions of society and is thus doubly suspect because most countries in Western Europe already have the makings of multicultural societies (see Chapter 6). Favoring such a traditionalist conception of society may help to scientize and thus to legitimize the very foundations for restrictive migration policies, instead of exposing "identity" for the social construct that it is—"the outcome of a labelling process which reflects a conflict of interests at the political level."[10]

The fact that Western European countries are confronted with immigrants with different cultural backgrounds does not represent a threat in itself. Rather, it is the political exploitation of these cultural differences that confers a security dimension to immigration, as is the case in the political instrumentalization of immigration and identity issues by extreme right-wing parties. The intensification of anti-foreign sentiments—of intolerance, xenophobia, and racism—has set the tone for the major social trends that have characterized European societies since the early 1980s. More recently, acts of violence against irregular migrants and asylum seekers or refugees have occurred in Germany, France, Switzerland, and Austria, among other places. Anti-immigrant sentiments have been usurped by extreme nationalist parties in some Western European countries to create a new political agenda. Electoral breakthroughs by the Front National in France, the Freiheitliche Partei Oesterreichs in Austria, the Vlaams Blok in Belgium, and the Alleanza Nazionale or the Lega Nord in Italy, as well as the ephemeral electoral success of the Republikaner in Germany in the early 1990s have helped raise the level of consciousness among European governments over the political costs of immigration. Greater pressure has been exerted on states to contain immigration; to reduce rights and entitlements granted to refugees, asylum seekers, and immigrants; and to expel irregular immigrants. The polarization that ensues from political debates over immigration in Western Europe has a major influence on the political system of receiving countries. Mainstream parties have become wary that overt stances on immigration could lead to a social and political backlash, which ultimately could even compromise the stability of existing regimes and lead to a dangerous societal polarization.

ETHNIC MINORITIES AND INTERNATIONAL POLITICAL TENSIONS

Members of some diaspora groups (see Chapter 9) play an important political role in relation to their homelands and to the receiving country. Through transnational channels, migrants and refugees can support domestic political parties, factions, or ethnic groups through representation, political lobbying, or, more directly, through recruitment and even flows of funds and arms. They often exert political pressures upon the receiving country's government in order to redirect its foreign policy toward their country of origin. For instance, migrants and refugees may try to convince the receiving country to support their cause against the home country regime, thus raising the prospects for bilateral political tensions.

Refugees in the United States are certainly not passive or dormant communities devoid of political influence on American domestic and foreign policies. The political lobbies by Cuban-, Jewish-, Armenian-, and Vietnamese-Americans are known to have been instrumental in the formulation of U.S. policies toward their countries of origin.[11] One of the most well-known examples is the political influence exerted by the Cuban-American National Foundation (CANF), created by Cubans who left the island after the revolution that toppled the Batista regime in 1959. In the early 1960s, Cuban refugees in the United States were trained to lead counterinsurgency activities in Cuba aimed at the overthrow of Fidel Castro. In the 1990s, through the CANF, Cuban-Americans lobbied intensely in the U.S. Congress to strengthen the more than 35-year-old embargo against Cuba through the Torricelli and Helms-Burton bills. They emerged as one of the major obstacles to normalizing of political relations between Washington and Havana. Other examples of migrant or refugee communities with a significant impact on political developments in the country of origin and on political relations between countries of origin and receiving countries include, among others, Turks, Kurds, and Croats in the Federal Republic of Germany; Algerians in France; and Tamils in various Western European countries.

IRREGULAR MIGRATION, TRAFFICKING IN MIGRANTS, AND INTERNATIONAL POLITICAL TENSIONS

Trafficking in migrants has recently been declared by some countries as a security threat. By accelerating and amplifying the phenomenon of irregular migration, traffickers of migrants undermine governmental rules of entry, as well as asylum and immigration procedures. Trafficking in migrants is now already a global phenomenon, which touches virtually every region of the world. Transnational criminal organizations—the Chinese and the Vietnamese Triads; the Japanese Yakuza; the Sicilian, Russian, and Turkish mafias among them—have expanded their range of criminal activities to include the smuggling of humans. The activities of these transnational criminal organizations unfold in spite of state regulations and represent a challenge to state authority and to national sovereignty as well (see Chapter 10).

Frequently, irregular migration flows and smuggled migrants provoke bilateral political tensions or bring about additional instability in already strained bilateral relations. In recent years, irregular migration flows and migrant trafficking have created political tensions between Northern and Southern European countries, as well as between the United States and Mexico, Morocco and Spain, Italy and Albania, Greece and Turkey, as well as other regions of the world. The trafficking of Chinese migrants is becoming a source of concern for many countries of transit and destination. Political tensions over this threat have developed between China and the likes of Russia, the Central Asian states, Japan, Taiwan, Singapore, Vietnam, and even the United States.[12]

Countries of origin can use irregular emigration as a trump card in interstate negotiations to force the countries of destination to make political, commercial, economic, or strategic concessions. By "pleading an inability to control the population outflow, or by demonstrating a willingness to manipulate it, the sending state is in a position to extract foreign policy and strategic concessions from the receiving state."[13] For example, the Albanian government has linked its cooperation in the control of irregular migration and human trafficking to its requests from the Italian government—and via Italy, from the European Union—for financial aid and for greater legal emigration opportunities. Also, receiving countries can choose to put the country of origin under pressure—whether by expelling irregular immigrants, by asking them to sign readmission agreements, or by withdrawing diplomatic, financial, and trade support. In recent years, political tensions arose between the United States and its southern neighbors (Mexico and other Central American countries), as the latter began to react strongly to every administrative and legal measure taken by the U.S. government to block more vigorously the irregular immigration flows from the south.

ECONOMIC MIGRANTS, REFUGEES, AND INSECURITY IN DEVELOPING COUNTRIES

Only a small fraction of refugees, asylum seekers, and economic migrants in the world move to the wealthier states of the North; the great majority of them wander from one developing country to another. Of the 14.5 million refugees and asylum seekers worldwide at the end of 1996, more than 11.8 million were located in the developing countries of Africa and the Middle East, thus amounting to 66 percent of that total. And except for the 1 million internally displaced people in Bosnia-Herzegovina, the greatest number of internally displaced people are found in countries such as Sudan, Afghanistan, Angola, Liberia, Iraq, Sri Lanka, Sierra Leone, and Colombia.[14] Flight is often the result of civil conflicts, rampant violence, state collapse, systematic violations of human rights, poverty, economic crisis, and environmental degradation. Forced population displacements and labor migration flows provoke a certain number of destabilizing effects not only on the security of both the sending and receiving countries, but also on the security of entire regions, as has been illustrated more recently by the situation in the Great Lakes region of Africa.

THREATS TO COUNTRIES OF ORIGIN

Population movements challenge the security and stability of countries of origin in at least three ways. First, refugees often use encampments in neighboring countries as logistical bases for their political and military activities against the home country regime. Usually placed near the border, these encampments allow members of minorities and of religious and opposition groups to find a relatively safe refuge from the persecution suffered in the country of origin. After their flight, refugee groups can at least partially reorganize their social basis in the receiving country, reformulate their political objectives toward the home country regime, and engage in military attacks intended to topple it. Often, the exodus is planned and organized by military and political leaders wishing to maintain control over the civilian population or to use it as a human shield. This was clearly the case in July 1994, when 1.75 million Rwandan Hutu were displaced into eastern Zaire, Tanzania, and Burundi—a displacement largely planned by the political leaders of those responsible for the genocide. Political and military leaders can also encourage their followers to harass and kill civilians in refugee camps, recruit children forcibly, obstruct and divert humanitarian aid, or even organize the traffic in arms or drugs in order to sustain and promote their objectives against the home country regime. In many instances, humanitarian aid—"unwittingly" or otherwise—aliments the guerrilla movements operating in refugee camps, thus fueling wars while attempting to extinguish their ravages.[15] Such was the case in the Sudanese refugee camps of Eritrea; refugee camps for former Contra combatants in Honduras and Costa Rica; the Mujaheddin in Pakistan; the Khmer Rouge along the border between Thailand and Cambodia; Rwandan political leaders, soldiers, and militiamen; and Burundian Hutu rebels in eastern Zaire. And while the jury is still out on Kosovo, reports warn of similarities.

Armed attacks launched from refugee camps can be tolerated or actively encouraged by the receiving country. By pleading an inability to control guerrilla activities in refugee camps or by sustaining them through the supply of personnel, arms, funds, or logistical facilities, the receiving country can choose to use refugee communities as strategic tools against the country of origin, thus raising the prospects of bilateral political and armed tensions. Such was the case in the backing given by Arab countries to Palestinian refugees in attacks against Israel; or in the military support provided by the Indian government to Sri Lankan Tamil refugees in the state of Tamil Nadu until the second half of the 1980s; or in Uganda's protection of the exiled Rwandan Patriotic Front, which eventually led to the overthrow of the Hutu regime in Rwanda in the aftermath of the 1994 genocide; or in the supply of arms to Afghan refugees by Pakistan, Saudi Arabia, the United States, and China during the Soviet occupation of Afghanistan. This instrumentalization of refugees was highly encouraged during the Cold War by the two superpowers as they sought to regain or consolidate their political, military, and ideological control over disputed territories. The United States armed Cuban refugees and Contra refugees, respectively, to help topple Castro and the Sandinista regime. And China, the United States, and the Thai government helped sustain the guerrilla activities of the Khmer Rouge after the invasion of Cambodia by Vietnam in 1979.

Second, origin countries usually are concerned about the way their nationals living abroad are treated by receiving countries. This is clearly illustrated by certain labor migration flows from developing countries. Many origin countries perceive in emigration a fundamental national economic resource, which can help improve the balance of payments through migrant remittances and also relieve the pressure exerted on their labor markets by a fast-growing population. Developing countries profit considerably from hard-currency remittances sent "home" by their labor force abroad. The World Bank's World Development Report notes that the net value of workers' remittances to their developing homelands rose from U.S.$15 billion in 1980 to U.S.$30 billion in 1994. Several developing countries such as Bangladesh, Egypt, India, Morocco, Pakistan, Jordan, Mexico, and El Salvador rely heavily on these financial flows.[16] It is therefore not surprising that admission restrictions and certain legislative changes or administrative decisions over immigration in receiving countries often lead to significant social, economic, and political problems in sending countries. Moreover, political tensions are also likely to arise between sending and receiving countries over decisions to tighten immigration laws, to limit the volume of migrant remittances sent home, to reduce foreign workers' entitlements, and eventually to expel them. Thus, receiving countries have considerable leverage through their ability directly and indirectly to exercise both socioeconomic and political pressures on the sending country.

Third, a massive return of refugees can place extra strains on the home country's already scarce economic resources, such as water and land, and extra burdens on the social services and infrastructure. This excerbates an already unstable social and political situation and leads to "repatriation emergencies." In many instances, refugees return to countries that have been, or still are, crippled by civil conflicts, violations of human rights, and economic recession. A repatriation emergency occurred in mid-November 1996 in Congo/Zaire, when the rebel movement led by Laurent Kabila succeeded in emptying the refugee camps set up in 1994 along the Rwandan-Zairian border. In a couple of days, a massive repatriation movement took place, which contributed to further destabilizing the already precarious social and political balance in Rwanda. Among the Hutus returning to Rwanda were many thousands of Hutu militia members and former soldiers, who, having taken part in the 1994 genocide, would also become responsible for the massacres of the local population and aid workers by the end of 1996. The return of Hutu refugees to Rwanda would also show that, where repatriation movements are not followed by—and included in—a concerted national and international effort aimed at rebuilding war-torn societies and at ensuring the transition from conflict to peace and stability, home countries are likely to suffer further instability and renewed waves of expatriation.

THREATS TO RECEIVING COUNTRIES AND TO REGIONAL/INTERNATIONAL SECURITY

It would be misleading to consider the impact of refugee and labor migration flows on the security of the receiving country in strictly negative terms only. Where forced population movements are at play, receiving countries can benefit from the presence of refugees in different ways. These include the inflow of emergency and development aid from the international community that also benefits the local population, whether by introducing novel agricultural techniques and products, or by developing local trade opportunities. Population movements in Sub-Saharan Africa show that refugees can act as enhancers of security for a receiving country,[17] even if some negative points apply here, too.

First, a large inflow of refugees in a poor area can strain natural resources such as wood, water, and land; place further burdens on education, medical care, housing systems, and roads; and exacerbate unemployment. Many developing countries simply do not have the financial and administrative resources to cope with the growing competition for scarce national resources.

This may lead to resentment by receiving communities over what is perceived as preferential treatment of refugees by the government and by the humanitarian agencies in the receiving country.

Second, an inflow of refugees or economic migrants can be perceived as a security threat by the receiving country when it changes the ethnic, religious, or linguistic composition of the receiving population, and destabilizes the social and political balances. Ethnic affinity often is a major factor in determining the perception and treatment of migrants and refugees by the receiving country. Thus, in South Asia, "the most common threat perception arises when migration changes the linguistic or religious composition of the sending or receiving locality."[18] And in Bhutan, fearing that a large inflow of illegal immigrants could alter the ethnic balance favorable to the ruling "Dropkas" majority in the North, the government, in the second half of the 1980s, began to take legal and administrative measures against the "Lhotshampas," the ethnic Nepalis living for generations in southern Bhutan, causing their flight to southeastern Nepal.[19]

Third, massive refugee flows can threaten the social order of receiving countries. Refugee camps are often characterized by high levels of violence and crime. The frustrations endured by people living in precarious conditions in quasi-permanent refugee camps can pave the way to various kinds of criminal activities, including murder, rape, harassment, theft, plundering, diversion of humanitarian aid, and life threats on local and international humanitarian staff. Violence and instability often spread outside the refugee camps and involve the local population, eventually leading to serious security problems for the receiving country. The militarization of refugee camps in eastern Zaire has had some important political and military repercussions in the Kivu region where violent clashes have occurred since the second half of 1994 between Hutu soldiers and militiamen controlling both the refugee camps and the local Tutsi population.

Fourth, refugees also can turn their arms directly against a receiving country's regime. Members of the Tamil Tigers responded to India's refusal to support their cause against the Sri Lankan government by turning their arms against India itself. The Sri Lankan Tamil Tigers were responsible for the assassination of Prime Minister Rajiv Gandhi during his visit in Tamil Nadu state in 1991. Problems of security also arise when refugee camps become targets for retaliatory armed attacks by the home country, as in the case of the raids perpetrated by the South African army against refugee camps in Angola, Botswana, Zambia, and Lesotho, all of which hosted anti-apartheid activists. The attacks by the Guatemalan army on refugee settlements in the Mexican region of Chiapas in the early 1980s and the raids by the Ethiopian army on camps harboring Eritrean refugees in Sudan are other examples.

Fifth, vast refugee flows into poor regions can cause severe environmental damage. The link between environment and population movements (environmental degradation as both cause and effect of population movements) was exposed in recent years by a number of refugee influxes in some of the poorest countries of the planet—Bangladesh, Sudan, Ethiopia, Zaire, and Nepal, for instance. The negative effects of refugee flows on a host country's environment could range from land degradation through overuse of fields to deforestation and the reduction and pollution of water supplies. The gravity of such effects depends on many factors (see Chapter 5), including the limited resources of a receiving region; the composition and the magnitude of the refugee wave; the length of its duration; the extent of materials, goods, and services made available by the government of the receiving country and by the humanitarian agencies. Ironically, the environmental consequences of massive human displacements have serious implications for the well-being of the refugees themselves, for their relations with the receiving country, and for the development potential of the regions in which they have settled.[20] In particular, refugees settling in a poor area may provoke resentment within receiving communities already facing a scarcity of natural resources. This may lead to clashes between them or to more or less violent protests against the receiving country's government.

Sixth, forced population displacements can have an important impact on bilateral relations and regional security, if receiving countries are drawn into conflictual relations with the sending country. For example, the political and security implications of population movements in Southeast Asia indicate that

population flows caused primarily by political or social strife carry some of the original conflict with them. Such flows have an inherently political impact in the receiving states, for by extending asylum the receiving state becomes at least indirectly a party to the conflict. Some actively utilize the refugees as instruments of foreign policy. For these reasons refugee flows typically appear in international adversarial contexts.[21]

The link between forced local population displacements and regional/international security has become evident since the end of the 1970s in conflicts in Central America, the Horn of Africa, Southeast Asia, Afghanistan, Sudan, northern Iraq, Somalia, and Liberia, if not least across the former Yugoslavia, for example. The implications of population movements for regional security are best illustrated by the forced displacements that took place in the aftermath of the Rwandan genocide in 1994. U.N. Security Council Resolution 929 of June 22, 1994, acknowledged that "the humanitarian crisis in Rwanda constitutes a threat to peace and security in the region." The security effects of successive mass displacements from Rwanda have been felt across the Great Lakes region, well beyond the two countries most directly involved—Rwanda and Zaire. Burundi, Uganda, and to lesser extent, Tanzania and Congo-Brazzaville have also been drawn into an increasingly destabilizing geopolitical situation.[22]

Mass population displacements in the Great Lakes region did not have significant implications for international security, because the great powers did not consider their interests to be at stake in this peripheral area. In spite of early ample evidence over the extensive preparation and planning for mass killings in Rwanda, the U.N. Security Council failed to take effective steps to prevent the genocide.[23] Per U.N. Security Council resolution 929, a humanitarian protected zone was established in July 1994 in southwest Rwanda under French military command to provide assistance and protection to displaced persons, refugees, and civilians under the code name Opération Turquoise. This operation contributed to the stabilization of the situation in southwest Rwanda, enabling thousands of people to survive, thanks to the humanitarian aid channeled into the region by relief agencies. But sadly, it also provided shelter for the perpetrators of the genocide. Instead of disarming and arresting the soldiers and the militia of the ousted Rwandan regime, French troops eventually allowed them to cross the border into Zaire. Once the exodus took place, those responsible for the genocide were able to sustain themselves for more than two years through the humanitarian aid channeled by a multitude of relief agencies into refugee camps in eastern Zaire. Calls for relocating refugee camps away from the border and for separating civilians from soldiers and militia of the former Rwandan regime somehow escaped the urgent attention of the U.N. Security Council.

COPING WITH THE SECURITY IMPLICATIONS OF INTERNATIONAL MIGRATION

The factual and perceived impacts of international migration on national, regional, and international security has provoked a reassessment of traditional immigration and asylum policies, in both industrialized and developing countries. In recent years, many governments and multilateral agencies have adopted new approaches or redefined traditional ones in order to cope with the security implications of certain kinds of population movements. Three main trends can be distinguished here: the progressive erosion of the traditional refugee protection principles enshrined in the 1951 Convention Relating to the Status of Refugees,[24] through stricter border controls and restrictive legal/administrative measures; the overemphasis on policy options aimed at changing conditions inside the country of origin; and the increasing involvement of multilateral bodies in such questions.

TIGHTENING CONTROL POLICIES

As a result of the 1973 oil crisis and the reduced economic growth that followed it, industrialized countries—especially in Western Europe—ceased recruiting low-skilled immigrants from the developing countries. They began to adopt stricter immigration laws. Since the beginning of the 1980s, arguing they were losing control over their borders, industrialized countries implemented a variety of legal and administrative measures in order to cope with an increasing number of irregular migrants and asylum seekers coming from distant and poorer countries. These measures aimed, on the one hand, at tightening admission procedures and, on the other hand, at preventing irregular migrants and asylum seekers from entering their territory and applying for asylum. The restrictive interpretation of the 1951 Refugee Convention; the rigid imposition of a visa requirement for nationals of refugee-producing countries; the penalties for airlines carrying people without valid identity or travel papers; the application of the "safe country" principle in relation to the country of origin and the transit countries; the increased deployment of border police and military troops on boundaries or high seas, to intercept and forcibly repatriate irregular immigrants and asylum seekers before they set foot; the accelerated asylum procedures, with limited or non-existent right of appeal; the detention of asylum seekers and the limitations set to their freedom of movement and to their entitlement to social services; the regional harmonization of immigration and asylum policies by the lowest common denominator, specifically through the Schengen and Dublin Conventions—regulating entry into the EU of third-country nationals and assigning purview for handling asylum claims are all part of this restrictive regime.[25]

For some commentators, industrialized states—by containing forced migrants in countries of origin or of transit—are in fact weakening their commitment to asylum.[26] Although they have reduced the number of asylum applications in Western Europe since 1993, these restrictive measures have imperiled the safety of refugees. According to the UNHCR, the major drawbacks of these measures include the threats posed to the individual security of actual and potential asylum seekers, the diversion of the asylum problem from wealthier states to other parts of the world, the growth in the trafficking of humans, and a greater public hostility toward refugees.[27] These restrictive measures by West European and North American states are also leading to an erosion of the traditional safeguards for the protection of refugees elsewhere in the world. "Expectations among governments are lowered generally, as are their voices, when the traditional leaders in setting standards of due process and generosity lower their own standards."[28]

TARGETING THE COUNTRIES OF ORIGIN

Since the end of the 1970s, large-scale refugee flows within and between developing countries (Central America, the Caribbean, Southeast Asia, Afghanistan, the Horn of Africa) and greater waves of south-to-north migration have altogether provoked a reassessment of traditional approaches to the refugee problem. These used to consist of post-displacement assistance to, and protection of, refugees in their countries of asylum. The exile bias, which used to characterize the traditional approach, has been slowly replaced by much greater focus on the domestic conditions of the countries generating—or likely to generate—human displacements.[29] Some of the countries exposed to economic migrant inflows researched the possibilities of stemming at their point of origin potential migratory flows caused mainly by economic, social, and ecological factors. In choosing to address the root causes of international migration, governments and multilateral institutions now pursue preventive and solution-oriented policies aimed at ensuring the security and dignity of potential migrants in their homeland. The purpose here is to leave them no reason to choose exile as a way of escaping persecution, endemic human rights abuses, civil war, extreme poverty, growing economic inequalities, or even ecological degradation. In recent years, states of destination have targeted the countries of origin by virtue of four main kinds of policy.

First, it has been shown that trade liberalization, foreign investment, and development assistance can reduce the pressures of emigration by creating income-generating opportunities, reducing unemployment, and improving wages in countries of origin. However, existing research indicates that economic growth is likely to increase emigration in the short run.[30]

Economic and financial measures are also used by governments of receptor countries to persuade countries of origin or transit to cooperate in halting refugee and irregular economic migrant flows. Thus, Germany gives financial incentives and technical help to Poland, the Czech Republic, and Hungary in exchange for their vigilant patrol of shared borders against any clandestine infiltration by westward-bound migrants and transients. To dissuade large-scale repatriation, the German government also offered economic assistance to ethnic Germans living inside the Russian Federation and in the other former USSR republics. Italy and the United States have provided economic assistance, respectively, to the Albanian and Haitian governments in exchange for their efforts to stem large flows of asylum seekers and irregular migrants.

Second, early warning and preventive action for potential refugee situations have gained in importance. Economic incentives to reduce migration pressures have been buttressed by timely and effective policies in preventive diplomacy, conflict resolution, human rights monitoring, and democratic institution-building, in order to strengthen civil society and to protect minorities, and thereby to prevent violence and massive population displacements. Methods of "soft intervention" are used when exerting diplomatic pressures to push a country of origin to adopt "good governance" policies—respect for human rights, protection of minorities, democratic institution-building, and sound economic policies—as a means of preventing or halting refugee and irregular migration flows.[31] For instance, the Italian government's support for Turkey's admission into the European Union has been pegged by Rome to the Turkish authorities' commitment to the respect of human rights in general—and those of the Kurdish minority in particular—as well as to its halt of the flow of trafficked migrants in the direction of southern Italy.

Third, armed intervention has taken place in recent years in countries affected by large population displacements—as in Iraq, Bosnia-Herzegovina, Somalia, Haiti, Rwanda, and Albania—to supply in-country humanitarian assistance and protection to internally displaced people and to war-affected populations and to prevent massive cross-border displacements that threaten the security of those at the receiving end. Acting on U.N. Security Council Resolution 940 of July 31, 1994, which authorized the use of "all necessary means" to restore democracy in Haiti, the United States sent 20,000 military personnel to the island, mainly to put an end to the exodus of Haitian boat people toward the United States, on the grounds that "If we don't act . . . we will continue to face the threat of a mass exodus of refugees and its constant threat to stability in our region, and control of our borders."[32] In April 1997, similar concerns over large migration flows from Albania pushed Southern European countries to play a key role through the deployment of a 5,000-strong multinational force on Albanian soil. In northern Iraq, Bosnia-Herzegovina, and Rwanda, national armies or U.N. peacekeeping forces were deployed to provide protection to civilians from internal conflict through the establishment of "safe areas," "safety zones," "no-fly zones," or "security zones." While, undeniably, safety zones did provide a certain degree of assistance and protection to war-torn people, their unenforced preservation has had serious security drawbacks for the very people they were intended to protect, if only for preventing them from seeking asylum in neighboring states.[33]

Fourth, many industrialized and developing countries contend that the increasing flow of economic migrants, asylum seekers, and refugees has become an unbearable burden. Growing pressures exist in these countries for the repatriation of unwelcome foreigners. Consequently, there has arisen increasing reliance on financial incentives and reintegration assistance programs to encourage the return of individual migrants and their reabsorption by emitting countries, as was the case in the handling of Bosnian refugees under the Dayton Accord of 1995. Since the 1980s, voluntary repatriation in the case of developing countries has been deemed to offer the most durable solution to refugee problems, which neither policies of integration nor efforts of resettlement have ever been able to provide. Thus in the 1990s, significant repatriations took place in Namibia, Ethiopia, Mozambique, Rwanda, Afghanistan, Cambodia, Vietnam, Myanmar, Guatemala, Nicaragua, El Salvador, and other countries. According to UNHCR estimates, more than 10 million people returned more or less voluntarily to their country between 1990 and 1997—of which 3 million returnees[34] were placed under UNHCR's direct global supervision. Figures will have to be seriously revised upward now that the Kosovo crisis has left the world with a dramatically altered landscape.

THE GROWING INVOLVEMENT OF MULTILATERAL INSTITUTIONS

The scope, nature, and geographical span of human dislocation have greatly preoccupied regional and international multilateral institutions. The forced displacements of unprecedented scale seen since the end of the Cold War have brought the UNHCR and the International Organization for Migration (IOM) to the forefront of the humanitarian scene. With demands for admission sharply up since the beginning of the 1990s, and with budgets, staff, and operations accordingly augmented, the UNHCR and the IOM have covered areas and contexts as diverse as northern Iraq, former Yugoslavia, Somalia, the Caucasus, Afghanistan, Rwanda, eastern Zaire, Mozambique, and Angola, among other countries. The new realities bring with them new ethical, legal, and operational dilemmas. UNHCR's activities on behalf of returnees, internally displaced, and war-affected people have raised serious and acute dilemmas in northern Iraq, former Yugoslavia, Myanmar, and eastern Zaire.[35]

Since the early 1980s, the proliferation of more or less formal multilateral instances allowed governments to discuss, negotiate, and adopt policies for international migration. In Europe alone, more than 15 different bodies have dealt with migration issues alongside such less informal entities as the Intergovernmental Consultations on Asylum, Refugee, and Migration Policies in Europe, North America, and Australia, all of which seek to improve policies concerning asylum seekers and irregular immigrants. Beyond UNHCR and IOM, other multilateral institutions which, so far, have been only marginally involved in refugee and migration issues, have expanded their agenda in order to address these concerns. They include inter alia the European Union (EU), the North Atlantic Treaty Organization (NATO), the Organization for Security and Co-operation in Europe (OSCE), the Commonwealth of Independent States (CIS), the Economic Community of West African States (ECOWAS), and the Organization of American States (OAS). The United Nations, via its political organs (the Security Council and the General Assembly), as well as the United Nations Development Program and the United Nations Center for Human Rights, has drawn heightened attention to the world's refugee and migration issues.

Governments in various regions of the world now recognize that the implementation of innovative approaches to the problems of human displacement necessitates the establishment of regional frameworks to replace ineffective unilateral initiatives. The Euro-Mediterranean dialogue, the binational discussions between the United States and Mexico on migration issues, the U.N.-sponsored 1979 and 1989 international conferences on the

Comprehensive Plan of Action (CPA) for Indochinese refugees, the conference on refugees and displaced people in Central America (CIREFCA, 1989), Southern Africa (SARRED, 1988), and the Commonwealth of Independent States (1996), provide excellent illustrations of these efforts.

CONCLUSION

The demise of the bipolar system after 1989 provoked a shift in focus toward the non-military sources of global and regional security. In this context, international migration acquired a new salience as a factor of insecurity, alongside other global issues such as the environment, human rights, democracy, civilian conflicts, broadening economic inequalities, uneven demographic growth, and transnational criminality. Both in industrialized and developing countries, certain kinds of migration flows—especially massive, irregular, economic migration flows and large refugee movements—gave rise to serious security concerns at subnational, national, regional, and global levels of analysis and synthesis.

Security implications of human displacement weigh not only on states but also on the asylum seekers, the refugees, and the economic migrants themselves. People abandon their countries of origin to escape myriad threats to human security—human rights violations, internal war and societal violence, poverty, economic inequalities, and ecological degradation. Some experience threats to their physical, material, and psychological security even in receiving countries, as demonstrated by violent xenophobic action against asylum seekers in Western Europe and by the armed attacks perpetrated against refugee camps in some developing countries.

In many instances, the flight of migrants seeking safety or better living conditions is severely limited by the restrictive policies adopted by the receiving countries. It would be absolute nonsense, however, to deny the right of sovereign states to seek to regulate such penetrations of their territory and to protect themselves from what they perceive to be an actual or potential destabilizing factor—"the crux of the matter . . . is not whether governments have a right to impose controls on the arrival and admission of foreign nationals, but the extent to which those controls are consistent with international refugee law and humanitarian norms."[36]

These considerations point to the need for elaborating and implementing asylum and migration policies that carefully weigh the humanitarian needs of people abandoning their countries of origin against the legitimate security concerns of the receiving states. Erecting legal and administrative barriers to dissuade asylum seekers and economic migrants from crossing international borders does not provide a satisfactory and consistent response to the security implications of international migration. Control policies respectful of humanitarian principles must be supported by effective actions to be undertaken inside countries of origin, in a manner to address the political, economic, and ecological root causes of international migration. A closer cooperation between the emitting and receiving countries and the regional and global multilateral institutions—such as the United Nations, the IOM, the World Bank, the EU, and the OSCE—can play a significant role in preventing forced migration and easing the economic pressures that compel human beings to leave and to seek refuge elsewhere.

It is through the enactment of a comprehensive framework of international cooperation that the destabilizing implications of international migration must be addressed, if movements of people across borders are not to constitute a source of insecurity in international relations but, rather, to be regarded as a factor contributing to the harmonious interstate relations and to the development of countries of origin, transit, and destination.

NOTES

Reinhard Lohrmann is an international civil servant. The views expressed in this chapter are his own and do not necessarily reflect those of the organization to which he is assigned.

1. James Purcell, Jr., Director General of IOM (International Organization of Migration), in "Security Implications of Mass Migration," at the Maxwell School of Citizenship and Public Affairs/Department of Political Science, Syracuse University, September 22, 1994, p. 6.

2. U.N. High Commissioner for Refugees, *The State of the World's Refugees: A Humanitarian Agenda* (Oxford: Oxford University Press, 1997), p. 2. Hereafter UNHCR, 1997 Report.

3. *World Refugee Survey*, Washington, DC, 1997.

4. UNDP, *Human Development Report 1994* (Oxford: Oxford University Press, 1994), p. 23.

5. See UNHCR, 1997 Report, chapter 1.

6. See Sarah Spencer (ed.), *Strangers and Citizens: A Positive Approach to Migrants and Refugees* (London: IPPR, Rivers Oram Press, 1994).

7. Russell King and Krysia Rybaczuk, "Southern Europe and the International Division of Labour: From Emigration to Immigration," in Russell King (ed.), *The New Geography of European Migrations* (London: Belhaven Press, 1993), p. 181.

8. Michael Tonry (ed.), *Ethnicity, Crime and Immigration: Comparative and Cross-National Perspectives* (Chicago: University of Chicago Press, 1997), p. 19.

9. Ole Waever, "Societal Security: The Concept," in Barry Buzan, Ole Waever et al., *Identity, Migration, and the New Security Agenda in Europe* (London: Pinter, 1993), p. 23.

10. Bill McSweeney, "Identity and Security: Buzan and the Copenhagen School," *Review of International Studies* 22, 1 (1996): 85.

11. See Kathleen Newland, "The Impact of U.S. Refugee Policies on U.S. Foreign Policy: A Case of the Tail Wagging the Dog?" in Michael S. Teitelbaum and Myron Weiner (eds.), *Threatened Peoples, Threatened Borders: World Migration and U.S. Policy* (New York, London: Norton, 1995), pp. 202–211.

12. Paul J. Smith (ed.), *Human Smuggling: Chinese Migrant Trafficking and the*

Challenge to America's Immigration Tradition (Washington, DC: Center for Strategic and International Studies, 1997), pp. 14–16.

13. Gil Loescher, "International Security and Population Movements," in R. Cohen (ed.), *Cambridge Survey of World Migration* (Cambridge: Cambridge University Press, 1995), p. 559.

14. U.S. Committee for Refugees, *World Refugee Survey 1997* (New York: U.S. Committee for Refugees, 1997), pp. 2–6.

15. See Ben Barber, "Feeding Refugees, or War?" *Foreign Affairs* 76, 4 (1997): 8–14.

16. See the Statement by Mrs. Narcisa L. Escaler, Deputy Director General of the International Organization for Migration, at the Twelfth IOM Seminar on "Managing International Migration in Developing Countries," Geneva, April 28 and 29, 1997, p. 3.

17. Karen Jacobsen and Steven Wilkinson, "Refugee Movements As Security Threats in Sub-Saharan Africa," in Myron Weiner (ed.), *International Migration and Security* (Boulder, CO: Westview Press, 1993), p. 219.

18. Myron Weiner, "Rejected Peoples and Unwanted Migrants in South Asia," in Weiner, *International Migration and Security*, p. 170.

19. See Michael Hutt, "Ethnic Nationalism, Refugees and Bhutan," *Journal of Refugee Studies* 9, 4 (1996): 397–420.

20. UNHCR, *The State of the World's Refugees: In Search of Solutions* (Oxford: Oxford University Press, 1995), pp. 162–177. Hereafter UNHCR, 1995 Report.

21. Astri Suhrke, "The 'High Politics' of Population Movements: Migration, State and Civil Society in South Asia," in Myron Weiner (ed.), *International Migration and Security* (Boulder, CO: Westview Press, 1993), p. 194.

22. Gérard Prunier, "The Geopolitical Situation in the Great Lakes Area in Light of the Kivu Crisis," *Refugee Survey Quarterly* 16, 1 (1997): 1–25.

23. Linda Melvern, "Genocide Behind the Thin Blue Line," *Security Dialogue* 28, 3 (1997): 333–346.

24. According to the 1951 Convention Relating to the Status of Refugees, a refugee is a person "[who] owing to [a] well-founded fear of being persecuted for reasons of race, religion, nationality, membership of a particular social group or political opinion, is outside the country of his nationality and is unable or, owing to such fear, is unwilling to avail himself of the protection of that country."

25. See UNHCR, 1995 Report, pp. 199–207.

26. For example, Andrew Shacknove, "From Asylum to Containment," in *International Journal of Refugee Law* 5, 4 (1993): 516–533.

27. UNHCR, 1997 Report, pp. 194–203.

28. Bill Frelick, "The Year in Review," *World Refugee Survey* (New York: U.S. Committee for Refugees, 1997), p. 14.

29. See Gervase Coles, "Approaching the Refugee Problem Today," in Gil Loescher and Laila Monahan (eds.), *Refugees and International Relations* (New York: Oxford University Press, 1989), pp. 373–410; UNHCR, 1995 Report, chapter 1.

30. See, among others, Commission for the Study of International Migration and Cooperative Economic Development, *Unauthorized Migration: An Economic Development Response* (Washington, DC, 1990).

31. Alan Dowty and Gil Loescher, "Refugee Flows as Grounds for International Action," *International Security* 21, 1 (1996): 43.

32. Quoted in Newland, "The Impact of U.S. Refugee Policies," p. 202.

33. See, among others, Karin Landgren, "Safety Zones and International Protection: A Dark Grey Area," *International Journal of Refugee Law* 7, 3 (July 1995): 436–458.

34. See UNHCR, 1997 Report, p. 146.

35. Nicholas Morris, "Protection Dilemmas and UNHCR's Response: A Personal View from within UNHCR," *International Journal of Refugee Law* 9, 3 (1997): 492–499.

36. UNHCR, 1997 Report, p. 195.

REFERENCES

Albuquerque Abell, Nazaré (1996). The Impact of International Migration on Security and Stability. *Canadian Foreign Policy Review* 4, 1: 83–109.

Braeckman, Colette (1996). *Terreur africaine. Burundi, Rwanda, Zaïre: les racines de la violence*. Paris: Fayard.

Castles, Stephen, and Mark J. Miller (1993). *The Age of Migration: International Population Movements in the Modern World*. London: Macmillan, 1993.

Ferris, Elizabeth G. (1993). *Beyond Borders: Refugees, Migrants and Human Rights in the Post–Cold War Era*. Geneva: WCC Publications.

Gordenker, Leon (1987). *Refugees in International Politics*. London: Croom Helm.

Jacobsen, Karen. Factors Influencing the Policy Responses of Host Governments to Mass Refugee Influxes. *International Migration Review* 30, 3: 655–678.

Joly, Danièle (1996). *Haven or Hell? Asylum Policies and Refugees in Europe*. London: Macmillan.

Loescher, Gil (1992). Refugee Movements and International Security. *Adelphi Papers*, No. 268. Oxford University Press for I.I.S.S.

——— (1993). *Beyond Charity: International Cooperation and the Global Refugee Problem*. New York: Oxford University Press.

Rogers, Rosemarie, and Emil Copeland (1993). *Forced Migration: Policy Issues in the Post–Cold War World*. Medford, MA: Fletcher School of Law and Diplomacy.

Stalker, Peter (1994). *The Work of Strangers: A Survey of International Labour Migration*. Geneva: International Labour Office.

Weiner, Myron (ed.) (1993). *International Migration and Security*. Boulder, CO: Westview Press.

——— (1995). *The Global Migration Crisis: Challenge to States and to Human Rights*. New York: HarperCollins.

Zolberg, Aristide et al. (1989). *Escape from Violence: Conflict and the Refugee Crisis in the Developing World*. New York: Oxford University Press.

CHAPTER 9

The Para-Modern Context
of Ethnic Nationalism

FRED W. RIGGS

THE FACES OF MODERNITY AND THE GAZE OF THIS CHAPTER

Modernity has two faces: its "ortho-modern," positive face includes all that we most admire and welcome; its "para-modern," negative face includes the side-effects that we most deplore and fear. These two aspects have accompanied each other from the very beginning of the main processes of modernity—which have included industrialism, democratization, and nationalism. Among para-modern aspects with far-reaching consequences are the imperial conquests by major powers, which not only competed with each other for the raw materials and markets required by their leading industries, but also imported some of the cultural treasures of the world's ancient civilizations. Nationalism, democracy, and economic growth were pursued in the imperial homelands. They were not practiced in the lands of imperial conquest—not until the very search for these goals led to liberation movements and made possible the rise of successor states whose often-haphazard boundaries were a sad legacy from the erstwhile imperial occupations. At the same time, interimperial rivalries (including the Cold War) led to global violence—in the process, weakening the empires and destroying their ability to hold on to their prized dominions.

Modern ethnicity has been shaped by para-modern processes. To date, widening ethnic cleavages—born from the artificiality of nations divided and from the multinationality of the states legated by the collapsed empires— have posed the most intractable problems, especially in states where anarchic conditions prevail and weak dictators cannot meet even the most basic needs of their subjects. By contrast, in modern democracies, usually—though not always—interethnic integration and harmonious relationships can flourish. As a para-modern phenomenon, ethnic nationalism creates deep cleavages. These cleavages can provoke civil wars, genocide, and terrorism. In the perspective offered here, there are a few foes but many victims. Modernity is easier to admire or to loathe than to fathom. It can have tragic consequences, one of which is bitter ethnic nationalism—the very subject of our analysis.

COMING TO TERMS WITH A MYTH

A widely accepted myth blinds us to the escalating and truly modern problematic nature of contemporary ethnic controversies. We allow ourselves to be puzzled by rumors of the revival of an ancient, non-modern phenomenon that—in our own imagination—was supposed to have been long since erased by the processes of modernity. Yet, and certainly in my view, the reverse scenario is more valid: Although culturally mixed, non-modern societies did not face insurmountable ethnic controversies. Rather, the very perception of multicultural problems as rooted in ethnicity and nationalism is, in and of itself, a remarkably modern phenomenon.

A recent essay rejects as myth the notion that contemporary ethnonational conflicts are rooted in age-old interethnic spite and rivalries. It dispels the belief that "ethnic groups lie in wait for one another, nourishing age-old hatreds and restrained only by powerful states. Remove the lid, and the caldron boils over" (Bowen, 1996: 3). While this notion needs to be rejected, it is necessary that we understand how modern ethnicity exploits such myths: Although Bowen does recognize that "global ethnic conflict" is a growing reality, he attributes it to leaders who are able to mobilize followers to help them cope with contemporary issues. And while this opinion is valid up to a certain point, we need to contemplate the phenomenon in greater historical depth. We need to go back several centuries into modern history in order to find a more thorough explanation.

Bowen's use of the term "ethnic conflict" is misleading. It suggests that ethnicity causes conflicts. I doubt that this is true. Instead, I think that many different kinds of conflict are seen today as "ethnic" when in reality they mask other problems—a fact that some other authors have recognized. One such author (Ryan, 1990: xvii) writes that "ethnic conflict . . . refers to the form the conflict takes, and is not meant to suggest that ethnicity is the cause of the conflict." Among these causes, he mentions expulsion from power, a sense of injustice, and fears that one's identity is threatened.

The term "ethnic conflict" is also misleading insofar as it implies conflicts between ethnic communities. In the modern context, the most fearsome of these conflicts arise when existing regimes are challenged by ethnonational movements. Actually, Bowen does acknowledge that most contemporary interethnic relations are non-violent and that many of them are even harmonious. But he fails to identify the forms of modern ethnicity that lead to the most dangerous conflicts. Although modern interethnic relations often do produce tensions, the most violent and devastating forms arise when members of an ethnic community claim sovereignty on the basis of self-determination—whether to reunite a divided nation or, rather, whether to secede from an existing state. Such claims produce tensions in any regime, including the most democratic, but their most violent results occur in weak states that are authoritarian. While strong authoritarian regimes can suppress dissent, weak ones cannot even solve the most basic problems of governance; they create immense spans of anarchy in which both the motives and opportunities for violent protests are, and remain, prevalent.

These conditions have become particularly widespread in the successor states of the modern industrial empires, namely, in the "third" and "second" worlds. But even the "first" world is not immune. The status and prospects of ethnic minorities in industrialized democracies are dreary. "Ethnic minorities currently participate in economic and/or political markets as disadvantaged actors . . . the intervention of the state and government in ethnic conflict is not always productive or benign . . . and such conflict will not significantly abate in the foreseeable future" (Rhodebeck, 1992: 279). But the existence or even the growth of conflicts rooted in ethnic diversity throughout the world does not contradict the fact that much interethnic integration and harmony exists and is on the increase, especially in the industrialized democracies.

The issues of ethnic conflict may be approached differently. The historical context of modernity may be a primary basis for ethnic nationalism. Yet, the prevalent interpretations regard ethnic conflict as a normal phenomenon throughout history. They see its contemporary manifestations to have merely become more visible since the end of the Cold War, because that event reduced the reach of the superpowers and enabled local conflicts to surface. But a few others (e.g., Gellner, 1983) do emphasize the links between modernity and nationalism.

It is often suggested that each local controversy has its own distinctive features. When we look at specific situations, whether in Bosnia, Rwanda, Somalia, Chechnya, Sri Lanka, Sudan, Cyprus, Northern Ireland, "Palestine"—or the Basque territory in Spain and the revolutionary movement centered in Chiapas, Mexico, for that matter—we can easily see that each of them does reflect its unique history, substance, and configuration.

The uniqueness of each case should not, however, obscure the shared features of many contemporary situations in which distinct politicized communal groups contend with each other or oppose the state. "Nearly three-quarters of the 127 largest countries in the world had at least one politicized minority in 1990 . . . 233 groups in 1990 had an estimated 915 million members, 17.3 percent of the global population" (Gurr, 1993: 10, 326). Gurr labels these groups as ethnonationalists, indigenous peoples, ethno-classes, militant sects, and communal contenders. Generically, he refers to them as "ethno-political" communities—most of which can be convincingly regrouped under "ethnic nationalism."

WOES OF THE PARA-MODERN

To explain the rise of ethnonationalist violence, we need an understanding of the global forces that have produced, during the last few centuries, our contemporary predicament. Although these long antedate the "Cold War," they are distinctively modern, or—in my own analytic-theoretical "languaging" of their reality (see Chapter 1), even more relevantly—"para-modern" in their making, character, and effect. Admittedly, I did coin this neologism to paraphrase the "negative side-effects of modernity." I offer it here in parsimonious focus on the negative aspects and side-effects of modernity, including those ethnic cleavages that tend to provoke local violence when driven by proliferating ethnonationalist movements. Its use helps me to insist on the irrefutably modern makings of contemporary ethnic controversies.

Since we are reluctant to recognize the unwanted results of modernization, we would rather attribute them to the past, to the hateful residues of "traditional" or "premodern" ways of acting and thinking. That is why the myth of primordialism persists. To recognize the negative side-effects of modernity is to confront a nemesis, to acknowledge the unavoidable consequence of our most vaunted achievements. Somehow, this threatens us. We would rather not create despair through self-indictment or self-recrimination, and not menace our highest achievements, or hurt our self-esteem.

In order to understand the modernity of ethnic conflicts, we need to recognize that, although multiculturalism is an ancient phenomenon, ethnicity was only rarely the focus of conflict in non-modern environments. It is modernity that has, relatively recently, pushed the notion to the forefront of our consciousness, turning it into a pretext, perhaps in order to rationalize the growingly bloody conflicts that today routinely plague the world.

Cultural Mixing

Going back thousands of years, all civilizations have been multicultural. Peoples with different cultural heritages have long coexisted and experienced acculturation. No doubt, primordial societies were monocultural, as hypothesized in many case studies by social anthropologists. But population movements, especially trade and urbanization, brought peoples with different cultural practices into contact with each other long ago, thereby generating multicultural relationships as the norm for exchange. In these contexts, cultural changes took place as the peoples in contact interacted with and influenced each other—sometimes by assimilating and changing their own cultures, often by becoming involved in conflicts based on economic, social, political, and other differences. However, they did not explain these conflicts in terms of ethnicity, nor would they have ordinarily resorted to ethnic nationalism or movements of self-determination for relief.

As kingdoms and empires arose in traditional civilizations, ethnic differences were indeed exploited by rulers, but rarely did they become a focus for organized competition and conflicts. When one people conquered another, sometimes they would establish systems of stratification. The strata created dominant elites and subordinates, conducive to conflicts between "masters" and "slaves" (subjects). Caste relationships became ritualized as each caste enforced and/or accepted traditionalized and/or legitimized rules of conduct. Those living on the margins of an expanding society fled to new lands, retreated to inaccessible enclaves, or resigned themselves to accepting assimilation. They did not conceptualize their intercultural relationships in terms of ethnicity. Indeed, contrasts would be drawn between civilized folks and barbarians, believers and infidels, settled peoples and nomadic groups. Yet, paradoxically, *ethnicos*, in its original Greek usage, identified members of one's own community. Only gradually did the attribute evolve into a slur reserved for outsiders: the heathen, infidels, barbarians, and aliens—also known as "foreigners."

In the manner of hierarchic ascriptive social relations and mystic beliefs in supernatural forces, marginalized communities typically accepted their fate (karma), trying to make the best of whatever opportunities came their way. They could not imagine the use of cultural difference as a pretext for organizing liberation movements or rebellions. Slave revolts were uncommon; and when they did occur, slaves rebelled as individuals against their masters, not as a racial or cultural community. Indeed, such groups were usually a mixture of peoples linked by their oppression. Even the Marxian slogan "workers of the world, unite!" relied not on some ethnic identity but on class solidarity. To fight their battles, kings often mobilized soldiers who were culturally different from most of their subjects. Monarchs would conceptualize or portray their conflicts with rival rulers in terms of different gods or rival domains, but not based on their cultural or national identities.

Multiculturalism in non-modern environments, therefore, involved social distinctions that were not based on ethnic differentiation or on differences between cultural communities. Sociopolitical strata and economic classes coexisted or fought each other, but not in order to assimilate minorities or to wrench their independence as nation-states. In historical terms, the Exodus of the Jews from Egypt might be viewed as an exception, but only when we superimpose our own ethnic categories on a community whose members sought escape from slavery under their religious leaders. In general, the wars, revolts, and conflicts found in non-modern environments involved rival elites, struggles against tyrants, nomads conquering settled peoples—

"causes" that are not conceptualized as ethnic struggles along cultural fault-lines.

Modernity

Modernity, by contrast, has imparted to ethnic identity and nationalism a live joint overlap with sociopolitical protest and action. By modernity is meant a way of life based on three major components: industrialism, democracy, and nationalism. Non-modern values and practices persist to the present day in all societies, and many contemporary societies are more non-modern than modern. Nonetheless, modernity has produced widespread ethnic cleavages.

Unfortunately, "modern" is often used to mean "contemporary," and therefore the two concepts need to be clearly distinguished: in a temporal sense, everyone on earth today is a contemporary, but in terms of lifestyle and values, many people are more non-modern (more "traditional") in outlook than they are modern. Of course, no sharp lines can be drawn: every contemporary has felt the impact of modernity to some degree. In an effort to maintain the distinction, I avoid using "modern" to mean "contemporary," and I eschew using "premodern"—although, admittedly, before the era of modernity, everyone was premodern, if in retrospect only. When thinking along the temporal dimension, we may speak of the past (as history) or of the present (as contemporary actuality). But modernity started only a few centuries ago (perhaps three at most), and its influence is now global in reshaping many ancient ways of life. Although they are ancient, only in our times have cultures been attributed self-conscious, self-propelling ethnic identities that can generate specifically modern forms of conflict.

To be more explicit about modernity, we may think of it as a way of thinking and acting, with innumerable causes and as many consequences. Modernity's skeletal structure comes into evidence when we focus on its fundamental constituents: industrialism, nationalism, and democracy. The underlying beliefs and material consequences linked with these features are all modern. In order to discuss their specific influences further below, we begin by distinguishing between three forms of modern ethnicity.

THE THREE FORMS OF MODERN ETHNICITY

Three modern forms of ethnicity have evolved, each important and distinctively different from the earlier (non-modern) forms of multiculturalism (ethnic differentiation) once prevalent, as described above. Each of these three forms is predicated on the post-Westphalian emergence and evolution of the modern state as of the mid-seventeenth century. Altogether, they constitute the three headings under which modern ethnicity can be intelligibly discussed: diversity, cleavage, and plurality.

In stressing citizenship for everyone living within their borders, modern states gave rise to notions of national identity and democracy. States grew strong through industrialism, a fruit of growing bourgeois power, which enabled capitalists to assure protection for their investments and, in some countries, even to create industrial empires.

Therefore, the three forms of modern ethnicity are shaped by the relationships of individuals to the state: *ethnic diversity* occurs when persons with different cultural traditions prefer to become citizens of the state wherein they live, usually accepting the ideal of a "national state" by which all citizens may share a common nationality. We may well identify this form of ethnicity as civic. Although prejudice and violence often mar relationships typical of civic ethnicity, congenial coexistence is possible.

Ethnic cleavages, by contrast, involve situations in which one or more than one ethnic community within a "national" state may choose to reject citizenship or to claim separate sovereignty, relying on the principles of "self-determination." Activists seek to mobilize members of their cultural community under the slogans of ethnic nationalism. Although the core membership of an ethnic nation normally lives on its ancient homeland, many are typically scattered outside that domain, in a diaspora. Some of them often even accept or assume leading positions in struggles seeking to establish (or reestablish) a national state for their people.

A third, fuzzier, concept—*ethnic plurality*—takes life and substance when cultural minorities are denied the opportunity to portray themselves as citizens and lack the territorial basis or solidary unity needed to claim status as a separate state. Once, typically, members of such communities migrated to wherever the need of industrial empires for laborers, miners, or plantation workers took them. As hired hands, they would be instrumental in the exploitation of new sources for the raw materials needed by the metropolis; as merchants, they would be able to establish their own subsistence communities despite outside market forces. Because of their precarious condition, they can be thought of as pariah communities. We might even use the term "limbo ethnicity" more correctly to characterize their marginal status in many liberated countries. Some of their members—intellectuals and workers—have discovered cause and inclination to join revolutionary movements, whereas others—some of them affluent merchants—have chosen to protect their property by collaborating with the dominant elites. In some countries, like Guyana, revolutionary activists have even become rulers; in others, like Uganda, they have been expelled.

In order to understand the origins of modern ethnicity—as expressed in diversity, cleavages, and plurality—we would need to consider the three underlying forces of modernity: industrialism, democracy, and nationalism. These three basic factors of modernity are like strands in a rope: intertwined into an end-product that is stronger than any of them on their own, each features its own distinguishing history and contributory characteristics. When twisted together, they create the foundation for modern states to evolve. Concurrently, they also create the very settings for modern ethnicity. Evolving in quasi-parallel fashion, they have reinforced each other. It makes no sense to ask which came first or "caused" the others. We could discuss them in any order, but they are discussed here in the following sequence.

INDUSTRIALISM

Historically, capitalism played a fundamental role in the rise of industrialism, but the two phenomena are quite different. Capitalism has existed for several millennia among traders and in market cities throughout the world. It is not specifically modern (Curtin, 1984). Capitalists did make the Industrial Revolution possible. But so did the kings who chose to endorse mercantilist partnerships with merchants in order to finance their ascendant statal power, after the treaty of Westphalia brought the feudal age to an end. It was the political empowerment of capitalists (the "bourgeoisie") during the period of mercantilism that permitted industrialism to emerge. Thereafter, industrialism would gain a life of its own, acquiring the capacity to expand in any modern state, with or without the support of capitalism. The technological achievements of modernity, modern science included, are the fruits of industrialism that could not have been produced by pre-industrial capitalists. Today, they are universally valued (Polanyi, Arensberg, and Pearson, 1957; Riggs, 1994) even in countries unable to support industrial production.

Traditionally, capitalists were members of ethnic minorities and, as such, politically marginalized. Although this phenomenon has often been described, its fullest significance (Zenner, 1991) has yet to be appreciated. They were not merchants because of their minority status: it is their economic priorities that marginalized them in societies where power—land ownership and an image of righteousness—were prized. Those who lacked such elite values could engage only in low-status occupations. Traders with external connections could engage in such functions for the purpose of acquiring wealth, provided that they accepted the need to abide by and assume the non-threatening status expected of all outsiders. Some could and did assimilate, even though this meant abandoning trade and adopting elite values. Outsiders who could not—or would not—assimilate, remained politically marginalized.

The evolution to modernity, therefore, involved the pivotal role of empowered capitalists. When, under conditions prevalent in Western Europe, entrepreneurs and inventors gained power but chose to remain capitalists, their ethnic particularism gave way to bourgeois nationalism. They fueled the struggle for democracy, and they led the Industrial Revolution. To recognize their pivotal role, however, is not to equate capitalism with modernity: They made industrialism possible—of which the fruits outnumber the causes by far, as detailed elsewhere (Riggs, 1994) at length.

Industrial Empires

Industrialism did not merely contribute to democracy and to nationalism. It also drove certain modern states into becoming empires. Each such empire expanded its industrial base by gaining secure access to larger markets but also to richer sources of raw materials. Industrialism enabled noncapitalist elites to acquire more of the treasured products of foreign civilizations—cotton, silk, chinaware, spices, and a host of other valuables—that they had been hitherto able to acquire only by paying for them in rare metals (gold, silver) or in raw materials such as opium, ginseng, or sandalwood. But industrialism also led to bigger and harsher conflicts between the industrial empires themselves. These would culminate in the "Cold War" waged between two superpowers who had survived the devastation of World War II. The contemporary world situation can best be understood, as a result of the rise of these modern empires, their prolonged and violent wars, and their final collapse.

The collapse of the empires, however, did not bring the end of industrialism. The successor states that emerged on the ashes of the collapsed industrial empires were determined to secure the benefits of industrialism for themselves, whether or not they had the capacity to sustain the modern processes of production needed to such ends. Development and modernity would be equated with the universal dream of economic success. (See Chapters 3, 4, and 6.) But the many obstacles left on site by the retreating empires would not permit industrialization to take root in most of the successor states emerging on the lands once spanned by these meanwhile fading former industrial empires.

Consider the ethnic consequences of imperial conquests: many tribes were mixed together in the new states even as some ethnic nations were divided between different states. Weak authoritarian rule competing with anarchy over expanses where despots could not even control their own provided incentives and opportunities for warlords and criminal gangs to thrive in many of these successor states (see Chapter 10). The more ambitious among the frustrated leaders would try to set up resistance movements. Anarchy has a way of motivating ethnopolitical revolts, even of legitimizing balky demands for self-determination and sovereignty and for the reunification of peoples divided by imperial conquest, as history books abundantly illustrate.

The inter-state causes and consequences of ethnic conflicts are still not widely recognized by specialists on international relations. Yet, "ethnic conflict can have a major impact on the interstate system" (Ryan, 1990: xv). Although some writings concern themselves with the beneficial role of the international system in resolving ethnic conflicts and in protecting minorities

(Ryan, 1990: 119–173), many do not explain the processes by which the modern inter-state system, centered on the ambitions of rival empires, has gone on to create the context in which ethnonatio..al conflicts have now emerged as a salient problem in world affairs.

Migrations

Another effect of industrialism is economically motivated migration. This increases the degree of multicultural mixing and ethnoracial marginalization. When the newly launched factories in Britain required large quantities of cotton to manufacture cloth, this generated a demand for plantation workers. And that drove the slave trade. Europeans aside, even the conquered masses would be unwilling to perform the arduous work on plantations and in mines that industrialism required. Yet they would not accept the poverty it entailed. When the American Civil War, followed by the emancipation, produced a large number of "freed" slaves, these groups turned into a marginalized racial (ethnic) minority that in time would create the United States' most acute ethnic controversy. Chinese would be brought to California to do manual labor in building railways. Plantation workers would come from Japan, Korea, and the Philippines to help grow sugar in Hawaii and elsewhere. In turn and in time, they, too, would create major contemporary controversies involving "Asian-Americans."

Throughout the domains of the modern empires, manual workers such as miners and plantation and construction hands were imported to help supply the factors of production and infrastructures most needed by expanding factories. Some became millers and processed agricultural products. Others became merchants operating village stores: peasants living on a subsistence basis could not become customers for factory-made products; they did become consumers when outsiders set up shops in their villages. But now they also needed to grow new cash crops in order to secure the money needed to buy goods at village stores. Traditional reciprocity in such societies would lead to the ostracizing of any community member who demanded money in exchange for merchandise. Merchants willing to lend money at high interest and to finance production would come to be seen as cruel usurers. Following independence, some alien minorities would become scapegoats and even face eviction—as did the Indians in Uganda or the Chinese in Indonesia. The causes and consequences of ethnic plurality need far more attention in the extant literature. In Chapter 8 in this volume, they emerge as a specific modern element among the many complex interactive dimensions of future insecurity.

Products of Industrialism

A third dimension of industrialism that contributes to the violence of ethnonationalist revolts stems from the goods and services that modern industry provides. The mass production and distribution of weapons of deadly violence arms both terrorists and ethnonationalists. True, the supply of assault weapons does not compel anyone to use them, but their easier availability does enable rebels to develop and sustain lethality.

Industrialism also created new modes of communication, not least of which was the Internet, which now eases the organization of resistance movements (see Chapters 3 and 7). It produced new modes of large-scale organization available to all—private enterprise, voluntary associations, political parties, multinational corporations, states, and ethnonational movements. Modern means of transport permit long-distance migration as well as greater mobility of labor, entrepreneurship, or cost-effective conveyance of manufactures and raw materials. All of these fruits of industrialism facilitate and invigorate the rise and revolts of ethnic nationalism. They are prime parameters that make ethnic nationalism possible. By themselves, they neither "cause" nor "determine" outcomes, however. A fuller explanation requires that we now look at the other major dimensions of modernity: democracy and nationalism.

DEMOCRACY

The most important rationale for the emergence of modern ethnicity may be the unintended consequences of democratization. When monarchic authoritarianisms gave in to democratic populisms, notions of human equality were to inform electoral practices that empowered citizens. That very project would end up angering those subjects who felt betrayed when promises of empowerment instead produced the bitter realities of marginalization and oppression. From the very start, the positive achievements of democratization were countered by the frustrations born of capitalist oppression and imperialist tyranny. The humiliations and hardships that were stoically tolerated under traditional monarchies could no longer be tolerated with the ascent and dissemination of democratic values.

Ideally, democracies promise to accommodate the true needs and just demands of all of their peoples. Undoubtedly, they best succeed when elected representatives uphold and defend the needs of enfranchised citizens. But these same democratic values also spur on the mobilization of marginalized peoples—the frustrated proletarians, the disillusioned peasants, the increasingly vocal cultural, and growingly self-aware racial, minorities among them.

For as long as sovereignty was vested in kings and emperors whose supernatural powers were thought to bring health, wealth, and peace to all peoples under their rule, revolts were viewed as sacrilegious provocations more likely to precipitate divine fury and retribution than to provide worldly benefits. If traditional hierarchic notions did legitimize gross inequities among varying cultural communities, castes, and classes, they were still unable to provide a rationale for self-determining ethnic nationalisms.

The shift from monarchism to democracy would propagate the acceptance of the new equalitarian norms—those proclaimed in the American Declaration of Independence ("We hold these truths to be self-evident: That all men are created equal"), for example. While this revolutionary doctrine has always clashed (see Chapters 6 and 11) with actual practice, it nonetheless offered inspiration, becoming an ideal for the marginalized peoples: Why, they asked, were they still so very "self-evidently" unequal?

As universal suffrage and social mobility progressed, so did the mobilization of oppressed minorities advance: starting with the "proletarians" under socialist/communist leadership; and then over the past 50 years, continuing with feminist, ethnic, and racial minorities as well. The leadership of such movements would simply proclaim democratic values to justify their protests and demands. In America, the civil rights movement—epitomized by Martin Luther King's "I Have a Dream" speech on August 28, 1963— would bring to a long-delayed, if still incomplete, fruition this most complex aspiration in the American Dream. And all around the world, Abraham Lincoln's "Emancipation Proclamation" continues to be celebrated as a call for marginalized peoples everywhere now to rise up and to demand their rights. Any discrepancy, therefore, between what the United States says and does, and how and why so, on human rights (see Chapter 11) can and surely will greatly affect transnational security in a globalizing international setting.

True, new social groups—identified by "ethnic, religious, or regional categories"—were recognized by the colonial powers, and many of those were given preferential treatment. True, this did provide a basis for self-identification, which subsequently would enable them to "act in concert, as political groups with common interests." And, equally true, "(t)hese shared interests have been those of political autonomy, access to education and jobs, and control of local resources" (Bowen, 1996: 7). However, "(f)ar from reflecting ancient ethnic or tribal loyalties, their cohesion and action are [mere] products of the modern state's demand that people make themselves heard."

Although these facts are true enough, they merely focus on the effects of imperialism, without so much as recognizing that democratic values were inculcated by imperial authorities. Modern empires did not create the ethnic distinctions. These already did exist among conquered peoples. It is the democratic principles available to their own citizens that acquired a new meaning when some subjects began to wonder why they could not enjoy the very same rights. It is aspirations of the kind that would inform the liberation movements of the 1960s and that are likely to continue to inspire ethnic minorities seeking equal rights for themselves in the century ahead. In the domain of ethnic conflicts, democracy is both motivator and resolution mechanism (Riggs, 1995, 1997).

Insofar as constitutionalism prevails and states are really democratic, newly mobilizing peoples can use non-violent methods to voice their demands through political parties and elections. By contrast, when weak authoritarians—especially members of a dominant minority—seize power, marginalized communities have both the opportunity and the motives to use violence. The efforts of weak dictators (to suppress dissent through terror, genocide, and police mafias) that used to uphold their rule now can only generate whiplash responses likely to reinforce wider dissidence.

Exponents of democracy "as a road to justice" for oppressed peoples need to see that the rhetoric and values of democracy, when not realized in practice, provide a rationale for protest movements. An even fuller understanding of modern ethnicity would require, however, that we now add the strand of nationalism to those of democracy and industrialism.

NATIONALISM

The most overt motivation for contemporary ethnonational movements, nationalism, was originally promoted by state elites and intellectuals who saw in it a motor for assimilation and nation-building. This goal also appeared to be a requisite for the success of both industrialization and democratization. The evolution of modernity was rendered possible by state nations able to promote the dream of a national state. Democratic leaders recognized that "majority rule" would be acceptable to minorities only when the minorities saw themselves as members of the nation, and industrialists wanted workers and managers to share those common values that benefit coordinated tasks in large-scale enterprises.

Once the need for raw materials and markets of the newly empowered capitalists led to the creation of modern empires, it would not be long before the dream of national independence would become the engine for liberation movements and for the throng of successor states that followed. But just as the democratization of the center areas reflected the urge to replace royal domain with popular sovereignty, so would anti-imperialist movements of liberation seek to link nationalism and equalitarianism in their drive for self-determination.

The colonial powers knew that "given their small numbers in their dominions, they could effectively govern and exploit only by seeking out 'partners' from among local people" (Bowen, 1996: 6). This tactic created "firmly bounded 'ethnic groups' "; but perhaps it also empowered privileged minorities who would often become rulers after independence. Too often, these new heads of state would quickly come to be viewed as oppressors by the newly marginalized majorities who, to their dismay, would discover they had exchanged exotic masters for indigenous authoritarians.

Ironically, the leaders of national liberation movements as well could quickly transform themselves into dominant minorities and begin to be feared as the new oppressors in many countries.

It would not be long before these ruling minorities became the target of second-generation self-determination movements that sought to partition multinational states or to reunite separated nations. Such protests and revolts fostered ethnic cleavages. The alienated members of marginalized communities mobilized to demand independence. In the absence of any democratic and effective governance, the preconditions of ethnic diversity based on a shared sentiment of solidarity with the new state simply failed to materialize. There are too few works on the influence of diaspora communities in world politics—an aspect that deserves much more attention than it has so far received.

Diasporas

Even the most authoritarian state cannot prevent some people from leaving, try as they may to block emigration. Living abroad, in dispersion (diaspora), refugees are able to escape the harsh rule of their homelands but do not forget those they left behind.

At the micro-level of family solidarity, "remittances" to relatives and friends, political activism designed to accelerate fundamental changes in the homeland—thus support of secessionist or revolutionary movements and sometimes of governments resisting such movements—are common. All the forces of modernity impinge on these activities, helping to shape diaspora politics.

In addition to their influence back home, diaspora members often intervene politically in their host country to influence its foreign policy on behalf of their allies and friends. Ethnic nationalism sometimes originates outside a home territory among members of a diaspora who feel obligations and see opportunities that arise as a result of their dispersal. The extent to which members of a diaspora involve themselves in the politics of their homelands is influenced to some extent by the level of acceptance or rejection to which they are exposed in the hostlands that may or may not help them to integrate or even repel them through mean discrimination.

Power plays between rival factions within a diaspora may greatly complicate the dynamics of diaspora politics. Dual, or overlapping, ethnicity is now increasingly also common and awaits to be recognized as a dimension of ethnic nationalism that will expand as the number of refugees and free migrants made possible by the evolution of the modern world system also grows.

The migration of peoples around the world is increasing as a result of all three active aspects of modernity: industrialism, democracy, and nationalism. This means that the number of ethnic minorities in almost every country of the world will accordingly increase. In addition to all the domestic problems created by this process, students of ethnicity need to consider the role played by diaspora peoples in the growth of ethnic nationalism.

The creation of Israel in response to the tragic experiences of Jews in many countries is a most notable example of a diaspora creating a nation. Today, the role of diasporas in international politics is becoming more important because "(s)tates that have close affective links with ethnic groups in another state will often not remain indifferent to the fate of these groups" (Ryan, 1990: 35). Diasporas warrant an active research agenda.

OVERLAPS

All three strands of the rope of modernity merge to produce modern ethnicity whose main forms also overlap. We cannot draw a sharp line between diversity and cleavages, they often interact and reinforce each other. For example, the violence generated by ethnic cleavages often generates torrents of refugees fleeing "ethnic cleansing." Some refugees settle as immigrants in a hostland where they can become naturalized citizens, eventually blending into a pattern of ethnic diversity. Looking back to their homelands, some may also join externally driven movements in order to politicize and reinforce ethnic revolts in the land they fled.

Migrants can also become accelerators: facing nationalist prejudice and exclusion in their hostlands, they become fierce nationalists in homeland politics. Facing a democratic acceptance that fosters cultural integration in the context of ethnic diversity, they may forget their anger and forgo extreme homeland activism.

Political transformations, especially those generated by the collapse of modern empires, can transform civic ethnicity into ethnic nationalism: Under Ottoman and British rule, Arab and Jew coexisted in relative harmony. The creation of Israel as a Jewish homeland in accordance with a U.N. partition plan, the armed opposition that lost its first war and led to the flight of some of the mainly Muslim Arab populace, the creation and sustenance in some Arab countries of refugee camps for the displaced and the self-exiled, and the role of these camps in creating a Palestinian national identity and in exacerbating the passions over several angry generations have not only intensified old enmities and led to several armed confrontations, but thereby have also hardened the bitter differences lingering since 1948 and still needing to be settled.

In Cyprus, too, the clash between Greeks and Turks is modern and follows from that island's independence from British rule in 1960. The dormant intercommunal tensions were accelerated, with armed support and nationalist rhetoric coming first from Greece and then from Turkey, and also from Cypriot activists on both sides, leading to physical partition and de facto separate governance.

Efforts by ethnic nationalists to create a national state can lead to violent repression of minorities. "Ethnic cleansing" became genocide in the hands of Serb militants. And the nascent Croatian regime "moved quickly to define Serbs as second-class citizens, fired Serbs from the police and military, and placed the red-and-white 'checkerboard' of the Nazi-era Ustashe flag in the new Croatian banner" (Bowen, 1996: 9) in former Yugoslavia. But the reverse process is also possible. Under the terms of the Dayton Accord, with international supervision, the now-fractured community of Bosnians may eventually regain the relative harmony it had before rival Serb, Croat, and Muslim leaders tore it down.

The dispositions of stay-at-homes also can fluctuate. The different cultures that have peacefully coexisted for generations in situations of ethnic pluralism may, under modern pressures, become mobilized and polarized by rival ethnic elites, producing cleavages marked by genocidal attacks—as in Rwanda, for example.

CLEAVAGES VERSUS DIVERSITY

The distinction between these two forms of modern ethnicity, based on attitudes toward citizenship in the place or country of residence, is often left vague. The three forces of modernity—industrialism, democracy, and nationalism—have somehow reconstituted relations between members of different cultural communities on the basis of ethnicity, using citizenship and the democratic norm of "self-determination" as root criteria.

Diversity is generated by migrations that bring people with diverse cultural backgrounds together—typically, in modern cities and in democratic states. Tensions and misunderstandings coexist with ethnic diversity, but they do not normally generate violence. Exceptions comprise pogroms, genocide, and urban riots directed against minorities or their persecutors. But these conflicts do not involve nationalist claims for sovereignty. Modern democracy can, and does, do everything possible to overcome the prejudices and conflicts that generate violence. Like traditional forms of multiculturalism, ethnic diversity need not become the cause or pretext for sustained violence.

By contrast, violence is a likely, if not always necessary, consequence of ethnic cleavages: The assertion that "(p)rotracted and violent ethnic conflict can be defined as conflicts between ethnic groups, which have been going on for some time . . . appear to be insoluble to the parties caught up in them, and . . . result in a significant loss of life or in a serious denial of basic human rights" (Ryan, 1990: xvii) fails to explain what it identifies.

Especially in countries with democratic inclinations, ethnic nationalism can be accommodated without violence. In the former Czechoslovakia, nonviolent means were found to permit the Slovak peoples to become an independent state by ceding their part of an existing state. When Bangladesh broke away from Pakistan, great violence occurred, even if peaceful relations have been restored since. The dissolution of the Soviet Union was accomplished with relatively little violence, though it was a highly traumatic and long-resisted transformation. In Cyprus and Somalia, there occurred de facto partitions, even if these received no formal recognition.

Conversely, divided nations can be reunited. Germany was reunited following the collapse of the East German regime. A hairier scenario may await the divided Korean and Chinese peoples: when and if they reunite, will it be through peace or violence?

AUTONOMY AND REVOLTS

Administrative autonomy within the boundaries of an existing state is an option that can permit different ethnic nations to coexist within the same boundaries. In 1980, the Catalans and Basques were granted autonomy. Some Basques continue to fight for independence, but Spain seems to have found a good accommodation with its national minorities. In the continental United States, many indigenous peoples have virtual autonomy as self-governing nations—but in other cases, as in Hawaii, the struggle for sovereignty on behalf of the Hawaiian people has intensified in recent years. Tensions between the Maori people and New Zealand also go on, unabated, albeit articulated in a non-violent way.

Comprehensive data on the "ethno-political" minorities now struggling for independence or autonomy can be found in the data compiled by Ted Gurr (1993). Almost all of the violence sustained and the civil wars waged on grounds of ethnic nationalism seem to concentrate in countries where ethnic cleavages linger or emerge, even if the existence of cleavages does not always yield violence and, overall, non-violent cleavages may outnumber violent ones. All ethnic cleavages could erupt into violence. But if adequate steps are taken to mitigate the needs and the sense of injustice that prevails among ethnic nations, much violence can be avoided.

Democracies are more likely to find non-violent ways to cope with their ethnic cleavages than authoritarian regimes. However, among the authoritarian states, there is a wide gap between those that are firmly governed by a single political party and those in which weak despotic rule prevails. In the former, police state disciplines can suppress ethnic nationalism and create a facade of unity. If and when such a state collapses—as was the case in the Soviet Union and Yugoslavia—ethnic cleavages surface in ways that resemble what has already happened in the successor states of all the other collapsed industrial empires.

CONCLUSION

Primordial rivalries between different communities do not explain the contemporary increase in violence attributable to ethnicity, but myths about them arm the activists promoting modern ethnic nationalism. It is wrong to imagine that ethnic conflict has always been a world problem. Multiculturalism is ancient. The deep cleavages generated by ethnic nationalism are modern and growing. Some contemporary manifestations of ethnic nationalism in the form of ethnic diversity have become increasingly problematic. These problems have complex explanations. Ethnicity is more a symptom than a cause. The following considerations may help explain the complex interactive dimensions at play here.

First, modern processes—industrialism, democratization, and nationalism—have created many post-imperial regimes that cannot satisfy the urgent needs of their national minorities. One tragic consequence has been the rise of ethnic nationalism as a violent force in contemporary world politics. Leaders of ethnonationalist movements often invoke ancient symbols and myths in order to mobilize their followers: these legends do not explain the movements that are rooted in modernity, even if they do help leaders to mobilize followers and to create deep-seated ethnic cleavages that defy peaceful resolution.

Second, the world today is increasingly crowded with peoples of diverse cultural backgrounds and histories who live peacefully together under conditions of ethnic diversity. Although frictions abound in these contexts, they normally can be overcome without violent confrontations. To the degree that states are democratic and responsive to the just needs of the peoples living within their boundaries, they will, I believe, find non-violent solutions for their ethnic problems, including ways to integrate cultural minorities into the mainstream of their political economies.

Nevertheless, many regimes are so inflexible about political boundaries and so undemocratic in their governance that they cannot satisfy the legitimate needs of ethnic communities under their rule. The rise of ethnic nationalism and terrorism (see Chapter 10), therefore, often results from the misguided policies of recognized states as much as from the angry claims of minorities for national unification involving boundary changes or for self-determination made possible only by secession from an existing state or through grants of autonomy within such a state.

Third, in addition to the cleavages from ethnic nationalism and to the diversity from civic ethnicity—the two most salient forms of modern cultural pluralism—an important third form needs to be studied as a different and very serious problematic dimension. It involves communities formed by colonial migrations ("plural societies") in which many minorities continue to experience prejudice and discrimination but cannot, because of their lack of territory and historical myths, make sustainable or acceptable claims either to a separate national identity or to total integration as citizens of the country where they reside.

Fourth, modernity has generated both the motives and the means for increasingly large numbers of people to migrate and live in diasporas. Although most of them do integrate within the societies where they settle, many retain sentimental, economic, and political ties with their homelands. And this leads them to become active in world politics and in their homeland's affairs.

Finally, it is an error to think of modern ethnic protests and ethnonational movements as a "revival" or "resurgence" of ancient struggles rooted in historic myths. We need to realize that "global ethnic conflict" is real enough to threaten world peace and to open a new chapter in world politics. Conventional theories of international relations focus on conflicts between rival states and empires. These conflicts have preoccupied the world for two or three centuries, during which the modern state—at once industrial, democratic, and national—developed and gave rise to a half-dozen globe-girdling empires, whose rivalries were a major reason for the great wars fought over the last 100 years.

The collapse of these empires in the aftermath of World Wars I and II, and in the wake of the Cold War, has radically altered the global arena, even if preoccupation with military security (see the Introduction) and with the risk of inter-state wars scarcely recognizes the new realities. In this late-modern era, the threats to world peace will more and more come from feuds between ethnic nations and states. These tensions will typically involve efforts by mobilized ethnonational communities to achieve their sovereignty, whether by secession or by autonomy within a state, or by changing state boundaries to permit national reunification. They will rarely involve conflicts between states or between ethnic communities.

Fueled by all three forces of modernity—industrialism, democracy, and nationalism—such ethnonational conflicts will, as generators of global tensions, become of growing major concern to the world community of states and to their leaders. They will serve as incubator for new forms of international organization and public policy, which will include humanitarian and military interventions in the world's most troubled zones of conflict (Riggs, 1996). Increasingly, regional and global organizations will assume functions hitherto monopolized by states and by substate entities, public and private, becoming more active and more important. For ethnonational conflicts are not only symptomatic of para-modernity; they are also able to reshape the modern world as only the fruit of our civilization's para-modern syndrome can.

REFERENCES

Bowen, J. R. (1996). The Myth of Global Ethnic Conflict. *Journal of Democracy 7*, 4: 3–14.
Curtin, P. D. (1984). *Cross-Cultural Trade in World History*. Cambridge: Cambridge University Press.
Gellner, Ernest (1983). *Nations and Nationalism*. Oxford: Blackwell.

Gurr, Ted Robert (1993). *Minorities at Risk: A Global View of Ethnopolitical Conflicts*. Washington, DC: U.S. Institute of Peace Press. Updated records available on the World Wide Web at: http://www.bsos.umd.edu/cidcm/mar.

Polanyi, Karl, Conrad M. Arensberg, and Harry W. Pearson (1957). *Trade and Markets in Early Empires*. Glencoe, IL: The Free Press.

Rhodebeck, Laurie A. (1992). Conclusion. Pp. 279–296 in Anthony M. Messina, Luis R. Fraga, Laurie A. Rhodebeck, and Frederick D. Wright (eds.), *Ethnic and Racial Minorities in Advanced Industrial Democracies*. Westport, CT: Greenwood Press.

Riggs, Fred W. (1994). Ethnonationalism, Industrialism and the Modern State. *Third World Quarterly* 15, 4: 583–611.

———— (1995). Ethnonational Rebellions and Viable Constitutionalism. *International Political Science Review* 16, 14: 375–404.

———— (1996). Turmoil among Nations. Available on the World Wide Web at: http://www2.hawaii.edu/~fredr/6-tan5a.htm.

———— (1997). Coping with Modernity: Constitutional Implications. Paris: UNESCO *MOST Policy Paper*. Available on the World Wide Web at: http://www2.hawaii.edu/~fredr/6mstza.htm.

Ryan, Stephen (1990). *Ethnic Conflict and International Relations*. Aldershot, UK: Dartmouth Publishing Co.

Zenner, Walter P. (1991). *Minorities in the Middle: A Cross-Cultural Analysis*. Albany: State University of New York Press.

CHAPTER 10

Terror and Organized Crime:
Old Fears, New Foes, Newer Threats

ROBERT J. JOHNSTON

BACKDROP

The political and economic spaces, which have burst open with the implosion of the USSR since the fall of world communism, have been exposed to a shift of power from the political to the economic arena. Across Eastern Europe and Latin America, authoritarian regimes have collapsed, taking with them the internal repression, foreign adventurism, and economic nationalism with which they were so often characterized. In China, Turkey, Mexico, and Indonesia, the old order is crumbling under the strain of global market forces. The new regimes in these emerging markets are in pursuit of investment capital and technology with the same fervor that their predecessors sought military might and diplomatic prestige. The changes in the nature of the world economy brought about by globalization have reconfigured the array of fears, foes, and threats that affect the ways and means of international security affairs (see Chapters 6 and 7 in this volume).

The transfiguration of the Soviet regime and of other Second and Third World autocracies into fractious, quasi-pluralistic emerging markets has shattered the East-West/state-state taxonomy that characterized the international security environment during the Cold War. Many of the actors in the Cold-War system have broken free of their superpower patrons: among them, terrorist groups, client states, arms brokers, and covert operators that pursue their own political agendas and interests, which are now increasingly commercial in content. These actors flourish in the emerging markets, where the rule of law is weak or inadequate and the disabled, often corrupt, collapsed or collapsing, remnants of the old regimes encourage the disdain, dismissal, or sacrifice of longer-term national interest for shortest-term individual gain.

The new taxonomy of international security includes more subtle linkages among suprastate, substate, and state actors, in varied combinations, at variable levels of aggregation. Unlike the Cold-War period, the transnational threats of today cannot be managed strictly within a state-state framework of international security relations. These threats do not merely challenge "the state." Like the broader process of globalization, they tend to disturb the world system of states as a whole (see Introduction and Chapters 3, 4, 5, 8, 9, and 11 in this volume).

This chapter integrally expands the complex array of international security concerns in the global political economy: The dual processes of democratization and marketization are now making it more difficult to fight terrorism and organized crime in many of the emerging markets. Within an interdependent global political economy, the consequences of terrorism and organized crime in the emerging markets cannot but impact the industrially advanced democracies through transnational networks. In their novel roles and relationships, democratized countries should gain in forming institutions of transnational law, along with networks of law enforcement and intelligence, in order more effectively to address transnational crime and terrorism. This process, already under way yet proceeding ever so slowly and prudently, is impeded mainly by circumstances where the vestiges of national interest in general and the exigencies of competitive commercial interests in particular may tend to discourage such transnational measures of international cooperation. The matter merits urgent attention.

GLOBALIZATION AND INSECURITY IN THE EMERGING MARKETS

The emerging markets are those countries that have recently begun to integrate into the global political economy (Garten, 1996). These countries face a dual challenge: overcoming their pasts and adapting to the future. On the one hand, the emerging-market nations are struggling to adapt to the requirements of the global political economy. They understand that in order fully to take part in the global political economy, they must commit to, and demonstrate, movement toward the established standards of the democratic countries for trade, arms control, human rights, and the environment, among other goals (Desai, 1997). On the other hand, in many such (re-) industrializing nations, the legacy of newly expired or now fading regimes has undermined such orientations.

Within some of the emerging markets, the collapse or the weakening of the old regime fuels new conflict and collaboration among domestic actors of dubious report—elements of organized crime, corrupt remnants of the state apparatus, rogue regional officials, members of the state's security apparatus, and some business sectors. The weakness of the political system in such emerging markets often fosters, and is sustained by, collusions and conspiracies among these actors, thereby further imperiling the growth of democracy and of free markets in these countries.

The central impediment to meeting industrialized nation's standards is that many of the emerging-market nations lack, to various degrees, institutions and mechanisms capable of enforcing the rule of law throughout the private sector, civil society, and even the government (Carothers, 1998). Economies-in-transition—those turning from communism to capitalism, as in Russia, Poland, Ukraine, Vietnam, and China—are struggling to replace or reform old political structures and to adapt to the norms, standards, and criteria that will help make possible their participation in the global political economy (Woo, Parker, and Sachs, 1997). Other countries—Brazil, Colombia, Mexico, Venezuela, Indonesia, South Africa, and Turkey among them— are struggling to shore up their fractious, nascent democracies, while yet others are still merely toying with the idea of taking a step toward democratic rule.

The underlying difficulty common to all of these regimes is their relative inability to enforce the rule of law. Most regimes in such emerging markets lack or reject the authoritarian power of their autocratic predecessors who could swiftly suspend civil liberties in the name of stable order, dominate and control civil society through martial law, impose censorship, resort to arrests and detentions, utilize death squads, and inflict other forms of intimidation, often principally to protect their own positions. Globalization has eroded the effectiveness of these tools and the power of the closed regimes that wielded them. Now, authoritarian regimes find it more difficult to hide their domestic repression in a world animated by faxes, E-mail, satellites, and the Internet linking the free to the liberated and the oppressed.

Authoritarian regimes also have been weakened through the expansion of global investment and production. Quite ironically, multinational corporations seriously considering investment in the emerging markets require more open regimes even as they insist on their hosts' concrete guarantees for the physical safety of their expatriate employees. As multinational corporations continue to shun authoritarian regimes for fear of bad publicity, boycotts, and media campaigns, early-authoritarian tools have been replaced by post-authoritarian, newly democratic governments like Poland, South Africa, and Brazil, or decreased by such late-authoritarian governments as Indonesia and China—for fear that overt exercise of such depleted means may generate a dangerous backlash, posited both in the form of domestic revolt and international opprobrium.

The weakening, and in some cases the collapse, of the prevalent authoritarian order in most emerging markets has left a "power vacuum" in many of them. In the emerging markets, the new regimes take on several forms, even if almost all of them have yet to attain the legally enforceable societal standards of the fully democratized nations. Most are discovering that not all the forces unleashed within civil societies upon the dissolution of the authoritarian order are benign and that many post-authoritarian social forces are even contributing to increased corruption and criminality. Emerging-market nations are finding that the absence of the rule of law is undermining political and economic development and is retarding accession to the rules-based political and economic system of the democratic nations. The country snapshots offered hereafter provide some representative examples and thus also a relevant basis for our specific concerns and related conclusions.

Russia

The collapse of the Soviet Union and world communism has been amply documented (Aslund, 1995; Matlock, 1995), as has the subsequent rise of crime and corruption in post–Soviet Russia and the Newly Independent States (Blasi, Kroumova, and Kruse, 1997; Handelman, 1994). Despite its high formal powers, the central government in Moscow remains vulnerable to the maneuvers of a "criminal syndicalist state": a "troika" of "corrupt officials, shady businessmen, and outright criminals" (Cilluffo and Burke, 1997: 26), which has come to imbibe the newer power structures that now control both the political and economic domains of activity in Russia.

These newer power structures combine the vestiges of the old authoritarian order with the country's ascendant elements. The Russian organized crime groups are controlled by gangsters who mastered criminal operations and formed criminal networks while in Soviet prisons. These gangsters formed relationships with corrupt officials during the last years of the Soviet era, when the black market was key to economic survival in Russia (Sterling, 1994). The collapse of the Soviet Union helped to solidify these networks and to extend them with veterans of the KGB and of the Soviet armed forces (Knight, 1996).

With the collapse of Soviet-era institutions, of their modes of governance and transactional practices, prospective political and business leaders struck alliances, establishing power centers where they could. Often, this led to arrangements with organized crime groups known as *krysha*. When and as needed, these *krysha*, or "roofs," provide armed protection, contacts to financiers, and privileged access to corrupt government officials, and bureaucrats (Cilluffo and Burke, 1997: 30). Legal forms of *krysha*—publicly registered companies employing "moonlighting" militia, offering bodyguards, and serving as legitimate conduits to nebulous power brokers—have also become very common.

Without proper enforcement of the rule of law, aggressive industrialists and avid bankers formed corrupt alliances with political insiders to obtain privileged access to the privatization of massive state industries. Efforts to crack down on corruption have done little, and even Russia's former President Yeltsin admitted that despite years of government efforts against corruption, "the problem of corruption remains acute" ("Yeltsin," 1998). Until corruption and criminality are contained, the pace of political and economic transition in Russia is likely to remain sluggish, even under Vladimir Putin.

China

If among the major emerging markets with a communist legacy, newly capitalist Russia displays great deficiencies in the rule of law, China shows that its voluntarily incremental transition to conditional capitalism may be exposing it to some of the great problems also faced by Russia. In China, the gradual lessening of authoritarianism and the growing transfer of economic power to the regions and to the private sector have helped the economic boom and the timid beginnings of a new political outlook (Lardy, 1994: 8–13). Like Russia, China spans a considerable geographic area. It is governed by an equally vast, multilayered bureaucracy. The willed, if still weak, loosening of the authoritarian grip of the central government in Beijing is creating room for corruption, particularly among businessmen and regional or local officials. As in Russia, there are growing indications of connections among organized crime groups, shady businessmen, and corrupt officials. The important distinction between China and Russia is that the state is far stronger in China. The "Strike Hard" anti-corruption campaigns in China have been more successful than similar efforts in Russia ("China: Supreme People's . . . ," 1997). Organized crime groups in China, particularly the secret Triad societies, maintain an understandably low profile. As evidenced by its use of flamethrowers against drug dealers in 1994, China's central government—despite reforms in other areas—has not been significantly inclined to lessen the brutality of its sustained crackdowns against criminals (Tyler, 1995).

Corruption is most problematic in the People's Liberation Army, wherein the central government has admitted to be facing "a long drawn out struggle" ("China: PLA's Efforts . . . ," 1997). Yet another problem, "local protectionism"—a term referring to the willingness of local officials "to consider local interests alone to the exclusion of overall ones" ("PRC: Local Party . . . ," 1997)—euphemistically captures the ease with which local officials and party cadres subvert national anti-corruption campaigns, expecting and accepting bribes from local interests.

In placing the Chinese state under strain, these forces also limit its ability to ensure civic order. The international and domestic pressures to liberalize the political system on one hand and the rising tide of corruption on the other jointly undermine the prospects for a system based on the rule of law. At the same time, the economic restructuring pursued by Chinese reforms is occasioning intense problems of poverty. For those deprived of the legitimate gains from growth through economic globalization in East Asia, trading in drugs or in counterfeit intellectual property is often a way of obtaining remedial compensation. In part, the appeal to the marginalized has always undergirded Asian organized crime. The Triads and Tongs[1] are especially attractive to poor 11-year-olds surviving in the streets of Chinese cities (Clement and MacAdam, 1994). As the stunning economic growth in China and Hong Kong keeps increasing the gap between rich and poor, so does the status of the Triads and Tongs ascend. The inputs of poverty and corruption, as well as the impacts of an onrushing economic restructuring and a retreating state, are sufficient to undermine any prospects for a successful economic and political transition in China.

Mexico

Mexico was formally launched into the global economy upon the implementation of the North American Free Trade Agreement in 1994. For some, this initiation precipitated Mexico's hasty accession to the global economy. In fact, the country had been radically modernizing its economy since the end of the debt crisis in the mid-1980s, under the leadership of President Carlos Salinas de Gortari. Salinas led the traditionally nationalistic Mexican economy through a major privatization drive conducive to an opening to foreign direct investment. These pursuits coincided with the emergence of Mexico as a major player in the hemispheric narcotics trade, first as a transit country, then as a producer country as well (Oppenheimer, 1996).

These parallel processes—of broader economic liberalization and deeper narcotization—were especially problematic because, Mexico, as a one-party state, remained under the control of the *Partido Revolucionario Institucional* (PRI). Without contradictory means of oversight, pluralistic accountability, and institutional transparence, this one-party system fueled corrupt undertakings at the highest levels. Most dramatically, the president's brother, Raul Salinas, stands accused—if not yet convicted—of laundering money on behalf of drug interests, particularly those of a close associate, Jose García Abrego, head of the powerful Gulf cartel. Corruption is suspected to have penetrated even law enforcement: in February 1997, the head of Mexico's anti-drug agency, General Jesus Gutierrez Rebollo, was arrested for entertaining close ties with one of the country's most powerful drug cartels.

Turkey

Turkey is one of the most promising emerging markets because of its potential for domestic consumption and its status as a "gateway" to oil-rich Central Asia. The formal accession of the country to the global economy is being delayed despite the discontinued rebuff of its renewed appeals to the

European Union for full membership. The EU member countries had rejected the Turkish request on several occasions, most recently in December 1997, on purported grounds of Turkey's uneven democracy and unequal human rights (Kramer, 1996). These concerns center around the treatment of Kurdish refugees and the ongoing counterinsurgency campaign waged by the Turkish military against the Kurdish Worker's Party (PKK). The Turkish government admitted in January 1998 that the Turkish security service had been using gangsters to form death squads that target Kurdish paramilitary leaders (Onaran, 1996). Turkish authorities fear not only the terrorist activities of the PKK, but also its growing involvement in narcotics trafficking and alien smuggling. Certain Turkish authorities have particular cause for concern as narcotics smuggling along the so-called Balkan route by the Kurdish national "mafia" is competition for the Turkish national "mafia," allegedly supported by corrupt ties to highly placed government officials. These long-suspected links came to light when a top Turkish police official, a leading Turkish gangster, and a former beauty queen were discovered sharing the same vehicle in a 1996 car crash. These corrupt links seem to flourish owing to the meager judicial and parliamentary oversight of the national political and military elites. In the aftermath of Kurdish leader Abdullah Ocalan's trial, the new chapter in Turkish-Kurdish relations will depend as much on Ankara's imaginative dispositions as on the irredentist Kurdish movement KKK's capacity for further conciliation.

South Africa

One of the most dramatic political transformations among the emerging markets is occurring in South Africa. With the *apartheid* regime now ended and democracy developing after the enlightened leadership of President Nelson Mandela, prospects for the future are good. The end of *apartheid* also put an end to the politically motivated economic isolation of South Africa, which is now reintegrating into the global economy. However, the opening up of the country is creating opportunities for both legitimate and illegitimate businesses. The Nigerian and Chinese smuggling networks have already made inroads into South Africa. President Mandela had called drug trafficking the "new universal threat" in 1994 ("South Africa: Mandela Says . . . ," 1994). He had vowed not to let the opening of the South African economy and political system make the country vulnerable to drug smugglers. But according to Colonel Neels Venter, the head of the police narcotics unit in Pretoria, drug traffickers swooped in "the moment things relaxed a bit" ("South Africa: Police Say . . . ," 1994). After *apartheid* ended, Nigerian and Chinese transnational organized crime groups began to establish themselves in South Africa, using the nation as a springboard into lucrative American and West European markets. The collapse of *apartheid*-era authoritarian police institutions has left a vacuum that waits to be filled by the country's newly democratizing, accountable, multiracial, but less effective police institutions.

The implications of these internal problems of the emerging markets for the vital interests of democracies are considerable. First, a transitional failure in any one of the major emerging markets would imperil regional stability and disrupt trade flows in the global economy. Second, while democracies have security interests, they also have commercial and humanitarian reasons that would require the successful integration of the emerging markets into the global political economy, without great further delay. One of the urgent reasons to press ahead with integration involves the need to stem the spread of transnational terrorism and crime from the emerging markets to the industrialized world.

TRANSNATIONAL THREATS IN THE GLOBAL POLITICAL ECONOMY

While the frailty of democracy and of lawful competition in the emerging markets constitutes a challenge to the international system, the instability of the states that embody those markets only compounds the uniquely "transnational" threats that directly target the industrialized democracies. Some of the more fractious emerging markets are virtual "safe havens" from which smugglers of arms, terrorists, and organized crime groups can expand their operations globally with near-impunity. Mimicking the ways of global corporations, these new transnational sources of threat exploit the opaqueness of multi-jurisdictional operations, the expanded reach enabled by travel and communications technology—the ease of moving money by electronic transfer, the flexibility bestowed by "market-hopping"—in order to maximize gains and minimize risks. The range of newer transnational threats facing the democracies includes two broad, yet intimately interconnected, categories of threat: terrorism and the proliferation of weapons of mass destruction; and transnationally organized crime and the boom in the world's narcotics industry.

Both categories of threats exacerbate fears because of their potential for cross-links with erratic government in weak states.

Weapons of Mass Destruction and Terrorism

Multinational security in the global political economy will be shaped primarily by a singularly difficult and transformative challenge: the use of weapons of mass destruction (WMD)—among them, nuclear and radiological materials, chemical weapons, and biological weapons—in terrorist attacks. The threat from WMD terrorism is growing because of increased accessibility to the knowledge, technologies, and materials necessary to develop and deploy these deadly weapons. One of the most salient examples is provided by the former Soviet Union. Poor "materials, protection, control, and accountability" (MPC&A) safeguards; questionable storage procedures for nuclear materials and weapons; and fears of a "brain drain" among unpaid Russian nuclear scientists have significantly increased the possibility for terrorists and other hostile actors to acquire the capability to produce a portable nuclear explosive. Concerns have been aggravated by the attempts of Russian organized crime to target the Russian military.

Potentially weak MPC&A safeguards and procedures in China, Pakistan, and India may yield similar opportunities for diversion of nuclear materials to terrorist groups. The barriers set to the acquisition, manufacturing, and deployment of a nuclear explosive are many and high—even after inventory relaxation since the end of the Cold War. Even a crude radiological device is not easy to come by. Yet the potential for abuse or "leakage" exists and can be exacerbated by way of the "nuclear black market" (Mullen and Raine, 1996). There are concerns about semiofficial as well as official transfers of WMD capability from Russia and China to unstable nations and terrorist organizations. These concerns are grounded on shoddy Russian and Chinese export control practices, a persistent lack of conformity to the norms of nonproliferation, and the complications of "local protectionism" already discussed.

Such observations underlie Western worries about the arms diplomacy entertained by the Russians and the Chinese with "rogue" states known to sponsor terrorism—Iran, Iraq, Libya, and, to a lesser extent, Pakistan. Russian arms deals with Iraq—including particularly alarming allegations about transfers of biological weapons technology—and with Iran, notably concerning aid for the Bushere nuclear reactor project, have been noted with opprobrium in the West. Chinese transfers of chemical weapons technology to Iraq and nuclear materials processing technology to Iran have caused much disquiet (Director of Central Intelligence, 1997) as well. It is feared that these transfers may allow such frustrated states to develop offensive WMD capabilities. An even greater fear is that terrorist groups may be ultimately able to acquire WMD materials and weaponry from these countries, through carelessness, help from sympathetic military, or collusion with scientific personnel, where not by an act of official policy. But no matter how "roguish" their behavior, "villain" states, too, are limited by their privileges and responsibilities as members of the world state system. They are equally subject to international sanctions, military pressures, and measures of deterrence. Thus, it is when the WMD materials pass into the hands of transnational terrorist groups that it becomes difficult for the democratized world to use legal instrument against "actors without an address" (Kupperman and Cilluffo, 1997).

As proven in the Tokyo subway attack by the Aum Shinrykio cult, terrorism involving chemical and biological weapons also is no longer in the realm of the hypothetical. Aum Shinrykio offered demonstrable reason for the world's concerns with WMD leakage: it imported biological warfare technology from Russia and received training from Russian advisors. The religious cult's use of Sarin also brought home the reality that WMDs can be produced and deployed by anyone in a matter of months. Sarin, and a number of other nerve agents, can be synthesized with primitive industrial equipment by individuals with a college-level grasp of chemistry. The same is true of biological weapons, including pathogens such as Anthrax, the continuous production of which can be secured by simple fermentation equipment such as is used in backyard breweries.

There are a variety of motivations for terrorist activity. Who are the "foes" likely to deploy WMD? Although ideologically motivated Cold-War terrorism is waning, terrorism motivated by extreme religious, nationalistic, tribal, and ethnic hatred is on the rise. Cold-War-era terrorist groups such as Sendero Luminoso and the Japanese Red Army were centralized and organized rigidly along paramilitary lines. They are now being replaced by loosely affiliated groups of like-minded extremists. The new entities are dangerous for several reasons. Their extreme beliefs give them an operating ethos that is completely, even fanatically, devoted to the success of any mission. As a result, their attacks are less discriminating and directed against casualty-intensive civilian targets of dramatic demonstrative value such as the Tokyo subway or the World Trade Center, not just ideologically symbolic ones.

Because these groups often form on a temporary ad hoc basis, their activities are difficult to identify and trace. Their very restricted membership entails an even smaller command structure, allowing for greater flexibility, easier adaptation to changing operational conditions in the field, and greater opaqueness to outsiders and law enforcement or intelligence agents. Penetration of and recruitment from these new groupings is very difficult. They involve long-term commitments to identifying and gaining the trust of prospective recruits. The small size and flexible nature of these transnational terrorist networks enable them to move on quickly, leaving little time for interface, let alone bonding.

Transnational Organized Crime and the Global Narcotics Industry

Another major fear of the world's democracies arises from the threat of transnational crime. Transnational crime involves a variety of activities, generally agglomerated around the control of various types of illegal transnational markets: from stolen autos to prostitutes, counterfeit goods, illegal aliens, weapons, and narcotics, including a panoply of illegal business schemes ranging from financial instrument fraud to counterfeiting, money laundering, and extortion. While actors engaged in transnational crime resemble their terrorist counterparts in their reliance on transnational networks of their own, they are no less inclined to form strategic alliances and joint ventures with the latter, the better to exploit each other's comparative advantages, as any of the world's legitimate international businesses would.

Those emerging market nations lacking the foundations and the mechanisms needed to promulgate and enforce the rule of law throughout the private sector, civil society, and the government itself provide the most fecund sources for transnational crime. Dictatorships like Nigeria and Myanmar (Burma), struggling democracies like Russia, Colombia, and Mexico, and weakly regulated privatizing economies like Brazil and Poland are no exceptions. They become virtual safe havens for transnationally organized crime groups. And the uneven economic development within their borders only fuels organized crime and corruption, multiplying their impact.

Looking outward from the emerging markets, the transnational crime groups view the citizenry and the companies of democracies to provide the major target for their primary goods and services. The major cities of democratic nations are the favored market for drugs, weapons, and illegal aliens. The citizens and companies of the democratic countries are targeted when they operate overseas: U.S. companies in Moscow are extorted by Russian organized crime groups, British businessmen are kidnapped in Colombia, and shipments of Japanese high-tech goods are now hijacked by pirates in the waters of Southeast Asia. Increasingly, however, such attacks are no longer confined to overseas. Shipments of high-tech goods are hijacked inside Japan. Asian immigrants in Vienna are targeted for extortion by Asian organized crime gangs. Investors on Wall Street are defrauded by Russian stock manipulators. And the traditionally open borders and relatively liberal immigration policies of the industrialized countries make the task of such transnational criminals an easier one. The great technological sophistication of these criminal networks empowers kingpins in Mexico or Russia to plan operations in the United States without the need to leave their home countries. Transactions by "encrypted" mail and electronic communications or by "cloned" cellular phones ensure utter privacy and speed. The winnings from these illicit ventures are wired in small sums or are physically smuggled out of the country, but the availability of professional money-laundering services helps streamline such tedious and difficult jobs at great profit. The two main structural factors within the global political economy that account for a global narcotics industry are virtual borderlessness and actual economic deregulation. These are two of the more prominent aspects of globalization. They reflect a shift in power from state-centric institutions to global networks. For some, it is this two-pronged broad process, not the failure of law enforcement or public health, that helps explain the growing power of the narcotics industry (Flynn, 1995). For others, the movement of narcotics is intrinsic to the "clandestine side of integration" (Andreas, 1996). The illegal drug trade between the United States and Mexico proves that "promotion of borderless economies based on free market principles in many ways contradicts and undermines . . . efforts to keep borders closed to the clandestine movement of drugs and immigrant labor" (Andreas, 1996: 51).

In NAFTA, increased trade flows have limited the ability of customs officials to inspect each truck and vessel that crosses the border or unloads its cargo in a U.S. port. This is a boon for narcotics traffickers, who are able to move their products more freely. The emergence of free trade agreements in East Asia, such as the broadening and strengthening of ASEAN and APEC (Asian Pacific Economic Community), as well as the creation of cross-border growth triangles, signify that the unintended consequences of NAFTA may be replicated in East Asia. Similar fears in Europe are delaying the expansion of the EU to include Turkey. There is a fear that Kurdish and Turkish criminal networks would take advantage of lowered borders to flood Europe with drugs, weapons, counterfeit goods, and illegal aliens.

Deregulation, another structural condition of globalization, is boosting the growth of the narcotics industry. Closely related to the twin phenomena of borderlessness and economic integration, deregulation lowers barriers in the transportation and financial aspects most crucial to the narcotics industry. In Mexico, the connection between NAFTA and the increased penetration of border-area shipping and trucking firms by narcotics cartels represents just a fragment of the "conscious choices" made by governments to "reduce restrictions of a growing volume of legal goods, capital and services" (Flynn, 1995: 5). If transportation deregulation is an obvious windfall for drug traffickers, so is deregulation in finance crucially gainful. Openness exacts a very high price.

The narcotics trade in Asia is fueled by *guanxi*, a Chinese term that denotes the preeminence of "contacts" by reflecting the networked quality of Asian organized crime—"favors" made and returned through a large circle—wherein the granter of the favor does not see the full extent of the network (Hart, 1995). *Guanxi* complicates law enforcement activities because no one within the heroin network knows its full size and structure. By definition, the network is fluid and diffuse—perfect for global enterprise, particularly when extended to ethnic Asian communities overseas.

Traditional *guanxi* connections in the heroin trade are often supplemented by sophisticated business practices. The influence of Hong Kong is particularly significant here. Hong Kong *Triads*, including the *14K*, the *Wo Hop To*, and the *Chaozhou* mob, bring much experience, great skills, and sophistication to fledgling criminal enterprises in the Guangdong coastal region of China. The groups in Hong Kong understand capitalism and are able to shepherd the Chinese groups into the global heroin trade. A report by the Royal Canadian Mounted Police finds these groups responsible for a significant percentage of the heroin trade on the west coast of Canada and the United States (Clement and MacAdam, 1994).

Collectively, these networks are best described as "global entrepreneurial webs" (Reich, 1991). They adapt to the process of globalization by emphasizing flexibility, by matching skills to tasks, and by displaying fluidity. Enhanced by *guanxi*, these traits form the basis for Asian narco-enterprises, empowering them to operate transnationally, well above the state. States are slow to match the transnational relationships of the drug smugglers. The full scope of the web of Asian narco-enterprise is exemplified by the heroin trade through the Burmese-Chinese-Nigerian connection. Burma, now Myanmar, has become the source country for over 60 percent of U.S. heroin (Greenhouse, 1996). Production is concentrated along the Chinese and Thai borders, a nebulous region when it comes to sovereignty and law enforcement capability. The area is largely controlled by dissident armies and rebel minorities who provide a safe environment for heroin production by leading industrialists such as Khun Sa. The Burmese organizations have the production capability but lack the know-how needed to smuggle heroin into the huge U.S. and European markets. So the Burmese form alliances with Chinese and Nigerian organized crime groups who have the contacts and expertise necessary for "product" to reach "market" (Greenhouse, 1996).

Global financial deregulation is a crucial facilitator for money-laundering operations. Money laundering is vital because "drug operators need to control their money, conceal its origin and ownership, and convert and legitimize the fruits of their labor" (Griffith, 1993–1994: 4). As with transportation, the sheer volume makes the clandestine movement of money considerably less onerous. In 1995, wire transfers totaled over $2 trillion a day in the United States alone (OTA, 1995). Increased utilization of information technology in the global financial industry, together with the integration of financial markets created by liberalized trade in financial services, produce vast flows of capital across borders. Wire transfers are but one potential path to abuse: other means include commodity transactions, credit cards, ATMs, and trading on secondary debt markets. The financial centers of Hong Kong, Tokyo, and Singapore, which are vital to the global financial community, also supply the inroads needed for money laundering by East Asian organized crime groups.

The transnational narcotics networks operating out of Latin America also rely on financial deregulation across the region. Inside the region, the economic giant Brazil has been ranked as a "medium-high money laundering priority" in a U.S. Department of State Report (1997). Foreign criminal proceeds flow into Brazil for laundering through "CC-5" accounts held by non-Brazilians and through "Annex 4"—a provision in Brazilian securities law that allows foreign investors to enter the Brazilian stock market. The Brazilian central bank reports that up to one-third of this capital is "suspicious money" from offshore havens such as the Cayman Islands ("Brazil: New BC Head . . . ," 1997). Money laundering at the Brazil–Paraguay border is estimated at $20 million per day, with much of it being generated through foreign exchange scams ("Brazil: Paraguayan . . . ," 1997). The Brazilian Federal Revenue Secretariat reports that the total of money laundered from 1990 to 1996, including financial fraud, drug smuggling, and grand theft, amounted to $28 billion ("Brazil: Report . . . ," 1996). Thus, an overabundance of financial regulation loopholes has made Brazil a major player in the regional narco-economy.

Like Brazil, Poland—an emerging market with weak financial oversight and promising investment opportunities—retains great appeal for legitimate and illegitimate businesses alike. Poland is an important hub within a transnational drug smuggling web and for alien smuggling networks. The country's strong bank secrecy laws and active role as a major transit country for narcotics (by land from Central Asia and by sea from Latin America) have led to the creation of front companies created for money laundering. The laundering outfits include convenient operations such as casinos, foreign exchange operations, and restaurants; more refined schemes may involve phony purchase orders for tricky software imports. The growing collaboration between Polish organized-crime groups with Russian organized-crime groups working out of St. Petersburg, the Baltic Republics, or Kaliningrad is already impacting security of transportation in Poland. Customs officials routinely accept bribes from organized-crime groups to let pass illegal aliens, drugs, and unlicensed or untaxed goods ("Poland: Report . . . ," 1997).

In addition to the seemingly distant problems of regional instability, brought about by the internal weaknesses of many of these countries, many of the emerging market countries are now safe havens for, and providers of, crucial services to criminals and terrorists—thereby contributing to the rise of transnational criminal and terrorist networks as well. It is in response to this threat that the democratic nations are now developing their own transnational networks.

NEW TRANSNATIONAL RESPONSES

The expansion of transnational threats in emerging markets by actors and intermediaries capable of damaging global peace and security has elicited a dual reaction from the democracies. In an effort to protect their territories from transnational threats and in order to preserve regional stability, democratized nations are now collaborating to raise adequate legal and political barriers so that these threats to and from the emerging markets can be limited (see Chapter 8). Proactively, democracies are also seeking to strengthen effective, accountable governance and rules-based commerce within the emerging markets in order to sustain the promising legitimate economic potential of the latter.

Such transnational fears and threats are now leading to the reconfiguration of relationships and responsibilities between the relevant organizations, within the law enforcement agencies, and among the communities of law enforcement, intelligence, national security, civil emergency, and diplomacy. Transnational terrorism and crime have created new roles for intelligence, interdiction, prevention, consequence management, investigation, and criminal prosecution. Democracies are beginning to turn to transnational coalitions of actors, in the public and private sectors, capable of managing these new roles. For instance, the European Union has created a transnational network of experts on terrorism, which will consult with any of the member governments (Nuthall, 1997).

The transnational security, law enforcement, and intelligence networks are still either tenuous or nascent, lacking the might and power of their criminal and terrorist counterparts. But the creation of so many networks by like-minded governments in recent years would suggest that the world's democracies have begun to admit the decisive value and role of transnational collaboration for combating transnational crime and terrorism globally.

Ironically, the creation of transnational institutions by nation-states does enhance suprastate globalization by putting in place a new group of actors endowed with an authority above that of any single state. These processes are perhaps furthest ahead in Europe. On paper, the European-wide police intelligence agency EUROPOL has gained considerable authority to target transnational crime and terrorism in Europe. In fact, lingering concerns over the transferral of police power and of sensitive intelligence to a multinational agency overseen by bureaucrats in Brussels have led to lukewarm national funding for EUROPOL, thus also hindering its role, performance, and success. As the widening and deepening of the European Union continues and the lowered border provisions of the immigration-restricting Schengen Agreement are adopted throughout a greater Europe, EUROPOL is likely to become far more powerful and decisively more effective (Dorn, Jepsen, and Savona, 1996).

At the international level, the Political Summit of the Eight (once known as the G-7 plus Russia), or P-8, is now taking the lead on issues of transnational organized crime and terrorism. In 1996, taking a strong interest in terrorism, the P-8 developed strategies to help Russia protect its nuclear stockpile. The P-8 has become a useful mechanism for encouraging countries to adopt the practices recommended by prominent expert groups such as the Financial Action Task Force (FATF), which set out 40 recommendations in 1990 to help banks monitor and control money-laundering activity. Although these recommendations were recognized to be successful among member countries, they failed significantly to impact the money-laundering problem due to their lack of universality. The Lyons Group on Transnational Organized Crime, a new group modeled after the FATF, is now also studying solutions and drafting recommendations for managing transnational crime. Transparency International, a Berlin-based coalition of business executives and academics concerned with corruption in the emerging markets, provides an example for private actors in a no less important role. The International Chamber of Commerce's Anti-Counterfeiting and

Business Fraud Units constitute equally meaningful sources of ideas for battling transnational criminals.

A crucial aspect of transnational responses to transnational crime and terrorism is at the operational level. Maritime and air interdiction does secure borders but is difficult to undertake without the help, at least the non-interference, of neighboring foreign government agencies. Maritime and air interdiction can disrupt shipments of drugs, weapons, or other illicit contraband. This type of maritime and air interdiction is one example of the importance of developing cooperative relationships with like-minded foreign governments, in support of mutual law enforcement and national security goals. Other important dimensions of this cooperation include extradition and agreements for joint cooperation on international investigations and prosecutions, referred to as Mutual Legal Assistance Treaties (MLATs) in the United States.

MLATs are indispensable to developing evidence supportive of prosecution of crimes committed against a nation from abroad, such as the foreign production of cocaine for sale on domestic markets or the external planning of a terrorist attack against internal targets. Through a wide range of assistance and training programs, including the International Law Enforcement Academy in Budapest, the United States is encouraging emerging market nations in Eastern Europe and Latin America to cooperate on law enforcement matters and to adopt similar investigative/prosecutorial practices.

Transnational programs for countering transnational crime and terrorism are beginning to reach the level of formalization exhibited in other areas of international cooperation. A treaty to ban bribes has been passed by the OECD countries in an effort to discourage corruption and criminal practices in the emerging markets. Such treaties need to be supported institutionally by a formal international secretariat—for which the Organization for the Prevention of Chemical Weapons would provide a good model—but also politically via the financial and diplomatic support of the major industrialized nations. As the next section shows, however, the vestiges of Realpolitik in the affairs of the major industrialized nations continue to undermine the fledgling prospects for transnational cooperation.

VESTIGIAL NATIONAL INTERESTS

The effort to counter transnational threats is undermined by conflict within and among the democracies. Within them, there is political resistance from economic actors reluctant to allow a remote security objective to disrupt ongoing commercial relations gainfully entertained with the emerging markets. Among them, the common security agenda is debilitated by economic temptations to "defect" from purportedly shared goals for the sake of lucrative contracts with, gains from, and influence over one or another of the emerging markets. Thus, economic temptation leads to disputes over which countries should be considered emerging markets and which should be considered transnational security threats. This, in turns, raises the question of which policies, sanctions, export controls, treaties, and incentives are most appropriate in addressing real fears and imagined threats.

Since the end of the Cold War, in 1991, U.S. foreign policy and that of its major G-7 allies toward the emerging markets has been plagued by a fundamental tension between political and economic aspirations. The accentuated salience of "geoeconomic trade advocacy" (Luttwak, 1993: 34)—the primacy of commercial interests in the pursuit of foreign policy objectives—as a major foreign policy priority by the G-7 countries, continues to impede the development of cooperative links against transnational crime and terrorism. Geoeconomic trade advocacy supports commercial interests through a broad range of foreign policy tools. As a result, commercial trade promotion practices are heightened by the use of instruments of state power—and those of the intelligence community. At the same time, the primacy of economic concerns in the democracies weakens the effectiveness of mechanisms such as export controls and sanctions for fighting transnational threats.

The use of communications intercepts to support the U.S. delegation in the 1995 automobile trade negotiations in Japan illustrates geoeconomic practices (Sieg, 1995). The clandestine collection of economic intelligence through espionage is a sore point in relations among the G-7 allies. France has been singled out many times. According to the American Institute for Business Research, "the French service has demonstrated that it is willing to use all the traditional tools of the espionage trade, from electronic eavesdropping, to . . . trash surveillance in its quest to obtain information that will support French industry" (A.I.B.R., 1992: 32). The French in turn have reprimanded economic espionage activities by the United States. For them, "the end of the Cold War left economic war at the top of the U.S. agenda" ("France: Article Examines . . . ," 1997). The German officials' call for a negotiated end to economic espionage among G-7 member nations ("Call for Ban . . . ," 1996), on the other hand, has produced no result. By creating mistrust at the operational levels of the intelligence community, such practices hinder the ability of nations to cooperate against transnational threats. For example, counter-terrorism cooperation was suspended between France and the United States following the March 1995 expulsion of five American diplomats from France—for alleged economic espionage. Diplomatic disputes resulting from economic espionage between the United States and its allies in Asia and Europe can and do jeopardize the strategic objective of building stability in those regions. Not least, economic espionage compromises G-7 efforts to construct an open global trading system, if only for fostering a form of unfair trade practice.

The pursuit of geoeconomic trade advocacy is not limited to economic espionage. Many states, particularly those with close government–business links, use bribery to advance the interests of their firms, creating diplomatically embarrassing situations when caught. This problem is particularly acute in the defense and aerospace sectors, as illustrated by a 1997 case involving French bribes paid to Pakistani naval officials in support of a bid for a $940 million submarine purchase (Bokhari, 1997). Like economic espionage, bribery is a geoeconomic trade advocacy of sorts that creates tension within the G-7 and impedes cooperation on the management of transnational threats. In a global political economy characterized by geoeconomic trade advocacy, should the G-7 countries view one another as economic competitors or as political allies?

U.S. attempts to enforce technology and trade embargoes on "rogue states," and the adverse reaction among the G-7 to such initiatives, illustrate the difficulty of fostering cooperation against transnational threats when foreign policy is dominated by geoeconomic trade advocacy. Opposition to the embargoes by the United States stem from both domestic and foreign commercial interests. In the area of export controls, the U.S. effort to replace the Cold-War-era Coordinating Committee on Multilateral Export Controls (COCOM) has floundered because of the new primacy of geoeconomic trade advocacy. One reason for U.S. allies to oppose strong export control measures by the United States has been, as a French diplomat put it, because "they would be effective," thus costing French firms hefty losses in arms sales (Sullivan, 1996).

With respect to sanctions, U.S. allies oppose the unilateral nature of the sanctions and the "secondary boycott" provisions of the Iran-Libya Sanctions Act, by which the U.S. government can impose sanctions on third-party states doing business with these countries. Thus, U.S. efforts to sanction Iran's WMD development programs and support for transnational terrorism are at odds with French, Russian, and Malaysian interests in obtaining gains from the development of Iranian oil and gas fields. These countries resent U.S. interference with their potentially lucrative designs and U.S. meddlings in domains deemed to be of sovereign purview.

The emergence of geoeconomic trade advocacy as a primary national aim in a country's foreign policy can result in a strong conflict between its commercial quests for global opportunities and its security pursuits against transnational threats. But the economic import of geoeconomic trade advocacy is hard to ignore: U.S. firms will be competing with their G-7 rival-partners for an estimated U.S.$1.5 trillion in Asian infrastructure contracts alone over the next 20 years (TPCC, 1996). At play are delicate choices.

CONCLUSION

International relations theorists and analysts of international foreign policy will have to take into greater account the role and effects of geoeconomic trade advocacy on a nation's ability to cooperate with its allies, to foster a stronger rule of law in the emerging markets, and to counter transnational crime and terrorism. Yet, even as policymakers and academics struggle to balance competing economic and political objectives, the networks of transnational crime and terrorism continue their exponential growth. The rule of law in emerging markets will not take root without the sustained support of democracies toward building and strengthening effective, accountable, and transparent mechanisms and institutions for law enforcement, the judiciary, and economic policy-making. Nor can the increasing threats of transnational terror and crime from the emerging markets into the democracies be stopped without stronger transnational cooperation. In the absence of transnational solutions, both the democracies and the emerging markets could retrograde: the democracies toward closed borders and restricted capital flows; and the emerging markets in the direction of newer authoritarianisms and restricted freedoms.

NOTE

1. Tongs are Chinese business associations, most prevalent in Hong Kong, that take on the characteristics of a secret society and often engage in mafia-type activities, particularly in enforcing cartels and exacting extortion payments.

REFERENCES

A.I.B.R. (1992). *Protecting Corporate America's Secrets in a Global Economy*. Framingham, MA: American Institute for Business Research.

Andreas, Peter (1996). US-Mexico: Open Markets, Closed Borders. *Foreign Policy* 103 (Summer): 57.

Aslund, Anders (1995). *How Russia Became a Market Economy*. Washington, DC: Brookings Institution.

Blasi, Joseph R., Maya Kroumova, and Douglas Kruse (1997). *Kremlin Capitalism*. Ithaca, NY: Cornell University Press.

Bokhari, Farhan (1997). Pakistan Naval Head Fired amid Bribery Claims. *Financial Times*, April 26/27, 1.

Brazil: New BC Head Grilled in Hearings (1997). FBIS-LAT-97-224, August 12.

Brazil: Paraguayan CPI Submits Dossier on Money Laundering (1997). FBIS-LAT-97-083, March 24.

Brazil: Report Calls for Stiffer Laws Against Money Laundering (1996). FBIS-TDD-96-022-L, July 2.

Bureau of International Narcotics and Law Enforcement Affairs (1997). *International Narcotics Control Strategy Report, 1996*. Washington, DC: U.S. Department of State. This report is also accessible at http://www.state.gov/www/global/na . . ._law/1996_narc_report/money 96.html.

Call for Ban on Economic Espionage (1996). FBIS-WEU-96-157, 12 August.

Carothers, Thomas (1998). The Rule of Law Revival. *Foreign Affairs* 77, 2: 95–106.

China: PLA's Efforts to Fight Corruption Viewed (1997). FBIS-CHI-97-118, June 6.

China: Supreme People's Procurate Work Report (1997). FBIS-CHI-97-059, March 20.

Cilluffo, Frank J., and Gerard Burke (eds.) (1997). *Russian Organized Crime Task Force Report*. Washington, DC: Center for Strategic and International Studies.

Clement, Garry W. G., and Brian MacAdam (1994). *Triads and Other Asian Organized Crime Groups*. Ottawa: Canada Customs, Employment and Immigration.

Desai, Padma (ed.) (1997). *Going Global: Transition from Plan to Market in the World Economy*. Cambridge, MA: MIT Press.

Director of Central Intelligence (1997). *The Acquisition of Technology Relating to Weapons of Mass Destruction and Advanced Conventional Munitions*. Washington, DC: Central Intelligence Agency, June.

Dorn, Nicholas, Jorgen Jepsen, and Ernesto Savona (1996). *European Drug Policies and Enforcement*. London: Routledge.

Flynn, Stephen E. (1995). The Erosion of Sovereignty and the Emerging Global Drug Trade. Paper presented at the Annual Conference of the International Studies Association, Chicago, Illinois, February 22.

France: Article Examines French Economic Intelligence (1997). FBIS-WEU-97-007, January 9.

Garten, Jeffrey (1996). *The Big Ten*. New York: Basic Books.

Greenhouse, Steven (1996). Burmese Lead in Heroin Supply and US Tries to Respond. *New York Times*, February 12.

Griffth, Ivelaw L. (1993–1994). From Cold War Geopolitics to Post–Cold War Geonarcotics. *International Journal* 44, 1: 4.

Growing Mafia Links to Poland Detailed (1994). FBIS-USR-94-095, August 30.

Haass, Richard N. (1995). Paradigm Lost. *Foreign Affairs* 74, 1: 47.

Handelman, Stephen P. (1994). *Comrade Criminal: The Theft of the Second Russian Revolution*. London: Michael Joseph.

Hart, M. Cordell (1995). "Guanxi": An Important Concept for the Law Enforcement Officer. Paper prepared for the 17th Annual Asian Organized Crime Conference, Boston, March 5–10.

Knight, Amy (1996). *Spies Without Cloaks*. Princeton, NJ: Princeton University Press.

Kramer, Heinz (1996). Turkey in the European Union. In Vojtech Mastny and R. Craig Nation (eds.), *Turkey: Between East and West*. Boulder, CO: Westview Press.

Kupperman, Robert M., and Frank J. Cilluffo (1997). Between War and Peace: Deterrence and Leverage. *Brown Journal of World Affairs* 4, 2 (September–October).

Lardy, Nicholas R. (1994). *China in the World Economy*. Washington, DC: Institute for International Economics, esp. pp. 8–13 and 106–109.

Luttwak, Edward (1993). *The Endangered American Dream: How to Stop the United States from Becoming a Third World Country and How to Win the Geo-Economic Struggle for Industrial Supremacy*. New York: Simon and Schuster.

Matlock, Jack (1995). *Autopsy on an Empire*. New York: Random House.

Mullen, Sarah A., and Linnea P. Raine (eds.) (1996). *The Nuclear Black Market Task Force Report*. Washington, DC: Center for Strategic and International Studies.

Nuthall, Keith (1997). Call in the Experts. *International Police Review* 3 (September/October): 35–37.

Office of Technology Assessment (OTA) (1995). *Information Technologies for the Control of Money Laundering.* Washington, DC: Government Printing Office.

Onaran, Yalman (1996). Report Confirms Turkey Murder Claims. Associated Press, January 28.

Oppenheimer, Andres (1996). *Bordering on Chaos.* Boston: Little, Brown.

Poland: Report on Eastern Border Smuggling (1997). FBIS-EEU-97-05, March 27.

PRC: Local Party Leaders on Local Protectionism (1997). FBIS-CHI-96-203, September 3.

Reich, Robert (1991). *The Work of Nations.* New York: Vintage Books.

Sieg, Linda (1995). Report of CIA Trade Spying Irks Japan. *The Washington Times,* October 17.

South Africa: Mandela Says Drug Trade "New Universal Threat" (1994). Reuters News Service, November 14.

South Africa: Police Say South Africa Now Part of World Drugs Trade (1994). Reuters News Service, July 27.

Sterling, Claire (1994). *Thieves' World: The Threat of the New Global Network of Organized Crime.* New York: Simon and Schuster.

Sullivan, Peter (1996). Export Controls: Conventional Arms and Dual-Use Technologies. *National Defense University Strategic Forum* 100 (December).

Trade Promotion Coordinating Committee (TPCC) (1996). *National Export Strategy.* Washington, DC: Trade Promotion Coordinating Committee, October.

Tyler, Patrick (1995). China Battles a Spreading Scourge of Illicit Drugs. *New York Times,* December 17.

Woo, Wing Thye, Stephen Parker, and Jeffrey D. Sachs (1997). *Economies in Transition.* Cambridge, MA: MIT Press.

Yeltsin: Corruption Still Acute Problem (1998). *Russia Today.* Found at http://www.russiatoday.com/rtoday/news/04.htm.

CHAPTER 11

Globalization, National States, and the Rule of Law

GEOFFREY C. HAZARD, JR.

PURPOSE AND PURSUIT

This chapter addresses the importance of a legal order in dealing with the fears and foes generated by the complex processes of globalization. It will consider the significance of a legal order in a social and political system; the characteristics of an effective legal order; the difficulties that globalization poses for traditional legal regimes based on the sovereignty to national states; and finally, the concept of a world federalist regime as an essential mechanism for controlling the social interpenetrations that globalization involves.

THE SIGNIFICANCE OF A LEGAL ORDER

A legal order is a system of governance and social control based on the promulgation of general standards of behavior (law), which is administered and enforced with reasonable efficiency and evenhandedness. Though closely associated with the political regime of a national state, a legal order is not inseparably dependent on political regimes. All developed countries function through a legal order. The very difficulties in establishing a legal order in the new Russian Republic are an indication of the complex requirements of a functioning legal system. It is hardly a coincidence that these difficulties are less severe in former communist regimes like the Czech Republic and Poland, which have less remote historical links to their precommunist political past. All underdeveloped countries in varying degrees purport to have a legal order, although their success in maintaining such a regime is uneven and typically poor. The People's Republic of China, for instance, is advancing legal order at the local level of municipal government and in production enterprises, even as it is adhering to a more authoritarian order at the national level of government. And, in contrast, Nigeria and Kenya inherited from the British colonial regime a system of legal order, which they were—by themselves—unable to sustain in the postcolonial era.

Legal Order and Private Property

A legal order is closely, though separably, connected with a national state's political regime; and with its economic order, which is based on private property, including private ownership of production facilities. The relationship between a legal order and private property is of a complex normative and empirical tenor. A system of private property places resources under the attentive management of their owners who guide and monitor the preservation and use of these resources in ways that seek to promote the most efficient means of conservation and of beneficial production.

A system of private property requires legal rules defining property interests of various kinds, in degrees of refinement commensurate with the complexity of economic development in the system: A modern capitalist system has legal rules governing ownership of homes; rental, sales, leases, and other forms of rights to residential and commercial property; rules governing financial transactions and conduct of corporate organizations; rules defining and regulating intangibles such as patents and copyrights, among myriad others. An important correlative of a system of private property, found in all political systems based on a legal order, are rules governing insolvency (bankruptcy, as it is called in American usage). The rules governing the insolvency of enterprises regulate the change in management and control of production facilities when an incumbent management has proved, by the fact of insolvency, that it is incompetent at sustaining the enterprise. The rules of insolvency procedure are legal rules enforced through legal procedures. The insolvency procedures are as important in the economic regime of private property as the rules of property themselves—they are a mechanism for legally changing the control of resources. The socialist regimes— once the Soviet Union and now the People's Republic of China—suffer chronic burden from inefficient enterprises surviving on debt.

The rules of property and of insolvency remain tightly, if indirectly, linked to regulation of the use of resources and of the factors of production. Regulations generally impose costs that managers of property would prefer to avoid. Plant managers with no accountability for preserving their property will have no incentive to adopt pollution controls, for instance. On the other hand, if financial penalties set the price for ignoring controls, and if the costs of those penalties must be borne by owners, then the owners will have reason to direct the managers to install the controls. The same logic for governance animates all regulations.

Other forms of ownership and control, village communism for instance, involve agendas beyond the conservation and productive use of resources. In this respect, "traditional" systems resemble socialist regimes: The efficient conservation and productive use of resources is typically compromised by concerns that discourage recognition by political authority of mistakes made in management in an effort to preserve the status inherited within that system. True, private property regimes, also suffer errors in management. But in a system of private property, management of production is separated from political control: Should management of production fail, it is possible for another element of the regime (say, the political order enforcing the insolvency laws) to effectuate a change of management.

Private Property and Constitutional Government

At the level of a regime's highest political authority, a system of private property provides career alternatives to those top political leaders who fail and must be replaced. A dethroned king or a failed autocrat has no comfortable vocation to pursue, whereas in a regime based on private property, a former president or prime minister can become a corporate board member or a media personality. A legal order provides rules governing transitions in political power, notably the constitutional provisions that determine the significance of losing an election or a crucial vote in Parliament. It is one thing to state that the government must fall when it loses an election and quite another for failed incumbents actually to exit peacefully. The rules governing such transitions are legal rules and as such are key parts of a legal order. A system of private property offers incentives that ease such legally required transitions. The symbiotic relationship between legal rules for constitutional transition and viable economic alternatives for the political losers is necessary to maintain what we understand as a constitutional regime.

The aforegoing concepts of a legal order place emphasis on private property and on legal procedures for change of control of production or for change of control of government. The salience of these basic elements, by implication, puts into subordinancy the matter of specific regulations and "police" law enforcement. Specific regulations and law enforcement are essential in any social order. Even primitive regimes must have controls on health (the relationship between a village's latrines and water supply), controls on distribution of food and other necessities (fixing the market days in a village), controls on presence of strangers (modern immigration controls), and "police" regulations (against homicide, violence, and theft). In authoritarian regimes, policing is pervasive and intrusive. In regimes of legal order, policing is more closely regulated than in authoritarian regimes. Because they are characteristic of all regimes, regulations and policing are not the distinguishing characteristic of a "constitutional" legal order. Rather, it is the existence of effective regulation of the regime's own regulatory mechanisms that distinguishes a constitutional order from any other.

An analysis of legal order must probe deeper into the close relationship between "law" and a social order. Many political and economic analysts of social order conceive of "law" in terms of the criminal law—regulations and policing. But criminal law is not the most fundamental aspect of a legal order, if certainly the most obvious and costly manifestation of regime authority. The most fundamental aspects of a legal order are the system of control and management of property and the system of control of highest political authority—constitutional law. More pointedly, the key elements of a legal order are the very rules that govern transition—of management of property, but also of incumbency in political authority—as well as the system's sustained potential for giving effect to those rules. This is the area where the most threatening of future fears and foes can exercise their effects.

Governance and Social Change

It is helpful to notice the characteristics of alternative forms of political governance, if merely because they reveal the special advantages of a regime based on a legal order.

The principal alternatives to a legal order have been an authoritarian regime—such as the Soviet system and various forms of militarily supported dictatorship—and the many historic forms of tribal government. Over time, both of these alternatives have proved unstable, particularly so during the modern era described in the chapters of this volume. Authoritarian systems concentrate direct authority intensely at a central control center, typically on a single individual or a small governing council. Such strong concentration of authority is not effective in modern settings.

A characteristic of modern conditions is the rapidity of technological change with ensuing shifts in economic, political, and social relationships that are also very swift and often quite unpredictable in their farther-ranging consequences. Concomitant to the accelerated rate of technological change is the increasing flow of information about technological change itself. Such fast-augmenting flows of information directly impinge on the exercise of managerial and political judgment, which at any given moment must be based on situational assessments (see Chapter 3 in this volume). The relationship between information flow and exercise of political judgment is perhaps the best explanation of why authoritarian regimes cannot effectively function in modern times. Simply put, the concentration of authority at a central control point is ineffective under modern conditions because no central control point can assimilate or effectively respond to the flood of information disseminated through the contemporary world. Although it could manage more limited and focused programs such as armaments production and space exploration, the defunct Soviet system found it impossible to create a consumer economy through central planning. Calibrating the balance between meat and potatoes, refrigerators and hotplates, clothing and shelter, and hundreds of other common modern human needs proved impossible compared to providing for the elite through special distribution channels routinely dependent on foreign supplies. The same proved to be true in the Argentine dictatorship and in the authoritarian regimes of Africa and Southeast Asia.

Both discernment of opportunity and adequate response to the "side-effects" that imperil society depend on information flows. The chapters in this volume address the complex impacts of such externalities on the security-relevant domains of the political economy. Such side-effects rarely occur on a sudden massive scale. Rather, they creep by increments. Human responses to threatening change pivot on the ability to perceive increments and on timeliness to adjust. One key problem under a system of centralized control is the failure of central authority promptly to obtain accurate information about such changes. A central authority's ordinary sources of information necessarily are bottom-up, usually from subordinates dependent on still lower echelons, each of which pursues its own rival agenda geared to hierarchical survival. Whether private or public, an effective system of governance must be more decentralized. Since a legal order is basically a means of coordination and of fixing responsibility, decentralization can pose serious problems when efforts must be coordinated and the loci of responsibility fixed: Participation becomes crucial.

Traditional kingships or tribal systems are ineffective in modern conditions, for reasons similar to the explanations that hold for authoritarian regimes. Both modes of power and their mechanisms of governance rely on legated precepts and practices for their basis of authority. Although this mode of authority can be effective in small communities and family circles that defer to their eldest, such archaic bases of legitimacy afford awkward and inefficient forms of governance in modern, large, and dynamic, societies. Because their basis of authority and their system of norms are based on the circumstances of a bygone era, kingships and tribal systems tend to be backward-looking. The high rate of social change in modern times makes such systems chronically and inevitably obsolescent. What modernity requires is a legal order stemming from a dynamic normative basis.

NORMATIVE BASIS OF LEGAL ORDER

A modern legal order maintains social control through norms generally promulgated and mechanisms put in place for altering the norms over time. Generally promulgated norms "speak to" every individual actor throughout the regime. Some of the norms under authoritarian regimes speak directly to the general population in this way. But many norms in an authoritarian regime, particularly those allocating authority, are highly confidential. In form, the constitutional norms governing authority purport to vest it in the leader or in the governing committee. In reality, however, authority downward and liaison upward in the hierarchy of such a regime is a product of—often covert—practice. All social systems entertain "informal" mechanisms of authority and control in addition to those officially acknowledged. But in a regime of legal order the informal norms must compete with the official system of rules—bending, then ultimately yielding to the rules.

The system of legal rules provides authoritative guidance to individual actors on conduct required and permitted in domestic interactions or public settings. As individuals can "consult" the legal rules in assessing their situation and in calculating their responses, they do not need permission from higher authority to guide their conduct. The system of rules includes not only the rules addressed literally to everyone in the community, but also many extensive subsidiary systems of rules. Moreover, the legal order includes rules governing change of rules.

Transparency of Rules and Dedication to Taking Rules Seriously

Although in reality an effective legal order may consist of an elaborate scheme of rules, it must make these rules transparent to all individual members and to every subset within its society. In an effective legal order, this transparency exists not only in principle but substantially in fact. Thus, societal activities can be pursued in light of a commonly understood set of normative expectations, maintained by participants in the widest variety of interactions that characterize a modern society. Coordination among these "front-line" circles of active participants requires additional institutional arrangements made through legal rules.

Realization of these expectations requires that the scheme of rules be adhered to with substantial seriousness. Regimes based on legal rules vary considerably in the degree to which realization is achieved in compliance. All regimes, including authoritarian ones, purport to adhere seriously to their system of regulations. All constitutional regimes are obliged to make such a commitment, for their constitution is the foundation of their regime's very legitimacy, which legitimacy is in turn the foundation of their authority.

A legal order's foundation is also bureaucratic, and unlike tradition-based kingship and tribalism or the charismatic rule of authoritarianism, bureaucracy rests on compliance to rules. Yet, many regimes purporting to be based on the rule of law are either under authoritarian control or merely chaotic, or yet in a mix of authority and chaos. There is a marked difference in this respect between the regimes in Germany or Sweden, for example, and those that have existed in Central America. What is required for the sustenance of an effective legal order is continuous commitment, at least acquiescence, by a substantial portion of the population in such a regime—a lack of which can pose threats to domestic stability, and the ensuing unrest can create its own fears and foes.

The modern history of many countries provides instances of the governmental authority's disregard of the plain requirements of law. Examples include the practices of abduction and murder by the recent military regime in Argentina and the events in Bosnia. A regime cannot function on the basis of the rule of law without consistent substantial adherence to law by government officials. But then, in a supranational regime, who is to govern?

To fulfill their responsible duty to treat legal rules most seriously, judges and executive officials must receive political protection from other centers of government authority and from nongovernmental power centers, including private enterprise. No less important, the judiciary must merit the confidence of the general public. That confidence can be maintained through regularity and consistency in administering the substantive law through the rules of legal procedure. But then, in a globalizing regime, what law is to be binding?

Experience has shown the value of also having a corps of legal experts—lawyers—to help the judiciary in administering the system; to provide advice and guidance about interpretation of the law to government agencies and to private organizations. In this context, the term "lawyers" refers to a group much larger than the licensed professional practitioners colloquially denoted by the term. In quantitative terms, resolving potential legal conflict on the basis of advice provided by lawyers and advisors is far more important than resolving of legal conflict through the decisions of judges. Legal advice addresses every possible legal problem: While lawyers often give advice permitting their clients to take action exploiting the limits of the law, exploitation of those limits does not include a disregard of them, nationally or internationally. For what fears and foes might yet arise under the threat of transnational crimes violating international law in a globalizing political economic system?

A legal order in modern circumstances must have the capacity for modification of the governing rules in order to address changing conditions and expectations. The basic mechanism for legal change is the representative assembly—"houses," parliaments of one kind or another. Though a central instrument for change, a reasonably efficient Parliament cannot but embody important characteristics of the existing legal order: Parliament is constituted according to law—along the rules governing elections and constituencies. Parliamentary deliberations need to have a reverse transparency, corresponding to the laws themselves: The assembled Parliament should be able to bring to bear the whole community's collective experience in assessing whether existing rules on a particular subject are so unsatisfactory that they should be changed.

Thus, a modern legal order requires general rules seriously interpreted by judges, conscientiously enforced by its executive officials, and amenable to modification by a parliamentary system or another. For what is a considerable organizational challenge to legitimacy of authority inside national borders can become a formidable source of threat and fear in a globalizing setting.

Property and Crime

Primary among institutions of a legal order are those of property and crime. Both of these institutions are immediately relevant to problems of globalization.

"Property" is a legal relationship between a person or set of persons and a specific resource. It encompasses specification of authority to direct the use of the resource. The resource may be tangible (such as water, oil, farm land, or an office building) or intangible (such as a patent, a copyright, a share of stock, a bond indenture, or the right to demand payment of a debt from another). The resource may be directly useful in production (just as a machine is) or indirectly so (in the manner telephone line connections facilitate whatever production is under way). Property may be "private" (authority over its use is vested in one person, in a family, or in a set of persons) or "public" (authority over its use is vested in a public agency—a police station, a highway, or the weapons of a national army). Socialist theory considered that "public" property is either a contradiction (because the public does not "own" property) or a truism (because resources controlled by government fall within that category). Still, property proved significant in the experience of the socialist regimes, whether a specific resource was controlled by one agency or the other. Such disputes over "turf" between agencies constitute yet another form of a property dispute that creates its own fears and foes.

Usually conceived as an affirmative authority—the right to control the use of a resource—claim to ownership of property can also consist of what might be called negative authority—a right to disclaim another's authority to use that resource in any way. This is one domain where the military dimension of security (see Introduction) finds swift and forceful expression.

Virtually all aspects of globalization analyzed in earlier chapters in this book are founded in concepts of ownership. For instance, "technology" (see Chapter 3) entails improved technique in the execution of a function. Technology also has to do with rights to use such improved technique to the exclusion of others. Authority over use is a form of property that may be "public" (protected by immediate policing efforts under a veil of secrecy, as in the pioneering space ventures conducted by the United States and Russia, or the national-scale development of secret weapons), or "private" (granted by internationally recognized patent systems.)

Economic power (see Chapter 4) entails the exchange of goods or services, including capital, where "exchange" consists essentially of "transfer of authority over use." And an economic problem, as well as a political one, is presented even by the most exiguous form of intangible property—that of an "idea." An idea by Salman Rushdie, say, in his *Satanic Verses*, can be a basis of royalties from sale of the book in most parts of the world and yet provide grounds in some other parts of the world for a claim of authority to liquidate him for propounding the very idea.

Environmental threats (see Chapter 5) may include manifold variations on potential conflict over negative authority, and migration (Chapter 8) may pose intensely human problems by questioning the authority of a specific people (the migrants) to occupy space in some different location—even though the problem of migration is not simply one of transborder, but also of intranational, movement as evidenced by rules aimed at domestic transients, vagabonds, and the homeless within states.

Indeed, almost all of the problems addressed in this volume have a legal dimension that can be expanded as a security problem threatening property if only for involving questions of authority over the use of resources. The source of conflict resides not so much on whether "property" is involved, but on what basis and to what extent such claims of authority are made and the extent to which those claims of authority by one set of actors (say, a government and its nationals) will be recognized and accepted by another set of persons (specifically, another government and its nationals). These questions can multiply the fears and foes.

The issues of one's claim to authority to control resources, and another's recognition or rejection of such an authority, are very much the essence of most of the problems of globalization. How is a world community to go about coordinating, "harmonizing," such—all too often violently contradictory—claims of authority? There are no pat answers to this question, and some proposals may prove less controversial than others (cf. Chapter 7).

The problems of coordinating authority are conventionally conceived in terms of law enforcement, here more relevantly in terms of policing wrongdoings that occur in transborder events. Such an interpretation necessarily entails the concept of crime—the very behavior to which policing is addressed—and necessarily, too, the concept of authority to intercept such behavior—police work itself. Here threats, fears, and foes become more salient.

Criminal Law

In this context, "crime" is a term referring to any behavior that a governmental authority seeks to prohibit by denouncing it as a crime or by subjecting it to a special regulatory scrutiny. Government regulation is pervasive in the modern world community and has a logical causal relationship to "crime." In the final processes of a government regulatory scheme, violation of a regulatory requirement is a crime for which the actor is subject to penal sanctions. The criminal sanctions usually are predicated on a pre-supposed regulatory scheme designed to anticipate and prevent harmful behavior—not on one meant to permit unrestrained conduct and to punish those violations with serious consequences. These regulatory regimes accrue over historical time and social experience. Hence, the criminal sanctions function as a "backup" of mandatory legal guidelines designed to canalize behavior at earlier stages of processes of relevant activity. Many forms of conduct that impinge on the security of others are regulated precisely because of their potential to be harmful.

All the antecedent regulatory regimes, which pervade modern societies, are formally part of the legal order. Functionally and especially in societies where government functions with a modicum of competence, they are even more important than the criminal sanctions which are their backup in addressing the "end-product"—specific anti-social behavior. Because attempting to control this specific kind of anti-social behavior is relatively expensive and inefficient, it has proved more effective to intercept paths of wrongful behavior rather than to punish their nefarious output.

Government regulatory investigation and intervention, in all forms, therefore should be considered as an aspect of prevention of "crime." By the same token, all forms of government regulatory investigation and intervention are forms of police work. The "police" are government officials with powers and responsibility for administering the manifold regulatory schemes of modern government. The powers and responsibilities of various police authorities are conferred by law. They are regulated by legal procedures. "Police work" should be perceived to include all forms of government-sponsored efforts to check legally regulated conduct, including the police, the prosecutorial and regulatory agencies, the information systems facilitating such efforts, and the agreements among such agencies to coordinate their tasks. Further reflection reveals that most "crime" and "police work" in this larger sense relate to control of property. From a security viewpoint, the challenges inherent in such locally interlinked complexities become even more formidable in globalizing settings.

THE DIFFICULTIES POSED BY GLOBALIZATION

Globalization, as seen in the other chapters, involves an interpenetration of activities among communities, transborder flows of information, trade, production, finance, population, and all other forms of human activity. These flows require controls.

All human actors discover more or less compelling incentives and strength to achieve their objectives at minimum inconvenience and cost to themselves. A means of realizing this objective in the immediate is to shift cost and inconvenience to others. Thus, at least in the short run—even among countries, via occupation or espionage—theft can be deemed less expensive for perpetrators than legitimate earnings. When such crimes become transnational, what national rules, international norms, or global institutions could effectively regulate and suppress them?

The social risks and costs of such opportunistic behaviors are familiar. Dealing with them is the task of government—no matter whether authoritarian, tribal, or one operating through the rule of law. The effective reach of government is limited in various ways. Principal limitations inside a regime include the difficulty of monitoring behaviors and the cost of intercepting violations of the community's norms. A global regime creates an additional problem, however—that of national borders: "Borders" constitute *the* essential problem in matters of globalization.

A governmental regime operates on its own exclusive terms, up to its territorial limits. This limitation exists regardless of the nature of the regimes. A ruthless authoritative regime such as that of Nazi Germany could not but accept limits on its authority over such countries as Sweden, Switzerland, and Spain. In the contemporary world, the United States, and more generally the Western community, must acquiesce in the national regime in Iran, even though that regime violates most of the modern precepts of political justice and of a legal order. These constraints are a consequence of the system of nation-states, which determines global political affairs today and is likely to do so tomorrow.

When, in a global setting defined by borders, behavior with anti-social effects originates in a community outside of one's own border—in the form of pollution, drugs, financial manipulation, fraud, or defamation—constraining or suppressing such anti-social behavior presents a special problem precisely because there is a border. In a globalizing system of national governments affording increasingly porous borders governed by national legislations grounded in rival sovereign interests, the problem threatens to become even starker. A border is a mutually recognized limitation on the territorial span (the "horizontal" scope) of a national regime's authority. In the classic language of political discourse, it is a tangible manifestation of the limits on sovereignty. In the legal phrase, a national regime's "writ does not run" beyond its borders. Whatever the regime's method of control, the regime itself is recognized as having authority only within its borders. As a sense of reciprocity underlies a system of national states, a national entity chooses not to purport to have authority over events in territory beyond its internationally accepted borders.

Much ambiguity plagues the terms "territory" and "beyond"—as applied to air space, navigable waters, and telecommunications. Allowing for these important ambiguities, all regimes prefer to recognize their own territorial limits. If they do not, they risk precipitating war or periodic border raids that enact governance through brute force. A more refined means by which a nation-state can exercise authority beyond its borders is diplomatic pressure supported by the threat of some kind of force. However, as in the example of Nazi Germany under Hitler and the relationship between the United States and Iran, this technique has practical limits. These limits arise inherently from the system of national states itself. But the reason why one country cannot ordinarily exercise unlimited diplomatic pressure on another stems from yet another aspect of tacit reciprocity: onlookers, nation-states standing by and not directly involved, would deem such inordinate diplomatic harassment as a potential, or impending, threat to themselves.

Short of such forms of international coercion, national regimes mutually defer in reciprocal recognition of each other's territorial domains of exclusive sovereignty. In the absence of the unimpeded means of governance wielded within national states, however, penal offenses, property abuses, and regulatory violations cannot be globally defined or recognized across national borders by the unilateral action of nation-states. Instead, varied forms of diplomacy are exercised—treaties, conventions, international understandings of cooperation, exchange regimes, and the like.

A more elaborate form of diplomacy is also achieved through international organizations such as the United Nations and its many agencies. International organizations are commonly accepted to be forms of "government." In some respects, a characterization of the sort is entirely coherent. The United Nations does promulgate rules of conduct. It employs bureaucracies to investigate, to intervene, and occasionally even to enforce sanctions that can much resemble those of domestic law enforcement. But the U.N. regime also recognizes a limitation—defined in terms of the "internal affairs" of member states. Here, "internal" ultimately refers one back to the "order" of nation-states. An "internal affair" beyond the reach of the United Nations is behavior in a national state, which that state determines to reserve for itself. Herein lies the weakness of the United Nations and similar international organizations. The same weakness attends all forms of diplomatic intervention across national boundaries. It is also here that, in the future, old fears may uncover new threats and newer foes.

Threats, Fears, and Foes in the Contemporary World Community

The impediments resulting from the world's organization on the basis of national states, and the corresponding limitations of mechanisms of international cooperation, can be illustrated by several "cases" in contemporary experience. These demonstrate the relationships between national states, regulatory authority, and police power as well as the problem of dealing with transborder threats, fears, and foes. The illustrative situations, in loosely descending order of menace, are nuclear weaponry, oppositional terrorism, the Russian "mafia," transborder drug trafficking, and financial fraud, as well as international piracy of intellectual property—specifically, copyright and patent infringement.

The case of nuclear weaponry arises in part from the collapse of central authority in the former Soviet Union and in part from the suggestive actions by small countries in tough neighborhoods that hint at their ability, if need be, to deploy a nuclear deterrent. The former Soviet Union's formidable arsenal of nuclear weapons was an instrument of its military and foreign policy, kept under close control and governed by treaties designed to discourage its use. Despite the less belligerent "ground rules" in place since, the successor regime in Russia is so disorganized that central authority may be unable fully to control the conduct of subsidiary organizations—such as the armed forces and the former KGB—in the preservation and status of these weapons. Yet, Russia and the other successor regimes have sufficient national identity and authority to preclude any external intervention seeking to impose more adequate controls. The global fear is that a militant successor regime or an extremist dissident group may insinuate, or intend, the use of nuclear weapons to elicit acquiescence in the likely event of some form of political exigency or another.

The smaller powers in disquieting neighborhoods, suspected of seeking to weaponize their nuclear capability, include Iraq, Iran, Israel, Pakistan, and India. These countries either deny having nuclear weapons or refuse to acknowledge possession. The global fear is that such countries may find themselves menaced, attacked, and overwhelmed with conventional weapons and that they may thereupon resort to deterrent or retaliatory use of nuclear weapons in an escalatory and ramifying war. If that contingency arises, the national authorities in one of these countries may find reason to "push the button." Alternatively, a subordinate authority in the country may find justification to do so instead.

The case of terrorism involves injury and danger of lesser magnitude but greater probability than that posed by the nuclear threat. "Terrorism" consists of local acts of violence against person, property, and community in one state, which emanate from a refuge inside or outside that state's borders. The problem of transborder terrorism is replete with examples in the Near East, and, more episodically, in the United States, Europe, and Asia. In cases where ambivalence is displayed toward such activity by the regime in the entity from which the threat emanates, the basic problem is similar to that concerning nuclear weapons. Where the regime from which the terror emanates is seen covertly to encourage, to condone, or to make little effort to interdict terrorist activity, it can be viewed to be complicitous in such activity, in terms of international law. Should the authorities in such a regime have reservations in interdicting terrorist activity, lest significant local political support for such acts of terror generate domestic opposition or even subversion to the regime itself, they may end up encouraging terrorism by avoiding confronting it—now becoming a foe to the targeted countries, who must act if only to assuage the fears of their own citizenry. The dilemma of the Palestinians is virtually a textbook example of this tragic dynamic.

The Russian "mafia" is alleged to be behind a wide variety of enterprises proliferating since the collapse of the Soviet Union, apparently by employing elements from the police agencies of the prior regime, and engaging in violent acts of profiteering. This is reminiscent of the warlord regimes active in Europe after the collapse of the Roman empire and at various periods in China. Organized crime exploits the enfeeblement of the government, in order to "supply" local order through intimidation and violence. But local violence may have transborder spillover effects as the victims and rivals begin to seek refuge for their families and a safe haven for their assets. In the modern world, local effects can become global. That dynamic may generate transborder threats abroad and insufferable governance at home. Yet, the conventions of international law, which safeguard a sovereign government's exclusive authority by limiting that authority to the contours of its national regime's internationally recognized borders, will by the same token also preclude the physical trespass of those very contours by any forces external to the so delineated territory.

The international drug trade can be considered a special form of mafia enterprise. In the contemporary scene, there is ambivalence toward law and authority on both sides of the drug trade. The nations of origin for such drugs as cocaine and heroin are ambivalent about suppressing the trade, which is a source of sustenance for poor farmers and a source of profit for domestic wholesalers. The nations of ultimate market also seem ambivalent about enforcement, if for different reasons. Some of the European market-countries have tried to contain their populace's recourse to these hard drugs by confining their use to designated locales. In the United States, whereas all levels of government are committed to suppressing the drug trade, local indifference or hostility by many sectors of the populace and indifference or corruption among law enforcement personnel have made it that much harder to trace the nation's new fears and to identify and locate its newer foes.

International financial fraud is typically a "white collar crime." Fraud can occur in all types of transactions: securities sold on the basis of misrepresentations, companies or other assets sold on the basis of inaccurate descriptions, insurance agreements unsupported by reserves, mining claims lacking support in the ground, and so on. In domestic transactions, fraud is inhibited by national regulatory laws and controls, as well as by the business and political relationships in which such regulatory regimes are embedded. In transborder transactions, the content of the rules may be less exacting. In any event, national regulatory officials can act against outsiders only via international cooperation and not on the basis of autonomous authority. Not least, constraints on cooperation may result from important local interests. These may include the confidentiality called for by bank secrecy laws.

International piracy of intellectual property is the use of technique or artistic product without disbursing the license fees predicated on the exclusive rights created by the national law of the innovator's country. Piracy is accomplished by production and sale outside the countries that recognize those property rights, or by sale in black or gray markets elsewhere. No one is hurt in a physical sense, but a complicated and socially useful system of commercial creativity is undermined. There exists an increasing asymmetry between the interests of countries where most technical and artistic creativity takes place and those of countries where that kind of innovation is lagging. There are also corresponding differences in official and popular attitudes toward recognition and enforcement of rights in intellectual property. One function of international relations in the last several decades has been to seek to reduce these differences and to achieve cooperation in enforcing intellectual property rights. These efforts have led to frustrations and fears in the "developed" countries and to appreciable antagonism between them and the "developing" nations.

In considering the legal order in a globalized community, it must be noted, however, that "cases" such as the aforegoing are exceptional in quantitative and qualitative ways. Even the cases of nuclear weapons, international fraud, and so forth are exceptional in the qualitative sense that they represent unusual and intensely distressing departures from normal everyday interactions. They are in this respect pathological manifestations of the hostility and disrespect that create the fears, which induce one community to regard an "other" as foe.

It would be a mistake, therefore, to present such cases as evidence that the legal order is generally ineffective or that general adherence to the rules of a legal order is not itself a generally recognized rule. Nevertheless, exceptions do "prove" a rule in the sense that they help test its inbuilt generalization. The exceptions illustrated in the aforegoing cases, which reality requires that we recognize, test the foundations of a legal order based on national states. Although they are exceptions, they help identify the absolute numbers of deviations of absolute threat to the world community. They justify a basis for a legal order that accepts the national state as the basic political unit of the world community, but that also transcends the national system. The essential problem with international cooperation is that an independent organization stands between the center seeking to exercise authority and the persons whose anti-social conduct is to be addressed. The center seeking to exercise authority is the agency of international cooperation—be it a telecommunications authority or one in charge of pollution control or banking. The organization standing between the actors and the international authority is of course the national state itself.

The national state, however much it may wish or profess to cooperate, has interests that are inherently at variance from those pursued by any international agency, if only because the interests pursued by a national state within its sovereign domain ultimately are those expected to coalesce to sustain the vigor, the autonomy, and the longevity of the national state itself. This conflict of interest in subgroup leaderships is inherent and, in varying degrees, ineradicable. The conflicts between the international agency and its national constituents typically can be more intense than those between groups and subgroups within a national community. This intensity results precisely because each national government, within its own statal domain, is relatively pervasive, intrusive, and enduring in the lives of its citizens.

In sum, the basic problem for social control in the nascent era of globalization is the national state itself. The national state is the font of legal, judicial, executive, and parliamentary authority. Whereas in domestic governance the national state can be argued to be a necessary pathbreaker, in the affairs of the global community it stands tall as a fundamental roadblock.

THE METHOD OF FEDERALISM

The problem of effective legal regulation in a global community can be approached by imagining a world in which there are no national states. Such a world would have one government whose authority and regulatory effectiveness would be immune to constraints by borders. Accordingly, the legal aspect of the social problems of globalization would disappear—whether they call for international treaties or cooperative arrangements or even for a United Nations. Regulation and law enforcement would hence amount to problems of administrative expediency, not of legal authority.

However, a moment's deep reflection would reveal that the problems of administrative implementation in a "one-world" legal system would be staggering. No sooner would "international" legal problems disappear than the very same ones would resurface—this time as "domestic" problems in a "world-government" regime. Such world government would have to contend with the same tired local differences in language, culture, religion, status of economic development, population density, societal composition, public morality, mores, traditions, and worldviews that have been and remain obstacles to cooperation in the present system of national states. It would be hard enough to obtain sufficient consensus in a world legislative body toward adopting elementary regulations—let alone a majority vote toward establishing a basic penal code.

Hence, in a realistic view of our condition, an improvement of legal coordination through "world government" appears to be a chimera. More modest arrangements would have better prospects. The appropriate pathway would seem to be the concept of federalism.

A federal system is one in which at least two levels of government function concurrently over the territorial limits of the regime in which the system is established. One level of government is universal, with authority over the whole territory; the other consists of regional governments. Many modern national states have federal systems of one configuration or another, as in Australia, Canada, Germany, India, Mexico, Switzerland, and the United States. Whereas among national states the division of authority is established along national borders, within federal systems there are two divisions of authority. One division is "horizontal"—along territorial lines delineating regions (say, states, provinces, or Laender). The other division is "vertical"—along constitutionally defined spheres of authority. In typical federal systems, the national government has exclusive authority over specified matters such as foreign and diplomatic relations; the regional governments' sphere of authority englobes education and the like; and authority over other matters is allocated along various demarcations.

Viewed more closely, many other regimes can be discovered to be endowed with a similar "federalist" character. Large central cities have privileged financial and administrative relationships with their central government, and special administrative territories (Hong Kong; and now Macau, too) enjoy special legal status. Many countries have distinct governments for specific regions—the Northwest Territory of Canada and the Commonwealth of Puerto Rico of the United States, for example. Remarkably, the division of authority between city and province antedates the national state. From this point of view, most forms of government can be said to have been somehow "federalist" in one way or another.

The problem of the national state can be moderated, if not thoroughly overcome, by a federal system of government such as the federal union in the United States: The system of government in the United States was not originally a federation, nor has the federal level of government forever been ascendant. The American colonies separated themselves from British imperial rule by the cooperative act expressed in the Declaration of Independence in 1776. The Declaration was a collective statement by the delegates assembled at Philadelphia, but technically, separation from Great Britain required affirmation by each of the 13 constituent colonies-become-states. When the British refused to go quietly, war ensued. The new state governments quickly concluded that full coordination of effort was required if the war was not to be lost, and so they formed an agency of international cooperation under the Articles of Confederation. At first, the agency was weak. It had a Parliament (Congress) but no executive other than General Washington, the military commander appointed by Congress. It had no power to tax directly. It depended on contributions from the member states. Except for the Articles themselves, there were no laws governing the citizenry as a whole and no judiciary. The result was incessant conflict between leaders confronting the menace of British military might and local interests reluctant or resistant to bearing the costs necessary for sustaining the war. Fortunately, uncertainty of purpose on the part of the British and intervention on the part of the French enabled the war to be brought to a successful conclusion. And the new states were born.

Even so, problems of cooperation persisted in circumstances continually posing new problems: the war debts, the contentions over ownership of property held by British subjects including erstwhile loyalists, confrontations with increasingly hostile and desperate Native American tribes, conflagrations with Britain, France, and Spain over the western borders; conflicts among the states over occupation and development of the western lands; and contestations over financial and commercial relationships, over debt and credit, among citizens within and between states.

A national leadership group was formed to address these manifold problems. It convened in Philadelphia for the authorized purpose of amending the Articles of Confederation. The leadership group—the Founding Fathers—produced a radically different form of government, the very federation expressed in the Constitution of the United States. And then another compound miracle occurred: not only was the Constitution ratified by a sufficient number of signatories, but also it let the new government go into business.

The U.S. Constitution expresses basic legal principles that can guide an effective response to the problems of globalization. The Constitution is based on an internal repartition of sovereign authority, a concept derided as an oxymoron by some theories of sovereignty. The division in question is between the authority conferred on the national government and that retained by the states. Article I of the U.S. Constitution constitutes the national Congress—an expression of parliamentary supremacy—but defines the powers of Congress primarily in terms of allocation of authority as against the states. It is within the domain thereby allocated to the national government that Congress is empowered to make laws—to legislate—for the whole community. Article II provides for an Executive and how that office is to be filled, but it says very little about the authority of the Executive except as regards military and diplomatic policy. Article III, in turn, provides for an independent judiciary—judges commissioned by the national government—and defines the scope of their authority. Next, the Supremacy Clause of Article V provides that the laws of the national government are to be the supreme law of the land and that all judges—including judges of the state courts—are to be bound by those laws. In that era, judges—quite distinct from administrative officials—were the principal and immediate authoritative voice of government. Hence, the creation of a separate system of federal courts was of major import to the constitutional system itself.

In a sense, the key to the whole constitutional scheme is the Supremacy Clause. The legal rule expressed in this Clause is addressed to the national community as a whole. However, the practical significance of the Supremacy Clause is its address to state officials and particularly to state judges. It pronounces that the Constitution as adopted, the treaties that have been made or that in the future shall be made, and federal laws as they may be enacted, are authoritative for state officials in the conduct of their state office. Thus, when the national law speaks (through constitution, treaty, or statute), it is that law—and not state law—that governs how a state official is to act. More to the point, the Supremacy Clause *pro tanto*, in fact, conscripts officials of the states into the governance service of the national government. By the same token and to the same extent, the Supremacy Clause withdraws the authority that state officials otherwise have in virtue of their offices as such. It is in that condition of mixed and subordinate authority that state judges and other officials must deal with individual citizens. By the same token and to the same extent, all individual citizens in the American federal union must guide their conduct by direct response to federal legal rules, not mediated through officials of polities—the states—who have legally independent agendas.

In this perspective, the federal system created by the Constitution was fully as revolutionary as opponents of the new system said it was. As it happened, the federal system barely limped along for another half century, until the Civil War. In that bloody conflict the question of legal supremacy was resolved by brute force. After the war ended, the victors adopted the "Civil War Amendments"—notably the Fourteenth Amendment. The political union nominally formed by the Constitution thereafter evolved into the American national government of today. That government speaks directly to citizens, enforcing its laws through judges and other officials whose fullest ultimate responsibility is to those laws and not to the legal mandates of subordinate units.

CONCLUSION

Globalization faces the same kind of legal problem. Would that it materializes without a world war, and, even better, in a prudent, purposive, and constructive way.

REFERENCES

American Law Institute (1994). *Principles of Corporate Governance: Analysis and Recommendations.* 2 vols. Philadelphia: American Law Institute–American Bar Association Committee on Continuing Professional Education.

———. (1987). *Restatement Third of the Law: Foreign Relations Law of the United States.* St. Paul, MN: American Law Institute Publishers.

Banco Nacional de Cuba v. Sabbatino (1964), Vol. 376, U.S. Reports 398. St. Paul, MN: West Publishing Company/West's Supreme Court Reporter.

Barnett, Randy E. (1995). *Perspectives on Contract Law.* Frederick, MD: Aspen Law and Business.

Bittner, Egon (1970). *The Functions of the Police in Modern Society: A Review of Background Factors, Current Practices, and Possible Role Models.* Rockville, MD: National Institute of Mental Health, Center for Studies of Crime and Deliquency.

British Nylon Spinners, Ltd. v. Imperial Chemical Industries, Ltd., U.K. Court of Appeal (1952), [1953] ch. 19, Vol. 2. All England Reports, 780.

Brown v. Board of Education (1954), Vol. 347, U.S. Reports 483–496.

Carter, Barry E., and Phillip R. Trimble (1995). *International Law: Selected Documents*. Boston: Little, Brown.

Currie, D. (1997). *The Constitution in Congress: The Federalist Period 1789–1801*. Chicago: University of Chicago Press.

Ellickson, Robert C., Carol M. Rose, and Bruce A. Ackerman (1995). *Perspectives on Property Law*. 2nd ed. Boston: Little, Brown.

Fallon, Richard H., Daniel J. Meltzer, and David L. Shapiro (1996). Hart and Wechsler's *The Federal Courts and the Federal System*. 4th ed. Westbury, NY: Foundation Press.

The Federalist: A Collection of Essays, Written in Favour of the New Constitution, as Agreed upon by the Federal Convention, September 17, 1787, special edition (1788). New York: J. and A. M'Lean; reprinted 1983, Birmingham, AL: Legal Classics Library.

Koh, H. (1997). "Why Do Nations Obey International Law?" 106 *Yale Law Journal* 2599. New Haven, CT: Yale School of Law/Yale Law Journal Co.

MacIver, R. M. (1926). *The Modern State*. London: Oxford University Press.

Missouri v. Holland (1920). Vol. 252, U.S. Reports 416–435.

Riensenfeld, S. (1947). The Evolution of Modern Bankruptcy Law. *Minnesota Law Review* 401:31M. Minneapolis, MN: University of Minnesota Law School.

Walzer, Michel (1983). *Spheres of Justice: A Defense of Pluralism and Equality*. New York: Basic Books.

Wood, Gordon S. (1969). *The Creation of the American Republic, 1776–1787*. Chapel Hill, NC: University of North Carolina Press for the Institute of Early American History and Culture at Williamsburg, VA.

Yakus v. United States (1944), Vol. 321, U.S. Reports 414–489.

A Hunger for Hope

JOSE V. CIPRUT

The insecurities that have buried the twentieth century and now pursue us into the new millennium are likely to continue to affect the world's security equations and military balance for some time to come. In so doing, they will also profoundly impact the lives of individuals and societies. Therefore, they raise some formidable questions of relative urgency for those who refuse to perpetuate or project the past and would rather step into a more positive future. Those who scan the horizon for alternate answers nurture a hunger for hope. But their hope cannot afford to be blind or devoid of reason. Such hope will need to be informed by a sense of history attuned to a sense of purpose.

We hope that what has been examined in this volume will help to shed our false certainties, to rid ourselves of unfounded fears, and to find justification for redirecting our destinies to more auspicious destinations. No amount of explanation, no extent of prediction, no method of planning can ever shield us perfectly or completely from our own selves, or endow us with parallax-free visions of alternate futures. Mustering the courage to face up to the unsuspected challenges of what we have yet to discover would deliver us from the very biases that we must still learn to shed.

Humankind's "insistence upon familiarity" and its Cartesian appetite for clarity conceivably will continue to boost its bent for wresting an understanding of the world simply "by reducing it to the human" (Camus, 1940: 17). Would that such lofty excuses no more be allowed to provide extenuating circumstances for those who tend to commit atrocities in the name of a "higher" cause, or are empowered to "simplify" the world in their own inhuman image, even as the many who should have known better and could have stopped the few at an early stage now wring their hands as they silently watch.

Would that social science rethink its theories, reorientate its gaze, and reinvent its approaches, in a manner to liberate new understandings, and elicit newer insights. Whether social theory treats the issues of comprehensive security from the interstices *"between* science and philosophy" or in the fuzzy space where "science *and* philosophy" (Keat, 1981) have learned to cozy up to each other, it is conceivable that human emancipation will pursue its unrelenting "movement from causality to freedom" (Habermas, 1974), even if there are by now ample reasons to ponder whether such a reality separating us from the world does exist or if our naive illusion of "freedom" is not merely (Prigogine, 1996) "our way of participating" in the reality of a world that somehow we have yet to understand.

Would that the destabilizing conditions that threaten the security of societies as a result of the disparities that fuel dissent within and between nation-states be earnestly addressed in ways to secure peace within countries and also to ensure stability around the world. When facilitated within the purview of social policy, the processes defined as urbanization, industrialization, modernization, and democratization can lead to self-actualization at all levels of participatory self-government. They can endow laggard societies with a novel dynamic of their own, ultimately helping to set free the masses unwittingly still enslaved to themselves. Much in contrast, the continued repression or convenient retardation of a populace will almost irrevocably thwart social progress and rob a society not only of its economic multipliers and sociopolitical purpose but of its innate humanity and of its ideals and hopes as well. The disillusionment of the masses ultimately will encourage violent upheavals and regime reversals, often backed or fomented by a dejected intelligentsia weaned from authority and empty of power.

Soon, the once centrally planned economies will begin to turn out their first- and second-generation capitalist proletariat. As those who were once gagged and resigned are now empowered to assume the lead in societies that acknowledge them as full participants, and as they move ahead to constitute the middle-class bourgeoisie of the land, newer paths will have been opened toward a somewhat juster and safer and more humane planet, in which famine, disease, and ignorance are defeated, premature death is overcome, familial unity is fostered, skilled employment is socially rewarded, and more dignified pursuits of happiness become wider-spread. Developments of the sort can spare the world encores of generalized strife and thus also discredit any lingering conspiratorial aspirations to install radical regimes whose communist powers in the recent past could not even manage to equalize poverty, let alone eliminate it.

Would that enlightened pursuits of principled pragmatism next enable to alleviate pain, and to eliminate deep asymmetries within and between nations, and across the world, in the robust mentality of a self-protecting altruism that shows an unswerving cooperative commitment to support continuity in the self-improvement of others.

We hope that this book will serve not only the specialist and the professional with the needed experience and disciplinary skills in the fields of social science most affected by compound/complex global change, but also the ecclectic reader motivated by a genuine concern for the future of the human condition.

May our modest collegial initiative through this volume inspire other scholars to engage in inclusive conversations of their own in the field of peace and security studies; that our example stimulate new harvests in the still arid domains of transdisciplinary theory, in the silent fields of interprofessional practice, and throughout the underdeveloped landscape of multi-governmental policy that rests on the fertile soil of intrasocietal action. May it encourage more footmarks in this less trodden, if not less virtuous, direction.

REFERENCES

Camus, Albert (1940). *The Myth of Sisyphus.* New York: Vantage Books.

Habermas, Juergen (1974). *Theory and Practice.* London: Heinemann.

Keat, Russel (1981). *The Politics of Social Theory: Habermas, Freud and the Critique of Positivism.* Chicago: University of Chicago Press.

MacCarthy, Thomas (1978). *The Critical Theory of Juergen Habermas.* Cambridge, MA: MIT Press.

Prigogine, Ilya (1996). *La Fin des Certitudes: Temps, Chaos et les Lois de la Nature.* Paris: Editions Odile Jacob.

Name Index

Subject Index

About the Contributors

CHRISTOPHER K. CHASE-DUNN is Director, Institute for Research on World Systems. His current research is on globalization and on the probability of future war among core states. A prolific writer, he is also the author of *Global Formation* (1989), *Rise and Demise: Comparing World Systems* (with Thomas D. Hall, 1991); *The Spiral of Capitalism and Socialism* (with Terry Boswell, 2000); and co-editor (with Volker Bornschier, 1999) of *The Future of Hegemonic Rivalry*. He is very active in fostering scholarly exchange across the electronic medium. A major contributor to the World System web of scholarly exchanges, he is also an online editor of its output and Distinguished Professor of Sociology, U.C.–Riverside.

JOSE V. CIPRUT is an independent social scientist who examines the geo-economic, ethnocultural, and sociopolitical dimensions of national, international, and transnational security in the countries and the regions of the Near/Middle East and East/Southeast Asia. He is a co-author and author of refereed articles in *Defence and Peace Economics* (1995) and *East Asian Economic Perspectives* (1996, 1999, 2000), author of chapter 20 in *Contributions to Economic Analysis: The Peace Dividend* (1996), and editor of *The Art of the Feud: Reconceptualizing International Relations* (Praeger, 2000). He is currently analyzing issues of indeterminacy, uncertainty, and risk.

F. HILARY CONROY is Professor Emeritus of History at the University of Pennsylvania. He has taught at Swarthmore College, the University of Hawaii, the University of Colorado, and the International Christian University in Japan. His research and writings have focused on the diplomatic historical aspects of conflict, war, and peace in East Asia. His many published works include *The Japanese Frontier in Hawaii* (1953), *The Japanese Seizure of Korea* (1960), *History of Asia* (1964), *China and Japan* (1977), *Japan Examined* (1983), *Japan in Transition* (1984), *Pearl Harbor Reexamined* (1990), and *America Views China* (1991), as well as numerous articles and book reviews.

SIMON DALBY is Associate Professor of Geography at Carleton University in Ottawa. His current research interests are in the areas of critical geopolitics and environmental security. He is the author of *Creating the Second Cold War* (1990) and co-editor (with Gearoid O. Tuathail and Paul Routledge) of *The Geopolitics Reader* (1998). He has written many articles on national and international security matters and authored several chapters, the latest of which is "Threats from the South? Geopolitics, Equity, and Environmental Security" in *Contested Grounds: Security and Conflict in the New Environmental Politics* (2000).

STEFANO GUERRA is a journalist for *La Regione*, an Italian-Swiss newspaper. Previously, he was a consultant to the International Organization for Migration (IOM) and to the United Nations High Commissioner for Refugees (UNHCR). His master's thesis, on UNHCR's new strategies for the 1990s, won the 1997 prize of the Swiss Association for the United Nations.

JEFFREY A. HART is Professor of Political Science at the University of Indiana–Bloomington and formerly an editor of *International Studies Quarterly*. His research interests include high technology, the diffusion of innovations, and international political economy. He is the author, co-author, editor, and co-editor of numerous publications. His more recent books include *Rival Capitalists* (1992) and (with Joan Edelman Spero) *Politics of International Economic Relations* (1998).

GEOFFREY C. HAZARD, JR. is Trustee Professor of Law at the School of Law of the University of Pennsylvania. He is also the Director of the American Law Institute. His recent works include *The Legal Profession: Responsibility and Regulation*, 3rd ed. (1994, ed. with Deborah Rhode), *The Law and Ethnics of Lawyering*, 2nd ed. (1994, with S. Koniak and R. Cramton), *Pleading and Procedure, State and Federal*, 7th ed. (1996, with D. W. Louisell, C. Tait, and W. Fletcher), and (translated into Japanese in 1997) *American Civil Procedure: An Introduction* (with M. Taruffo, 1993).

ROBERT J. JOHNSTON is Manager, Political and Sovereign Risk, at Enron North America. His particular focus is the impact of crime and corruption on Western businesses operating in emerging markets. He was research analyst for the Russian Organized Crime Task Force at the Center for Strategic and International Studies. His articles have appeared in *International*

Economy (1998, 1999), *Thunderbird International Business Review* (1998), *Financial Post* (1997, 1998, 1999), *The Nonproliferation Review* (1998), *Jane's International Police Review* (1997, 1998, 1999), *Global Governance* (1999), *Asian Survey* (1999), and *Journal of Commerce* (1998, 1999).

SANG-BAE KIM is writing his doctoral dissertation in the Department of Political Science at the University of Indiana–Bloomington. He specializes in international relations, with a particular emphasis on the politics of science and technology and its role in national security. He has conducted field research in East Asia and penned and published many papers on international security, serving also as research assistant in related academic fields and as editorial assistant to the *International Studies Quarterly*. His dissertation reassesses U.S.–Japan rivalry in the competitive computer industries.

KLAUS KRIPPENDORFF is Professor of Communication at the Annenberg School for Communication of the University of Pennsylvania. He is interested in the role of language in the social construction of realities and in the unsocial consequences of objectivist language in social inquiry. He is the author of *Information Theory* (1967) and *Content Analysis* (1980), and editor of *Communication and Control in Society* (1979) and *Design in the Age of Information* (1997). He has written many articles in scientific journals and a few books on communication theory, cybernetics, system theory, constructivist epistemology, methodology in the social sciences, and design.

REINHARD LOHRMANN is Chief, Division of Research & Forum Activities at the International Organization for Migration (IOM) in Geneva, Switzerland, where he has worked in various capacities since 1975. The IOM's role in Balkan-type emergencies is of humanitarian effect but also of analytic, prescriptive, normative, informative, and not least, educational import on a regular basis. Since his 1974 work, *Auslaender Beschaeftigung und Internationale Politik*, his analytic-theoretical audits of empirical data gathered all over the world on a regular basis have permitted him to write about such problems as international migration, imported labor, and European integration.

KRISTIN M. LORD is Assistant Dean and Adjunct Assistant Professor of Political Science and International Affairs at the Elliott School of International Affairs, George Washington University. Since receiving her Ph.D. in Government from Georgetown University, her research interests and conference papers have remained focused on the field of international political economy. In addition to her panel presentations, she has co-edited (with Bernard I. Finel) a volume titled *Power and Conflict in the Age of Transparency* (forthcoming).

FRED W. RIGGS is Professor Emeritus at the Department of Political Science of the University of Hawaii in Honolulu. Although he spent most of his professional life teaching at American universities, he has also conducted field research and taught overseas, particularly in Southeast Asia. His main focus in teaching and research has been on comparative governance, with special emphasis on bureaucracy and politics in the countries of the Third World. His writings and his field work have concentrated also on the more rigorous redefinition of concepts loosely used across the social sciences.

HENRY TEUNE is Professor of Political Science at the University of Pennsylvania. Since 1990, he has directed the Democracy and Local Governance Project, an international research program involving local political leaders and governments in 26 countries. His books include *The Integration of Political Communities* (ed. with Philip E. Jacob and James V. Toscano, 1964), *The Logic of Comparative Social Inquiry* (with Adam Przeworski, 1970, 1982), *The Developmental Logic of Social Systems* (with Zdravko Mlinar, 1978), *The Social Ecology of Change* (ed. with Zdravko Mlinar, 1978), *Growth* (1988), and, more recently, *Democracy and Local Governance: Ten Empirical Studies* (ed. with Betty M. Jacob and Krzysztof Ostrowski, 1993).